Women Pirates

OMEN PIRATES

AND THE POLITICS
OF THE JOLLY ROGER

ULRIKE KLAUSMANN
MARION MEINZERIN

GABRIEL KUHN

TRANSLATION BY TYLER AUSTIN (CHINA SEA)
AND NICHOLAS LEVIS

Montréal/New York/London

Black Rose Books No. AA251
Hardcover ISBN: 1-55164-059-7
Paperback ISBN: 1-55164058-9
Library of Congress Catalogue Card No. 96-79522

Canadian Cataloguing in Publication Data

Klausmann, Ulrike
Women pirates and the politics of the Jolly Roger

Translation of Piratinnen.
ISBN 1-55164-059-7 (bound).-
ISBN 1-55164-058-9 (pbk.)

1. Women pirates. I. Meinzerin, Marion
II. Kuhn, Gabriel III. Levis, Nicholas I. Title.

G535.K5313 1997   910.4'5'082   C96-900779-5

Translation by Tyler Austin (China Sea), and Nicholas Levis
Cover Design by Atlas Stucco Design Group
Cover Image: "Judith" 1885, by Benjamin Constant (1845-1902)
les lettres et Arts, 1886
Book Design and Layout by Darcelle Hall

**BLACK
ROSE
BOOKS**

C.P. 1258	250 Sonwil Drive	99 Wallis Road
Succ. Place du Parc	Buffalo, New York	London, E9 5LN
Montréal, Québec	14225 USA	England
H2W 2R3 Canada		

To order books in North America: (phone) 1-800-565-9523   (fax) 1-800-221-9985
In Europe: (phone) 081-986-4854 (fax) 081-533-5821

Our Web site address: http://web.net/blackrosebooks

A publication of the Institute of Policy Alternatives of Montréal (IPAM)
Printed in Canada

Table of Contents

Women Pirates

by Ulrike Klausmann and Marion Meinzerin

Life Under the Death's Head:
Anarchism and Piracy

foreword

ho were the pirates? What motivated men and women to become pirates or sea robbers? What was it like, what did it mean, to be a pirate in different parts of the world, at different times? The two works gathered here, which originally appeared in separate German-language editions, approach these questions in very different ways. What Ulrike Klausmann's and Marion Meinzerin's *Women Pirate* and Gabriel Kuhn's *Under the Death's Head* share is a hope that the history of piracy and sea robbery might still show to us a liberatory moment: What can we or should we learn from pirates and sea robbers of times past? What, if anything, does being a pirate mean today?

Ulrike Klausmann and Marion Meinzerin take a comprehensive and historical approach. They side with the women of history—with women who were driven to, but did not shrink from, extreme acts. In a wealth of detailed narrative reports, plundered from four seas and three millennia, they reveal glaring inconsistencies in the standard histories of some well-known events. No wonder: patriarchal history, they argue, has always denied women (seafaring or otherwise) the quality of will, and has reduced them to objects of fantasy, to monsters or victims. In their search for more plausible interpretations, Klausmann and Meinzerin piece together—from surviving trinkets and gems—what must have really happened, using a vivid, though logical imagination. The resulting feminist overturning of male-dominated history is compelling, and unapologetic in depicting its subjects honestly.

Some of the woman pirates and sea robbers told of here may have been heroic in the best sense; clearly others were themselves tyrants or scoundrels. All fought consciously, however, to live and get by as well as they could. This recognition restores full-blooded agency to the female subject in history.

The role of women as fully participating agents in the activities around them is also a theme in the concluding essay by Gabriel Kuhn. Like the narratives in the fourth section of *Women Pirates*, Kuhn focuses on the Caribbean during the "Golden Age of Piracy" at the turn of the seventeenth century. But his approach is more theoretical, looking for general principles of pirate life that might also serve in the struggle against contemporary oppressors and exploiters. Like it or not, this thirteen-gun broadside is certain to rekindle the debate about what it means to be an enemy of the State.

At times the two works reach strikingly different conclusions—even in their understanding of the term "pirate"—and in translating them into English we have taken pains to preserve that sense of difference. Any tactical errors we may have committed in our efforts are fully ours; the strategic flourishes belong to the authors; but how to spend, invest, or be robbed of the booty is up to the reader. Sail forth, if you dare.

Tyler Austin and Nicholas Levis

WOMEN PIRATES

Acknowledgements

For their information, cooperation, and support the authors wish to thank Ursula Ahlborn, Daniela Aleccu, Gabrielle Alioth, Angelika Behm, Alessandra Coppola, Christopher Davies, Carla Despineux, Hinrike Gronewald, Uschi Ketterer, Barbara Kistner, Sabina Lebmann, Barbel Lotter, Beate Mathias, Prince Wolfram zu Lowenstein und Mondfeld, Ute Mohring, Molly Gold, NININ, Johanna Sohn, Regina Speulta, Je Siung Tjoa.

Our special thanks to Hildegard Eisenmann, who discovered and translated French sources for us, and manoeuvred us safely into the cliff-encircled harbour of Morlaix.

Introduction

Rhine Pirates in Cologne

Ulrike Klausmann

It is Weiberfastnacht 1990. This is the first day of the Rhineland Carnival, the day when women traditionally assume control. The large and sprawling buildings of Cologne's Rhine Island harbour shine under a bright February sun. Gulls circle about the pointed towers of the old Customs House. There is a smell of gasoline and foul water.

Bobbing in the river as always is the *City of Cologne*, a beautiful old luxury steamer, anchored here for many years and used only occasionally to ferry city councillors about, or bring prominent visitors to, Loreley. Just a few hundred metres away, on Old Market Square, the opening festivities are being held for the Carnival of Cologne. But there is no sign of that here.

A big crew of wild-looking women suddenly appears on the western horizon. Wearing eye patches instead of the traditional jester's caps, carrying a double-axed Jolly Roger and armed with a drill, they move towards the harbour; however, they wait for the green signal to cross the heavily-trafficked riverside road, as they have children with them.

While the police are busy clearing the first of many prostrate drunks with clown's noses from the curbs of the Old City, about two hundred women occupy the ship.

A short time later, fax machines in Cologne's editorial offices and city agencies start spitting out a leaflet, headlined "WEIBERFASTNACHT EVERY DAY—THE SHIP IS OURS, NO QUESTION!"

"We finally found a place for ourselves. It just stood there, bobbing up and down in the water," the Pirate Women Against Patriarchy declare. Their leaflet condemns the catastrophic housing shortage in Cologne, which especially affects women, and sets out demands, including: "spaces for women who discuss and work out their own goals and ideas, and want to undertake their own initiatives." The ship is supposed to be a beginning; they demand its conversion from a prestige piece to a cultural and communications centre for women.

The Ship, *City of Cologne* [Stadt Köln] on Weiberfastnacht, February 1990. Photo: NININ

But who in Cologne bothers to read faxes on the first day of Carnival?

The law enforcement agencies take no action at first, and the pirates have time to get settled into the ship. Word spreads like a prairie fire to all of the city's carnival-free enclaves. Ever more women come on board. They bring giant pots of green corn soup, sleeping bags, instruments. There is dancing and drumming on deck.

The pirates really picked out a nice ship for themselves. Decorated with thick blue carpets and expensive crystal chandeliers, the steamer is a designated landmark. It was built in 1938, under the code name "Fireboat," specifically to hold a reception for Hitler. But he never came. After the war the boat was confiscated by the Americans for a while, and later passed back to the City of Cologne. Since then it has wasted its days as a "city council ship" under the aegis of the Cologne mass transport agency. Anyone with the money can rent it for 800 marks per double hour.

Now the old ship sports a black death's head, and banners with slogans like: "Women, fly your flag: come aboard!"

There is great confusion on land. The responsible authorities have in the meantime appeared. Since the pirates are not talking with them, they first work out their jurisdictions among each other. This is a complicated affair. The Cologne Harbour Police is responsible for the harbour itself, but anything that happens on the water is a matter for the Waterways Police in Duisburg. As long as the pirates are on the ship itself, the Cologne authorities have no right to intervene. Not that they are too thrilled about the prospect.

The property relations are about as clear as the brackish waters of the Rhine washing incessantly against the white hull of the ship. The ship belongs to the Harbour Association, ten percent of which is owned by the City of Cologne, ninety percent by the City Department of Works. Who should proclaim their householder rights, and where? And against whom? The pirates have already announced that they don't negotiate with men.

Early in the evening, as the sun disappears behind the

roofs of South City, the fire department approaches the scene.

One of them calls out: "Hey, where is your boss, we want to talk with you."

"There's no boss here, piss off," many voices cry at once from the deck rail.

"People, don't get so worked up, we only want to turn on the lights! We're from the fire department," the leading uniform insists.

"We don't need it, now get lost," the pirates reply.

"But we only want to help you. What happens if one of you has a baby?"

"Watch out or you'll get a baby yourself." Raucous laughter echoes from all decks.

Hours go by. The mood rises on board, puzzlement still reigns on land. The City Director cannot be reached. Apparently he's boozing it up somewhere with Prince Carnival himself. And at the moment the office of High City Director is vacant.

Finally Li Selter, Director of the City Women's Agency, is located. With confetti in her hair and cheeks painted bright red, she begins the negotiations between the pirates and the City of Cologne.

These last for the duration of the six-day carnival. No agreement is reached. The city fathers offer to pay the pirates 500 marks and drop any criminal investigations, in exchange for an immediate abandonment of the ship. They also offer a broken-down bus as a replacement. The pirates refuse. Finally, attending a banquet at the classy restaurant Bastei, the City Director lets on that he intends to have the ship cleared by force.

On Ash Wednesday the Rhine Pirates have disappeared. The "council ship" again bobs empty in the harbour. It has been deprived of a few decorations and enriched by a couple of wall slogans. "Lesbians Devastate Luxury Steamer," scream the headlines the next day in a major Cologne tabloid.

After that I was never able to stop asking myself: Were there once women pirates? Real pirates, commandeering ships and not just handing them back? I began searching, put up sail and travelled into the past, but against the current.

Sooner or later, anyone who sails the Rhine upriver from Cologne will arrive at Karlsruhe, where Marion Meinzerin had been researching the subject for some time. She promptly shanghaied me into an unsuspected world full of pirate women, water sprites, sea serpents, and other water-bound monsters.

Introduction

The Woman and the Old Sea

Marion Meinzerin

riting about the women of times past is difficult. The sources of patriarchal tradition contain little more than the sorry remnants of a very different past, mere hints of a reality that has been denied for thousands of years in a society structured and dominated by men.

The history of sea travel is a male domain, but this is by no means true of sea travel itself. Nowhere is the feminine as present and as feared as on the sea. The danger seems to be contained in the element itself: currents that cannot be tamed, dangerous depths and reefs, sea monsters devouring hapless sailors, sirens, harpies, sea hags, giant polyps. Terrible beings that stalked and stalk seafarers at all times. Little wonder that in statistics of mental illness, the profession leading the list is that of the sailor.

"The sea is the mother of all things," Thales of Miletus wrote in the sixth century B.C. Today we know from evolutionary history that all life originated in the sea. According to the anti-lesbian ideology of patriarchy, everything bad also comes from the sea. Filled with evil, with slimy occupants, wet mermaids, polyps vacuuming everything away, the incomprehensible wet element is home to strangling sea serpents, monsters that cause whirlpools. The sea as a giant placenta. Like a mother, the sea determines life and death. Reason enough for men to want to subdue its power.

That was not everyone's thing, and it often took truly exceptional heroes. Men feared being out of sight of a coast.

Introduction

Herodotus reports of an Egyptian captain who chose to be skewered alive by his Pharoah, rather than follow orders to sail out from Gibraltar and over the Great Ocean. He preferred certain death to that challenge.

Columbus was only able to start his journey over the Atlantic with men condemned to death. A few chose to be executed rather than sail into the unknown, while others were brought onto the ships in chains.

If the sea "breaks out like a riderless or rabid mare," as the Bretons say, then only one thing can help: the ship has to be inaugurated by a virgin. Only she can saddle such an animal. In western France and in the Basque country around the stormy Bay of Biscay, there is a traditional and terrifying story of the "Three Waves." They rise up, high as houses and white as snow, and swallow ships whole. The Basques believe that the three waves are the wives of seamen, who transformed themselves through witchcraft in order to take revenge upon unfaithful husbands.

For Christian sea travellers, an element as laden with sin as the sea serves as the repository and medium for any number of evil spirits. Pierre de Lancre, "the executioner of the Basque country," swore that he had seen whole armies of devils on his sea journey to Bordeaux at the beginning of the seventeenth century. He speculated that they had been driven from the Far East by missionaries, and were now on their way over the sea to France.

The ships themselves provide evidence for the fear and discomfort that accompany the supposedly fearless men who sail the seas. Apparently they have always had an urgent need to put themselves under female protection. Ships were often dedicated to a goddess, so that the sea traveller could feel like her hero. Ships carried and still carry female names, or wooden sculptures of the goddess on the bow. These galleon figures have the task of guiding a ship safely over the

sea. In ancient times the dedication of a ship was conse-
crated by a priestess; today the custom of the "maiden voyage" is still in force everywhere. Fishing boats in the
Mediterranean still carry the eye of the Goddess on their
bow, just like the ships of antiquity. The eye is supposed to
ease the ship's way over the sea.

Aristotle described woman and her egg as cold and wet,
associating man and his sperm with aridity and heat. "Heat"
was decisive in determining a life-form's degree of soul. It
follows that women were short on soul. The attributes "cold"
and "wet" recall sea animals. The association of fish with
woman is nothing new. Piscine symbolism was always feminine and equated with the vulva. The image of "Vesica pis-
cis" appears in various old cultures; the "vessel of the fish" or
vessel of life, it depicts female genitalia.

The profile of boats shaped like a quarter moon, as they
were built in prehistoric and ancient times, corresponds to
the oval of the vulva. The Indian Goddess of Truth is occasionally described as the "virgin called fish-smell." The goddess Matsya, worshipped in India as the "cosmic fish," carried
the ark Ma-Nus out of the chaos of the intermediary worlds.
In Egypt, Matsya was called "Maat." Translated, both names
signify "truth." Maat-Isis means "the fish of the abyss," and
conjures up the journey of Death through the subterranean
world and into a new life. Ships were always considered the
appropriate means of transport for that particular voyage.
Ships running into sharp ends, pointing up at bow and stern,
correspond to the vulva-fish symbolism representing a
threshold into the cycle of life. The ships' profiles also depict
the waning or waxing quarter moon, another sign for the
coming and going of life. Death does not signify the end, but
the beginning of a new life.

When they set sail over the ocean from Penmarch in western Brittany, Tristan and Isolde were by no means the first to

go over the water and into the world beyond. Egyptian pictures from the time around 2700 B.C. show expensively equipped ships, most of which also carry the Goddess Isis herself, sailing into a new life. There are similar images in Celtic and Etruscan grave frescoes, as well as some in Asia Minor.

The idea that the dead are carried into the subterranean world by a ship is the likely reason for the terror seafarers felt whenever they had corpses on board, or when someone died during the journey. Would their ship be lead forthwith into the world beyond? This is why the dead receive a fast burial at sea, lest the ship slow down and be hit by a storm. Thus are the sea ghosts turned away. But even thousand year-old corpses in balsam might cause such a misfortune. Even today, many sailors refuse to transport the mummies of pharaohs on their ships.

Shakespeare referred to this superstition in his drama *Pericles*, where he had the Queen of Tyros die while giving birth on a ship.

> First Mate: Lord, your Queen must go overboard. The sea works high. The wind is loud, and will not lie till the ship be cleared of the dead.
> Pericles: That's your superstition.
> First Mate: Pardon us, sir; with us at sea it hath been still observed, and we are strong in custom. Therefore briefly yield her, for she must overboard straight.

The spirits that create fatal whirlwinds or dead calms are female. They live in the sea, among the other sea monsters.

Athenian whirlwinds arise near the Mount of Nymphs. Old Greek women still make the sign of the cross when they see the dusty spiral of a whirlwind on the coast, and they say: *Meli ke gala sti strata sas*, "honey and milk, go your way."[1] Milk and honey are the usual sacrifices to the Nereids, the nymphs that arose from the union of the sea and its currents. They live in a palace on the ocean floor and are honoured as moon priestesses, or beseeched for a good catch of fish. Nereids summon the whirlwinds that pull men, who are seduced to approach by their siren-like sisters, into the depths. Charybdis is another example of whirlpools and whirlwinds. No ship can escape her. Not to mention Scylla: a sea monster with six mouths yelling in many voices, crying and singing, waiting for seafarers. Even today she still takes ships into her arms and carries them down into the depths amid a great din of rustling noises.

Encounter with a water sprite. Woodcut from a German version of the *Navigatio Sancti Brendani*, 1499. Source: Gerald Sammet, *Der vermessene Planet*, Hamburg 1990.

The Romans felt a terror before Seelamia, who set off water spouts. She is a demon with the head and breasts of a woman and the torso of a snake. Her form is coloured in green, blue, and gold. Or striped like a zebra, with one red band. Black, white, red: the colours of matriarchal cultures. Seelamia also takes men down to the ocean floor.

Water spouts were dragons to Arabian sea travellers. According to legend, these "tannins" crawled out of the sea and stretched into the clouds during storms, extended their heads into the water, and drank so greedily that they swallowed ships in the process.

Christian seafarers attempted to handle the whirlwinds and waterspouts with help from the Bible. In a loud spectacle they would recite the Gospel of John and stab the water with a knife in the direction of the danger, or shoot at it with their cannons.

The worst of all stormbringers was surely the nymph Echidna, together with her multi-headed offspring: Cerberus, the five-headed hound of hell (a masculinized version of Scylla), the eight- or nine-headed Hydra, and the Chimera with its three heads.[2]

These creatures could be avoided with help from the oracle of Sena on the Ile de Sein. Nine virgin priestesses, the Barigenae, lived on this island near the coast of Brittany. They could influence the wind, and helped those who sought their counsel. This island was inhabited entirely by women. The priestesses on Ouessant, the island just across the way, held much the same function. They were even more famous than the Barigenae; sea travellers did not dare set forth without their blessing.

There were also mothers of the winds. Hera, for example, held the four winds in her hands, "a blessing for humanity," as Hesiod put it. On the coast of Estonia she was called Tuule-Amma. When hearing the cry of a storm, people there still say: "The mother of winds is crying; who knows what other mothers will soon also cry?"

In England, the storm swallow is called "Mother Carey's

chicken." Mother Carey is a sea witch who rides on waves. The small birds with dark wings are her followers. Christians believe that "Mother Carey" is a misspeaking of *Mater Cara* ("the beloved mother"), i.e., a synonym for the Virgin Mary. Are Mother Carey's chickens merely a careless translation of "les oiseaux de notre dame," the French appellation for storm birds? In either language, these expressions inevitably suggest the undisputed patron saint of Christian seafarers. "Santa Maria" was and remains one of the most popular names for a ship. Columbus's flagship carried the same name. Ship chapels all around the world attest to the power of the Holy Virgin. She restrains storms, stamps down sea monsters, saves lives. Colourful, elaborate paintings show Maria protectively holding her broad white cape over ships and sailors. She is called the star of the sea, the queen of the heavens, harbour of hope, lady of the world. Sea travellers tormented by storms pray to her and sing "Salve Regina." But what if Mother Carey really is a sea witch? Then praying is of little use. In that case captains are left with no alternative. They have to buy the wind from their good partners, the witches. And that is exactly what they once did. In England and elsewhere, sea men bought magic hawsers tied in three knots. By the end of the sixteenth century, wind selling had grown into an international trade.

The witches in Finland and Lappland possessed a remarkable sense for business. They had an international reputation, and could call up winds for the most remote areas. Hardly an industry could compete in annual revenues. While the Finns and Lapps ruled the market and worked in a highly commercial fashion, it was said of Scottish and English witches that they did their work merely out of pleasure in the ancient art, or simply for revenge. They sold only enough wind to cover their costs of living. These witches were thus much more feared. They cursed ships, causing them to sink or run out of provisions. Among those who reported on this evil, Shakespeare also set it in verse, in *Macbeth*. The first of his three witches takes revenge for an insult by summoning opposing winds, keeping the ship of

Selling the Wind. Source: A. Hall and J. Kingston, *Hexeri und Schwarze Kunst*, Mannheim 1979.

the gentleman whose wife cursed her at sea until its crew starves.

A Scottish witch called Margaret Barclay sank a ship by making a wax model of it and throwing it in the sea. The legendary repertoire is replete with countless stories of witches who took revenge on seafarers by this or other means. Joan of Arc was considered a witch because the winds turned when she appeared on the coast of the Loire near Orleans, forcing the English to lift their siege.

The last European wind-seller was Bessy Miller, resident of the Orkney Islands. Sea travellers were still paying her tribute in the nineteenth century. But the industry suffered in the age of steam-ship travel. Nonetheless, witches left a few signs that can still be detected on modern ships. The cat, whose form the witches themselves often took on, especially when casting storm spells, is still very much present in the language of sea travel. The various tools required for raising anchor are called a cat-head, cat-hook, cat-back, cat-block, and so on. In German these are also called *Kattdavit, Katthaken, Kattseil, Kattblock*. Thin tea on board is derogated as "cat-lap."

The wise women of the ancient arts of magic and mythological female figures were not the only ones thought to possess powers as stormbringers. In German there is a well-known saying: "girls who whistle and hens who crow need to have their necks wrung in time." This expression still has its force, especially in areas where activities originally carried out by women became professions for men. Women are not supposed to whistle in hotel kitchens. While male cooks whistle and warble away at the oven, whistling can serve as grounds to fire a female cook.

Sea travellers have a well-guarded superstition that women should not whistle while on board. "Every time that a woman whistles," according to Christian seafaring tradition, "the heart of the Virgin bleeds." And why? Because every time a woman whistles, a sailor drowns.

The whistling of women entices storms to come and throw ships up against cliffs. In the nineteenth century, sea travellers still claimed they could hear an echo from the song of the sirens in the whistling of a woman. Many beautiful virgins sitting on cliffs were seen turning into sirens or harpies—giant birds with women's faces and fish tails. Their song was always fatal. In sea ghost stories there are three sirens, each fulfilling a different function: Ligaia, who sings, Leukothea, the white one, and Parthenope, the lovely one with a virginal appearance. Rationally this can only be explained through the white, booming surf that attracts such dreamy and distracted looks.

Loreley was active on the Rhine. She caused whirlpools near Goarshausen, the deepest point of the river bed, and sank ships there. She sang while combing her golden hair, and no man could resist her look—until he fell into the whirlpool and oblivion. The "wonderfully powerful melody" of Loreley also has its logical explanation; it sounded from the deepest part of the Rhine, where there is in fact a pronounced tendency to whirlpools.

Mermaids were seen at all times and on all seas, however, even by the most enlightened of captains. Thus all of these stories must surely have some other, common basis. Water sprites were encountered especially often up until the seventeenth century, mostly around England, Scotland, and Brittany. They were more seldom in points south, but are still seen there nowadays.

In Greece, where the water sprite is now called Gorgo, her original significance can still be determined. The Gorgons, Titan goddesses comparable to the Furies, describe three aspects of the wise Goddess of yore. As original goddesses, the Gorgons are residents of the sea. They decorate the walls of taverns in the form of virgin mermaids. They can still be found as protective galleon figures on ships in all harbours. A captain we met reports of them in all seriousness as living, contemporary beings: "Their main haunt seems to be the eastern Aegean and the Black Sea." Whoever runs into a storm in these areas nowadays still meets them face to face, the captain reports. They supposedly cling to the bowsprit of the ship while it is tossed to and fro, and ask questions of the ship's captain in echoing voices. If he answers correctly, the Gorgons disappear and the waves even out. At a false answer, the waves strike upon the deck, and Gorgo promptly pulls the bowsprit down to the sea floor. Ship, man, and mouse are destroyed. The captain's description strongly recalls the practices of the Sphinx.

Medusa is the Gorgon's head threatening to emerge from the sea. This terrible monster was once a beautiful woman who was raped in a temple of Athena by the sea god Poseidon. According to Ovid, Athena was so enraged that she turned Medusa into an ugly creature, transforming her hair into a thousand snakes. After that Medusa was so ugly that any man who caught sight of her would turn to stone. Very much in keeping with modern-day court procedures in cases of rape, Athena let the rapist go unpunished.

Why was Athena so hostile to women? Actually she was a very ancient wise goddess, of far older origin than the male Hellenic gods. But after the arrival of male gods to the mythology, she was transformed into a being birthed from Zeus's head, who had swallowed her mother Metis, the Goddess of Wisdom, who was pregnant with Athena by parthenogenesis. Afterwards, Athena became the protective goddess of many a hero. One of them was Perseus the Destroyer. He was sent to kill Medusa. Athena gave him a perfectly reflective bronze shield, so that he could see Medusa without looking at her. Thanks to this device, Perseus was able to behead Medusa, with Athena guiding his hand. He stuck Medusa's head in a sack and gave it as a gift to Athena, who thereafter carried the snakes on her breastplate so as to strike fear into her enemies. The symbol of the snake always belonged to Athena, whose mother Metis was called "the wise counsel." In prehistoric times the snake was a symbol of feminine wisdom, and not just of growth and fertility, as was

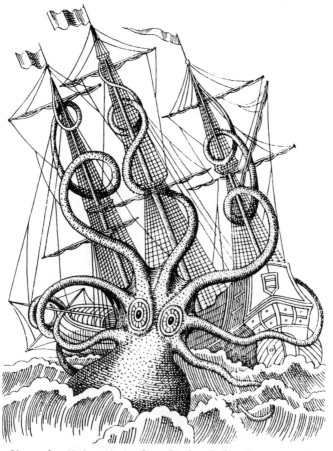

Giant polyp. Votive painting from the chapel of St. Thomas in Saint Malo. Source: P. Werner, *Lange, Seungeheuer. Fabeln und Fakten.* Leipzig 1979.

later assumed. Metis and Medusa represent one and the same power. The name Medusa, a feminine form of *medon* (ruler), derives from the Sanskrit root *medha* (wisdom), which is also the root for the Greek *metis* (good counsel).

The grimace of the grey-skinned snake's head expresses the fury of those women who still remember. The Latin word for causing someone to think of something, to remind or to warn, is *monere*. Etymologically a "monster" is thus the "emblem of the gods in terrifying manifestation." The monster Medusa reflects countless obsessive ideas about sea monsters. In mythological terms, the Medusa story relates the destruction of female culture; in psychoanalytic terms it describes the hero's murder of his mother, and femininity as a psycho-symbolic monstrosity.[3]

In the end Perseus failed to achieve his goal, despite divine protection and all manner of magical assistance, and although he killed his enemy in her sleep with his hand guided by Athena. Medusa lives on, the Gorgon's head has grown back, and its fury has by no means burnt out. The terror of men before Gorgo, who pulls ships into the depths by their bowsprit in the midst of a tempest, is fully justified.

Gorgo is the Greek name not only for Medusa—petrified through "ugliness"—but also for the mermaids, who are known to be beautiful and lovely. This may seem like a paradox, but corresponds to the ambivalence with which men view the female.

Aristotle's hostility to women is far more consistent, and serves to clarify the connection. The relationship between femininity, fish, mermaids, and sea monsters lies in the attributes "wet" and "cold." These beings all have a shortage of "heat," and are thus also lacking in soul and reason. According to Aristotle, a mother only provides the passive material, while the father contributes the active soul endowed with reason. He bears the true species of humans (man). If a mother nonetheless brings a female being to the world, she has circumvented the reasoning species, and once again set loose upon the world a monster lacking in soul. In the legends of seafarers, mermaids also have no souls—but might be able to occasionally acquire one by adopting a respectable way of life among people, and falling in love with a man.

Patriarchal stories of dragon-slaying show two different images of the female: the powerful, threatening mother in the form of the monster, and the desirable, submissive virgin. In the killing of the dragon, psychoanalysts like C.G. Jung and Erich Neumann saw the liberation of the man from his terrible mother, and the conquest of a new image of the female in the form of the lovely virgin. The man becomes a hero by freeing the virgin from the claws of the mighty monster, in order to subordinate her to himself.

In his book on the origins of consciousness, Erich Neumann writes: "the transformation of the male that occurs in the course of battling the dragon includes a change in his relationship to the female, symbolised in the liberation of the hostage from the power of the dragon; meaning a dissolution of the image of the female from that of the terrible mother."[4]

Neumann ignores that in antiquity, the life-giving femininity of the Earth and the cosmos was worshipped in the form of the Great Mother. In all her monstrosity she threatens the male need for recognition. That which psychologists understand as the liberation of man from the overwhelming power of mother is actually a desire in the collective male consciousness to subdue nature itself.

The story of our hero Perseus goes on to show how pointless these acts of violence actually are. Flying high on the trip home after his "glorious" beheading of Medusa, Perseus encounters a beautiful, naked virgin chained to a cliff. On the horizon a sea monster approaches. The unhappy girl is the daughter of an Ethiopian queen, who had boasted that she and her daughter were as beautiful as the Nereids. The Nereids promptly lodged a complaint with Poseidon, who sent out a flood of storms and a female sea monster in retribution. An oracle declared that the queen's daughter had to be chained to the cliffs. Perseus, a man of action, did not dilly-dally. After quickly negotiating the dowry with the parents of the princess, he killed the monster in a bloody battle, and "as prize and cause of all the trouble the virgin strides up, released from her chains," according to Ovid. Here Perseus seems to have won the battle of his life, acquiring a kingdom and a lovely princess. But closer observation shows that the action has gone subtly awry. The lovely and passive princess is called Andromeda: *andro-meda*, meaning the "ruler of men." The information that her mother is an Ethiopian suggests a likely relationship to the Libyan Medusa. Apparently the beautiful virgin and her monstrous mother relate one and the same femininity.

Leviathan poses the biblical counterpart to the Greek myth of Medusa. He is a sea serpent, appearing in the legends of sea travellers as the worst of all sea monsters, crushing ships and swallowing seafarers.

In many creation myths, the snake is worshipped as a world-creating divinity embodying feminine wisdom. Leviathan is male, but so similar to its female predecessors that we can safely assume his identity refers to the cult of the Great Goddess. In the Canaanite language, in which Leviathan is also called Lotan or Lawtan, *lat* means "goddess."

Leviathan is among the most despicable beings in the Bible. "In that day the *Lord* with his hard and great and strong sword will punish Leviathan the fleeing serpent, Leviathan the twisting serpent, and he will slay the dragon that is in the sea." This is how Leviathan's fervently anticipated destruction is described in Isaiah 27, under the chapter title "Israel's Salvation." Surely the Lord is not just thinking of saving the poor imperilled sea travellers. One passage from the forty-first book of Job allows further conclusions: "Can you draw out Leviathan with a fish-hook, or press down his tongue with a cord?" The forked tongue of a snake recalls a symbol of ancient female civilisations. Perhaps Leviathan can still reveal something about his struggle with Yahweh, back when the latter was still but a hero destroying a female culture.

The importance of Leviathan's bloody destruction of patriarchy is revealed when we consider that Yahweh was not at all the first to kill Leviathan. Apparently Leviathan had to be killed many times, just as in Greek mythology the Amazons had to be exterminated at several points in different periods. Some time before Yahweh appeared, Baal had done away with Leviathan at Ugarit, an area south of Canaan. Baal was a mountain and storm god, a favourite son of Ashtoreth, and thus a classic hero. Like Medusa, however, Leviathan seems to perpetually regenerate, for he continued attacking sea travellers ever after.

The primal snake in old Nordic mythology is called the Midgard serpent. Odin's son Thor attempted to kill her. According to the earliest conceptions, Odin owed his life and power to the Norns, the goddesses of fate in Celtic mythology, and for a long time he was the god of a matriarchal culture. Thor fought vehemently against this female position of power. Thor used an ox as bait to fish up the Midgard serpent. "Ably the valiant Thor pulled the poisonous worm up on to his ship. With his hammer he struck the repulsive head... Cliffs resounded with thunder, mountains droned, the old earth was pressed together, and the snake again descended into the sea." Here we see a destructive attack on Terra Mater. But the serpent apparently survived, for she has been encountered by many mortals since, especially in the Middle Ages.

A final example of violence by a male God against feminine wisdom, as symbolised by sea snakes in creation myths, is provided by the terrible and arrogant act of Marduk, who killed Tiamat. *Tiamat* signifies "the primal water, the chaos before creation, salt water, the ocean." The ambitious young god Marduk dismissed the efforts of the council of male Gods, who wanted to negotiate with Tiamat peacefully. Marduk gained the other gods' sympathy by describing Tiamat's femininity as a weakness. Marduk insisted on a preponderant position among the gods as the price for killing Tiamat. In a grim battle, and with cunning, he killed the divine sea snake and divided her into two parts, from which he created the heavens and the earth.

Tiamat derives from Babylon. Her Hebrew sister is Tohuwabohu, goddess of the depths, of heavenly ocean-chaos. Tohuwabohu, according to the etymological dictionary, is an "Old Testament description for the condition of the earth before the creative and ordering intervention of God." That implies creation as destruction. And what is destroyed?

In *Symbolik des Bösen* [Symbolism of Evil] Paul Ricoeur writes: "Creation is a victory over an enemy who is older than the Creator. This original enemy of the divinity receives its historical form in all enemies whom the King, the servant of God, is authorised to destroy. The act of violence is included in the origin of all things, in the principle that builds by destroying."[5] Catherine Keller adds the essential point: "Ricouer ignores that the original enemy is a woman, and that the cosmos created through her destruction is by no coincidence a patriarchy."[6]

And what does this all have to do with women pirates? They move on the water, the element in which the primal feminine is at home. It seems that at sea, women have the home advantage. Women on board ships were either feared,

Introduction

or regarded as bringers of luck. Pirate women were considered especially dangerous, and accepted as leaders at a time when women on land had long been robbed of their rights and dignity. Pirate women were often compared to furies or sea snakes.

In 1672 the Governor of Jamaica, Sir Thomas Lynch, said of piracy: "This accursed trade has existed so long and is so widespread that it shoots up again, like weeds or the Hydra's heads, as quickly as we can cut it down."

NOTES

1. Milk and honey are synonyms for a women's civilisation based on agriculture and livestock breeding.
2. Echidna may well be Echidne, sister of the snake Ladon, who could speak human languages. Ladon guarded the golden apples of the Hesperides, until Hercules killed him with an arrow. Echidne was a daughter and guardian of the sea.
3. See Catherine Keller, *From a Broken Web* [*Der Ichwahn*, Stuttgart 1989], Chapter 2.
4. Erich Neumann, *Ursprungsgeschichte des Bewußtseins* [Origins of Consciousness], Frankfurt 1986, p. 162.
5. Paul Ricoeur, *Symbolik des Bösen* [Symbolism of Evil], Frankfurt 1986, p. 162.
6. Keller, p. 101.

CHINA SEA

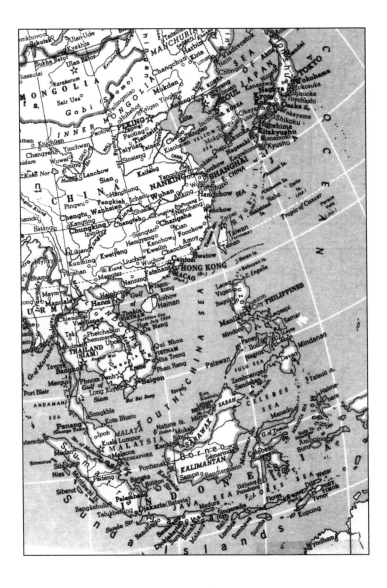

Introduction

Our journey begins in the Sea of China. Up until our present century it was home to numerous women pirates. Perhaps it still is. We find ourselves, according to Western chronological reckoning, at the threshold of the nineteenth century A.D.

The multitude forces its way through the dirty streets of Shanghai, moving past mat-covered kiosks and various other places of commerce. Dancers swirl their ropes through the air above the heavily-loaded donkeys being drawn through the crowd. Street vendors meander through the masses, their baskets laden with sweets, needles, tea, and fans. Artisans sit, busily patching porcelain with rivets. Barbers deftly shave the brows of their customers, braiding the remaining hair in a long plait as a sign of Chinese submission to the foreign rule of the Manchu Dynasty. Soothsayers peer into the future, guided by the I Ching, and sell calendars marked with the lucky days of the upcoming month. Beggars loiter about.

In the port, the junks of fishermen and tradesmen, and pirates and their families, rock gently along the water's surface. The small cabins, which also serve as homes, are invariably overcrowded. The scent of fried fish and garlic predominates, except for the occasional waft of opium smoke winding its way through the harbour.

On land the Mandarins are carried through the streets in sedans, the different colours of which display rank. The colour green denotes those of the first and second order, while blue represents the mandarins of the third and fourth order. Imperial yellow is reserved exclusively for the "Son of the Heavens" and his retinue.

Nearby, an old, scar-faced man sits, selling Chinese ink

drawings. Three paces further is a storyteller. Upon closer inspection, she is revealed to be a woman disguised as a man. She is seated on a low stool and the audience has gathered around her, idly searching their heads for lice as they listen. She is telling the story of P'ao and the yellow rose briar.

Ch'iao K'uo Fü Jên

Women's Liberation in the Age of the Yellow Rose

An old legend, dating from the year 600 B.C., recounts the story of P'ao and the yellow rose briar. At that time pirates were already making the Yellow Sea unsafe. Some originated from the group of islands we now call Japan. They sailed to the coasts of China, abducting women to sell when they returned home. Once, a horde of these sea bandits captured a young girl named P'ao on the shore of Ho-ang-Ho, and carried her onto their ship. The pirate captain took a liking to P'ao and attempted to take advantage of her. His efforts were in vain, however, for P'ao wore a shawl that served as her protection. Each time he came too near, this shawl transformed itself into a briar of yellow roses with a thousand thorns, and she was thus able to ward off his advances during the long journey. Upon reaching their destination, P'ao was put up for auction, as were the other captured women. However, because word of the legendary rose briar had spread, P'ao was considered to be of exceptional value, and consequently fell into the possession of the son of the Sun Queen.

One day P'ao was on the beach, as always under close surveillance, when a ship suddenly came ashore and the armed occupants sprang out and slew the guards. P'ao recognised the leader of her liberators, the infamous Ch'iao K'uo Fü Jên, a woman pirate from P'ao's homeland. She freed P'ao and returned with her to their country.

China remained immune to western influences for a very long time. This can be accredited to the Chinese conception of self, a mixture of pride and self-sufficiency. China considered itself the "Middle Kingdom." Seeing themselves as the point around which the rest of the world revolved, they saw all other peoples as barbarians and of no significance.

Ch'iao K'uo Fü Jên. Painting on silk, late sixth century. Source: Philip Gosse, *History of Piracy*, London 1954.

The Chinese refused to allow the entry of Western colonisers for a long while—up until the nineteenth century, when the French and English entered by force. Until then, European merchant powers had found it difficult to build up trading relations in the Middle Kingdom. The English East India Company had succeeded in establishing itself in Canton in 1786, but the Chinese did not look kindly on the idea of purchasing goods from the "barbarians of the western sea," as the Europeans were referred to in official documents. Commonly they were called "hairy large-noses" and "foreign devils."

Trade in the Chinese seas was limited and relatively balanced. The English brought tin, lead, and wool material to the East, the Chinese sold them silk and tea. Nevertheless, this was not enough to satisfy the East India Company, who began to export large quantities of opium from India to China. The Emperor placed a strict ban on the opium trade, but the large-nosed dealers paid him no heed. Among the corrupt Mandarins they found plenty of willing accomplices. A lucrative field thus opened up for smuggling, extortion, and piracy.

Lady Ch'ing

We are but smoke in the wind, mere swells of the sea in a typhoon, like broken bamboo canes flowing thither and sinking, up and down, with no thought of rest.
—Ch'ang P'aou, lieutenant to pirate captain Ch'ing

Admiral Tz'uen Mao Szün leaned against the railing of his flagship and lit up an opium pipe, feeling he had earned this little indulgence. After all, he had managed to deliver a not-inconsiderable blow to the most dreaded demon of the Chinese seas.

Tz'uen had just forced Ch'ing Yih Szaou, captain of the largest pirate fleet, to beat a hasty retreat. Tz'uen had embarked with a hundred imperial warships to put a stop to the ferocious female sea robber. He hadn't exactly looked forward to this venture with anticipation; indeed he had been seized with dread at the contemplation of the fate of his predecessors.

Admiral Kwo Lang had been the first to attempt to destroy the foundation of Lady Ch'ing's remarkable rule. But he had been no match for her cunning strategies, and the battle ended with many deaths among the imperial marines. The Admiral, who couldn't bear to be a prisoner at the mercy of Ch'ing, had committed suicide.

General Lin Fa had launched the second attempt. However, his courage had failed him at the first sight of the immense pirate fleet, numbering six hundred armed junks.

He promptly ordered his fleet to turn around, and fled in the direction of his home port. Nevertheless, Ch'ing's squadron quickly overtook him. As the sea was calm, the pirates sprang into the water and, swimming with their daggers between their teeth, boarded the enemy ships and took all of them, without exception.

Tz'uen's was now the third attempt this year, and he had to admit that the heavens had granted him a most favourable day. During the battle the pirate ships' rigging had caught on fire, and Ch'ing was forced to withdraw. Although Tz'uen had not been able to catch the notorious captain herself, he had succeeded in taking many of her people prisoner.

One of the women pirates had fought with exceptional fervour. Tz'uen could still envision her, sabres in both hands, attacking the soldiers like a wild beast, wounding many before she was finally overpowered.

The Imperial Admiral was now looking forward to his return. He would surely receive numerous honours, and perhaps even be allowed to wear the ostrich feather with two eyes in his silk cap.

Tz'uen Mao Szün hadn't even time to finish smoking his pipe when terrified cries rang out from the neighbouring boat. "They're coming back, the pirates are closing in from behind!" A few hours later, only the remains of a hundred imperial warships drifted upon the swells.

One of the few soldiers who survived Ch'ing's vengeance described the massacre: "Our fleet was completely demolished, ripped to pieces, and thrown into a mangled chaos. The uproar tore the heavens asunder. Everyone fought to save their own skins, and scarcely a hundred people survived."

According to Western chronology, this occurred shortly before the eighteenth month of the eighth moon, in the year 1808.

Lady Ch'ing was the most notorious pirate of her day in

the Sea of China, her command numbering more than 70,000 people. She had taken over her husband's fleet following his death. Her husband had gained so much power and renown that the Emperor had given Lord Ch'ing the title "Golden Dragon of the Imperial Staff," in effect a promotion to the rank of a prince. In doing so the Emperor had hoped to divert Ch'ing's attacks.

Nevertheless, this honour didn't prevent Ch'ing from extending his operations to the coast of present-day Vietnam, which he terrorised until a typhoon reportedly carried him away. According to another source he was seized in a raid and tortured to death. Supposedly, as his fleet fled, those on Lady Ch'ing's flagship heard her announce: "Under the leadership of a man you have all chosen to flee. We shall see how you prove yourselves under the hand of a woman."

Lady Ch'ing was a bold and extraordinarily successful sea robber. It was said that she had the wisdom of a Mandarin in his seventh incarnation, and the authority of an Emperor.

She most likely came into the world on board a pirate ship; indeed, sea piracy was a family undertaking in China. The pirate clans lived on their junks, contrary to the practices of those in the Caribbean and other seas. Large, many-member families lived in close quarters. All were present during combat, and from the moment they could walk, girls and boys had no other choice but to learn their trade. The women on a warship first served in duty to their fathers. The wife of a pirate captain would hold the rank of first lieutenant, and was often chosen as his successor in the event of his death. The circumstances surrounding the widow Ch'ing's assumption of leadership were thus by no means an exception. Her success, however, was unique.

An impression of typical life aboard a pirate ship was placed on record by the English officer Glasspoole, relating his three-month imprisonment aboard Ch'ing Yih Szaou's ship:

Lady Ch'ing in action. Source: Gosse.

In the back lives the captain, together with his family, who in most cases has five or six wives. Each man, along with his wife and children, has a four-foot square room at his disposal. With so many souls in so little space, one can imagine how dirty it was, and the ship was swarming with every possible insect. There was also a multitude of rats, purposely bred as they were considered a delicacy, there being at any rate hardly a living thing the pirates didn't eat. During my imprisonment I lived on rice cooked with caterpillars. The pirates love games, and spend their free time playing cards and smoking opium.

Mr. Glasspoole must have endured still more unpleasantness, having survived various hold-ups and shoot-outs.

When combat became especially intense, Ch'ing would sprinkle her precious garlic water in the faces of her hostages, as it was believed to protect them from being shot. After drawn-out negotiations, Glasspoole was set free in exchange for two bundles of costly fabric, two chests of opium, two chests of gun-powder, a telescope, and 7,654 dollars in ransom.

The Lady Ch'ing held up everything that crossed her path. If she seized a ship belonging to the Imperial Navy, then all those aboard would be killed. Trade ships, on the other hand, only shared this fate if they offered resistance. Captives who lacked the money to purchase their freedom would be given a choice: conversion to piracy, or an excruciating death. Women and children who brought in no ransom would be sold to the slave handlers at the Portuguese trade station in Macau. From here they would be smuggled to the black markets of Singapore, Bombay, and San Francisco as likely prey for the harem and brothel trades. Europeans, women as well as men, were particularly desirable hostages, since they could usually be ransomed for a nice sum.

In traditional Mafia manner, Ch'ing Yih Szaou also collected "protection" money from the people along the coasts. She raided and pillaged the estates of the Mandarins, but not those of the farmers, to whom she even gave reasonable compensation for the provisions she took.

At that time, anyone caught aiding a pirate or buying his loot was sentenced to an orderly thrashing, and deported either to military service or hard labour. Those who gave evidence against the pirates could reckon with a more moderate penalty, according to the Chinese version of a "crown witness" protection program. Pirates themselves were beheaded if they fell into the clutches of the imperial guardians of the peace, with their heads put on public display.

This was a particularly severe penalty, because according to Confucian teachings it was important that one's entire body be buried in the same place so that the spirit could enter the next world intact.

The prospect of death by beheading did not stop the 70,000 pirates under Ch'ing's command, however, from causing the southern Chinese coastal waters, from the Yellow Sea to the Straits of Malacca, to remain perilous for travel and trade. In any case the pirates had few alternatives. Since the beginning of the nineteenth century, the Chinese people had experienced increasing poverty. The number of births continued to rise, along with a developing food shortage. While the imperial court in Beijing still revelled in luxury and the mandarins secured a comfortable life for themselves through extortion, dissatisfaction grew among the people towards those in power.

Ch'ing, wishing to avoid the fate of her people on land, had organised her fleet with efficiency in mind. Her fighting ships were divided into six squadrons. Each sailed under their own flag of varying colours, and was commanded by a ship's purser who was outfitted with costly clothing and given a title such as "Jewel of the Crew," "Mealtime of the Frog," or more ominously, "Knife in the Neck" or "Scourge of the Eastern Seas."

The fleet was set up like a sort of constitutional monarchy, except Her Majesty Ch'ing was the absolute sovereign at its head. There was a council, whose members were chosen by the pirate captain herself, and a prime minister. This post she entrusted to her foster son, Ch'ang P'aou.

P'aou had been captured and brought onto Ch'ing's ship along with many other children intended for sale. Something about the child must have caught the notice of the young pirate captain's wife. She took him aside and proceeded to raise him as her own. After the death of her husband, Ch'ing appointed P'aou leader of the "red squadron," and bestowed upon him the title "Steady of the Steadiest."

Together with Prime Minister Ch'ang P'aou, Ch'ing built up a clever intelligence network that enabled her to be informed at all times as to the happenings in the harbours, as well as about potential prey and the plots of her pursuers.

She had drawn up strict regulations concerning the conduct that was expected in her fleet. "Not even the smallest object may be privately removed from the common loot. Every piece must be accurately registered. From every ten pieces, the individual receives two. The remaining eight parts go to the warehouse for common stock. Whosoever takes from this common supply without permission will be sentenced to death." Contrary to her predecessors, who had lived from hand to mouth, Ch'ing took care that there were provisions enough to ensure that her squadrons were always well armed and in good condition. The use of the word "plundering" was forbidden. Lady Ch'ing referred only to "transferring shipment of goods."

Another paragraph decreed: "If any member of the crew should go on land without authorisation, their ears will be lanced before the entire fleet. If the violation is repeated, the penalty will be death."

In addition, Ch'ing attempted to regulate the common use of violence against women; the pirates were no exception there. Her orders read as follows: "No one shall satisfy their lust with captured women in the villages or public places. On board, the permission of the squadron leader must be obtained for this purpose, and the act performed aside, in the ship's hold. Those who employ the use of force against a woman without permission will be penalised with death."

Ch'ing Yih Szaou did away with the cruel practice of hanging captured women and children by their hair on the ships. Women and children "who had a high standing or reputation" were not sold, but rather held for ransom. If no ransom was forthcoming, then pirates themselves were permitted to buy them for a low sum; however the purchasers were obligated to "treat them like respectable wives." Whosoever did not abide by this rule would be killed on the spot.

These reforms most likely originated from tactical considerations rather than out of an interest in kindness to women. Presumably Ch'ing reasoned that without these clauses, many women would have jumped over board in order to bring their life to an end.

Ch'ing Yih Szaou never made important decisions without first consulting a particular guardian spirit, whose likeness was represented by a statue found on each of her ships. When he gave the order to attack, the fleet responded even when the decision appeared irrational. The spirit communicated with Ch'ing through inspiration, and his commands were always obeyed. Indeed, she fared well; the advice always proved strategically sound. Thus she was able to raid and plunder for ten years undisturbed, the Imperial Navy helpless in all attempts to capture her.

As we see, communication with the spirit world, especially the use of oracles, was and still is an important element of political as well as everyday life in China. No emperor married without first calculating the horoscope of the bride under consideration. Before plans were laid for an important political act, astrologers were consulted to determine the most favourable day. That Ch'ing had such a good connection to other-worldly powers increased her authority, and the success of her rapacious enterprise grew and grew.

At the same time, British trade ships were increasing their activities in Chinese coastal waters. To the pirates, the British were suitable both as prey and as potential customers for opium smuggling and the slave trade. Once the imperial authorities realised that they could accomplish nothing against the powerful fleet of Ch'ing Yih Szaou, they were forced to ask the foreign barbarians for help. However, even the British with their heavy gunboats were no match for the unpredictable pirate squadrons, who would seemingly emerge from nowhere and disappear just as quickly. The British were not particularly troubled by this. In fact the pirates, who helped them bypass the restrictive imperial trade laws, were as welcome as the corrupt Mandarins at the harbours. What took place in Chinese waters was a battle without any clear division among sides. Whether pirates, imperial officials, or European customers, each dealt unscrupulously in the service of their own profit.

In spite of Ch'ing's continued success, there nevertheless emerged a point of dissension among her subjects. The lieutenant of the green squadron could no longer tolerate P'aou's continuing rise to predominance. Their competition grew increasingly fierce, until one day when the green squadron succeeded in sinking sixteen of P'aou's red-fleet junks, along with their 300 crew members. As a result, the leader of the green squadron applied to the governor of Macau, expressing his remorse, and begging for amnesty. The governor complied, granting the green squadron's 8,000 subjects indemnity, and laying at their disposal arable land upon which to settle. This was a heavy blow to Ch'ing. She had lost a squadron with 160 fighting ships, 500 large cannons, and 5,600 weapons. In light of this defeat, Ch'ing began to contemplate if perhaps it wasn't also in her own best interest to enter into negotiations with the governor. She consulted her spirit, and was persuaded to go on land and speak with him.

It must have looked like a mammoth the giant fleet of Ch'ing Yih Szaou appeared in the delta of Hsiang Kiang. Accompanied by music and gun salutes, the pirate captain boarded the governor's ship, where she was treated as though she were the monarch of a very powerful country. Ch'ing Yih Szaou and her people capitulated, and prepared themselves for the transition to life on land, receiving amnesty and provisions from the governor: a piece of pork, a litre of wine, and monetary compensation for each pirate.

The stories about Lady Ch'ing's subsequent fate vary. One maintains that she married the governor and became an honourable lady. The other suggests that she established herself in Macau, and was responsible for one of the most successful smuggling operations of that time. Perhaps both are true, for the one certainly does not rule out the other. On the contrary, possessing more than enough "business" contacts and the necessary connections with justice officials, it was no doubt quite simple to run a successful smuggling operation and still remain a lady of society.

from the Galley:

Shark Fin Soup

The English officer Glasspoole, quite upset by pirate cuisine, obviously didn't know what was good for him. Today this has changed. Gourmets throughout the world appreciate the culinary specialties of China. In New Zealand, roasted maggots are a delicacy, while European gourmets pay horrendous prices for toast with ants. Nevertheless, Chinese cuisine has more to offer than maggots and ants. The pirates were partial to seafood in all conceivable variations.

Ch'ing not only possessed 600 war ships, but also many hundreds of supply ships equipped with galleys, whose business it was to keep the fleet well-fed. At the harbours and surrounding areas, they attended to the rounding up of foodstuffs, which were then prepared en route back to the fleet. On the high seas they peacefully devoted themselves to fishing, even as the crews of the warships practised their "trade." Not without reason were Ch'ing Yih Szaou's squadrons considered to be the best-organised of their kind. On the Chinese seas, much like in the rest of the world, pirates maintained a much higher standard of cooking than that of merchant and naval ships. The pirates, whose societies were less hierarchic than those of military and commercial navigation, were more intent on the physical well-being of their entire community, and provided for this as long as circumstances permitted.

Chinese culture, in general, attaches a much higher value to the preparation of good food than in the West. Indeed, much time and love is devoted to the making of a meal. An interesting comparison: while the pirates in the Caribbean prepare shark meat as minute-steaks (p. 189), the Chinese use it to make a soup that takes at least four hours to prepare.

Stewed Red-Boiled Shark Fins

Ingredients:

400 grams shark fins
100 grams dried, ground shrimp
10 large dried Dongu mushrooms
50 grams dried bamboo shoots
1 slice ginger root
2 tbsp. bacon fat
1 tsp. salt
2 tbsp. soy sauce
4 tbsp. Chinese white wine
3/4 litre chicken broth
Fish stock from red-boiled fins
1 tsp. sesame oil
1 tbsp. corn starch

Preparation

Clean the fins, place in lukewarm water. Soak ground shrimp and dried mushrooms for thirty minutes in 1/4 litre of warm water. Water can then be discarded. The dried bamboo should also be soaked until soft, then cut into thin strips.

Thoroughly clean and scale the shark fins, place in a litre of water. Simmer for one hour. Afterwards set the water aside.

Place fins in a fresh litre of water and bring to a boil. Reduce heat and simmer, covered, for an hour and a half. Afterwards strain fins.

In a separate pot, add chicken broth and bring to a boil. Add ginger and shrimp, simmering for thirty minutes. Remove from heat and strain the broth, discarding the shrimp and ginger. In a separate pot, heat the bacon fat, adding the bamboo shoots and mushrooms together with salt. Sauté for one minute, then add soy sauce, wine, broth, fish stock, and fins. Boil under low heat, stirring frequently, for twenty minutes. Remove from heat and slowly stir in the corn starch, in small increments. Sprinkle sesame oil on the soup.

Serve in a large bowl. The shark fins should remain on the surface.

*L*otus Feet and Henpecked Husbands

*C*hina is the land furthest from Europe on our journey, not just geographically, but also culturally.

How can we fathom a land that, in the twentieth century, placed a three-year-old child on the Royal Dragon's throne, before whom all were obliged to kneel? A land whose corrupt practise of overtaxation was not only legalised by officials, but termed the "Cultivation of Incorruptibility"? In what kind of language is the disfiguring disease smallpox called a "visit from the heavenly flowers," while a lieutenant receives the title "Mealtime of the Frog"?

The history and culture of the Chinese are so foreign to us as Westerners, that, both fascinated and disconcerted, we are only able to observe with curiosity. Indeed, we can only marvel at our distorted perceptions, restricted by a Western point of view.

Our standards limit us when we attempt, for example, to deliver an assessment concerning the social position of women in China. We are repeatedly confronted with contradictions. On the one hand there are references of oppression that find a particularly brutal expression in the maimed lotus feet. Conversely, we encounter countless stories of women who fought to maintain their individualism. We have established, for example, that since the notorious pirate king Koxinga in the seventeenth century, nearly every single one of the famous pirate captains was a woman.

The sources upon which we build our knowledge are Western sources, books written by Europeans. Thus, only the reproductions from Chinese silk paintings and book illustrations are truly authentic. Nevertheless, without explanations they cannot be fully comprehended.

For example, there is the picture in a book by Marina Warner.[1] In a room decorated with flowered draperies and large-patterned wallpaper, a man lies half naked, his blood flowing onto the floor. Beside him lies a woman, dressed as a man in wide-cut pants, a kimono, and heavy boots. Her cap has fallen from her head. Around her are standing men with sticks, looking on with triumphant expressions. A man has removed one of her boots and is holding her crippled foot in his hand.

Mysterious Occurrences in a Brothel in the Nineteenth Century, says the text written beside the picture. "A girl had murdered a customer and stolen his clothes, in order to disguise herself and flee. However, she was discovered by her pander, who first killed her, then removed her head from her corpse."

The lily feet or lotus feet, as the women's maimed appendages were called, were a contrivance of the upper class. Small feet were considered attractive, a guarantee that a woman was bound to the house. The binding of feet, which began at seven or eight years of age, handicapped a woman's ability to move freely. Some were unable to walk at all, and were either reliant upon others to carry them, or forced to "walk" on their knees. In China, "large-footed girl" was an insult. Starting in the nineteenth century, the women's movement fought against the lotus-foot custom. This, among other movements, is what finally freed the women from their foot-fetters.

To be born a female in China was no blessing; indeed it was believed to be the penalty for a previous life of sin. The birth of a girl was commonly termed an "unfortunate delivery"; in fact, many female new-borns were killed. According to Confucius, whose doctrine dictated the way of life in

China, a woman must adhere to the threefold "Rule of Obedience": she was subjugated as a daughter to her father, as a wife to her husband, and as a widow to her son. That she didn't always adhere to this rule in practice is verified not only by our information concerning women pirates, but also in stories such as that of the henpecked husbands, translated by Gudula Linck:

> One day, as all the henpecked husbands assembled in order to discuss how they could enforce their innate rights as men, some took the occasion to play a joke. In order to frighten the men, they told them that their wives had caught wind of the meeting, and were on their way to give them all a good thrashing. The men took to their heels—all except one, who remained seated, with no apparent sign of dread. Upon closer examination, however, it turned out that he had died of fear.[2]

This henpecked husband-movement is a contrivance—fantasies are known to reflect fears. We wish to indicate another movement here, that of a women's and lesbian movement that existed as early as the nineteenth century in southern China.

The silk spinners of the Canton River delta had consolidated themselves into a sisterhood, choosing to live communally. The women, who provided for themselves through their work in the silk industry, took an oath of fidelity for life, refusing to enter into marriage with men. If a family attempted to force a daughter who had "gone astray" in this manner to marry, her "sisters" helped to defend her. If a woman was nevertheless forced to marry, she refused the sexual advances of her spouse and returned to the sorority after the wedding. The rebellious women of the Canton River delta decided for themselves when they would enter into a love relationship. Many of them preferred women and entered into lesbian partnerships.[3]

However, before we drift off into a boundless topic, lets hold our course for the women pirates.

The English had come to realise that piracy was also proving to be a hindrance to their interests in the Chinese seas. The numerous raids made travel dangerous, and decimated the Chinese market's purchasing power. This, in turn, had a negative effect on the English trade balance, persuading the British to support the Emperor in his battle against the pirate nuisance. In 1834 a widespread international manhunt began, and a high price was fixed on each pirate head.

This gave many English traders the notion of earning a little on the side, so to speak, by capturing innocent Chinese and delivering them over to the authorities as pirates. British officers, on the other hand, supplemented their salaries by entering into business with the pirates themselves. They lay convoys with British flags at the pirates disposal, assuring them of protected raids and quick escapes.

Nevertheless, English traders could barely keep their heads above water. All of the British attempts at expanding their market in China were in vain. The Imperial government would not allow them to conduct "free" trade in the "Middle Kingdom." British traders were only permitted to negotiate before the walls of the city of Canton, and there only with the Emperor's agents. The Chinese were simply not very interested in buying British wool, luxury articles, or technical devices. They didn't need them. In 1839 the Emperor once again cracked down on the illegal trade of opium, and sent his commissioner Lin T'zê-hsü to Canton to put a stop to the smugglers.

The English response: "If you don't want to buy the superfluous things of our civilisation, then we'll just have to use force." According to this maxim of colonialism, the English began the Opium War. They bombarded the southern coast of China, penetrating the mouth of the Yang-Tze up to Nanking. The Emperor was forced to surrender, relinquish Hong Kong to England, and open up numerous cities to colonial trade. He was required to pay reparations for a war the British had started.

A second war broke out when Chinese officials inspected an English ship they believed was engaged in smuggling. This time the British marched together with the French to Beijing. On the way they pillaged and laid to waste the Imperial summer palace at Yüan-ming-yüan. The treasures they looted surpassed a pirate's wildest dreams:

> "[The] French encampment overflowed with silk and jewellery," observed an envious British soldier. "One French officer had a splendid pearl necklace, each pearl the size of a marble... others had paint-boxes inlaid with diamonds, timepieces, and vases inlaid with pearls."[4]

But the English also helped themselves to the treasures of the Chinese people, as we learn from the account of an English chaplain, Reverend M. Ghee:

> "What's this here, hardly likely that it's gold?" said S., as he struggled to raise the statue of an idol, almost a metre in height. "Gold, my most esteemed, do you really believe that gold in China is so abundant that such a remote temple as this would pos-

sess a deity of real gold, where anyone could walk off with it?' "But it is rather heavy" he said, "we can attempt to break it and, if it isn't gold, then we shall surely see." The deity fell with a dull thud as it impacted upon the marble floor, but there was no crack to be found. "I'm certain it is gold" said S. "Then take it home with you," I said, laughing.[5]

The war resulted in the Europeans obtaining even more rights to trade, property, and jurisdiction in China, along with permission for the opium trade and Christian missions. Subsequently, the Chinese people suffered growing poverty due to the financial distress of the state and its increasing dependency upon foreign powers. Piracy once again flourished.

In the Bias Bay

We now travel forward in time to the 1920s. It is evening aboard the *Solviken*. The Norwegian coastal ship rolls gently over the swells of the southern Chinese seas. The store rooms have been converted into dormitories packed with people. Women, men, and children are sitting on mats between bundles and sacks, some preparing something to eat, others doing their wash even as others sleep. A few first-class passengers stand on the front deck, watching the sunset.

Shortly thereafter the passengers gather in the dining hall for dinner. Suddenly an unusual noise resounds: three blows of a gong, promising trouble. On the command, some of the Chinese passengers stand up and draw pistols. "Put your hands up," orders one, who up until that moment had been a stewardess. The travellers let their silverware fall and raise their arms, knowing they are in the presence of pirates who mean business.

The operation is executed quickly and with the utmost discipline. All over the ship, from the engine room to the bridge, travellers, sailors, and other employees on board are revealed to be pirates. "Hold your course on the Bias Bay," they order the helmsman. "Nothing will happen to those of you who offer no resistance." They force Captain Jastoff to open his cabin. His hesitation proves fatal. He is shot, and the passengers are locked in their cabins after being relieved of all that they possess.

The ship glides along as if nothing has happened. The navigation lights and other illuminations have been turned off. In complete darkness, the steamer, like a ghost ship, heads towards the Bias Bay. The water in the bay is dead calm and smooth as glass, and surrounded by sand dunes, between which Chinese huts peek forth.

As soon as the pirates lower the anchor of the captured ship, the shore begins to stir. Numerous barques are untied and head towards their prey. The people in the boats greet the pirates, come on board, and take everything that isn't nailed to the floor: chronometers, graphometers, and other technical devices, furnishings and other household objects. The hostages are brought on land and held for ransom.

This scenario was typical of pirate raids in the first half of the twentieth century. They were elaborately planned operations that exhibited, in almost every regard, the structure of a modern commercial undertaking.

First a dummy company would be quietly set up, to facilitate raising the necessary capital. Then someone would be commissioned with the role of leadership. In most cases this was a woman. Her task consisted of finding suitable prey and recruiting the right people to carry out the operation. She was responsible for making the necessary inquiries as to whether the ship in question was inconspicuous, while at the same time worth the trouble in terms of money, goods, and prisoners on board. When she had found such a ship, the chief went on board with some of her fellow pirates and acquainted herself with the layout, the work routine, and other various details. Then the armed pirates smuggled themselves on board as passengers of every class and crew members of every station, and the operation ran its course.

Almost all of the names of such chiefs entered into the history of piracy are female. It is repeatedly stressed how beautiful these pirate captains were, whether referring to the dreaded Ki Ming or P'en Ch'ih Ch'iko, who in 1936 still commanded over a hundred bandits; or T'ang Ch'ên Ch'iao, who had proclaimed herself the mortal enemy of the West and bore the nickname "Golden Grace."

Huang P'ei-mei, leader of 50,000 people and seventy ships, plundered up until the 1950s. She had the nickname "Two Guns," for she was known to carry a gun in each hand as she jumped onto a ship, opening up a two-handed line of fire. For Huang P'ei-mei, who began her career in 1937, piracy played a role against the political backdrop. She was a Nationalist and fought first against Japan, then later against the communists. In the Second World War she worked together with the American secret service. In May of 1950 the wire agency United Press announced: "Huang P'ei-mei, the most famous pirate in China, has arrived in Formosa, not only to take charge of the defence of the island, which she considers unconquerable, but also to prepare a counter-offensive in order to enable the Nationalists to gain back the Chinese continent."

There were also women pirates who supported the Chinese Revolution, for example Honcho Lo. She had worked her way up to the rank of colonel in the Revolutionary General Staff, uniting her sixty-four junks with the fifty-ship fleet of the female pirate Wong. Before she disappeared in 1922, she bequeathed twelve junks from her fleet to Lai Sho Sz'en, another notorious lady corsair.

Lai Sho Sz'en

On land she appeared in a worldly guise, wearing garments of white silk and costly earrings, her hair twisted in a knot and fastened with a green mignonette needle at the nape of her neck.

As soon as Lai Sho Sz'en boarded her ship, she brushed her sandals aside with a brisk gesture. On board she preferred to remain barefoot, and wore a simple fighting uniform on raids. Lai Sho Sz'en had a small fleet in comparison with her predecessors. With her twelve junks, which she had inherited from the sea robber Honcho Lo, she raided smaller freights in the waters around her private island, and collected extortion money from the fishers. Nevertheless, she must have been immensely wealthy. She dreamed of buying a skyscraper in the United States for her eldest son, intending her younger son to become a pirate and her successor.

At any rate, Aleko E. Lilius, a journalist from Manila who was permitted to accompany the pirate for a while on her privateering expeditions, claimed that this was the case. After long negotiations, Lai Sho Sz'en had allowed him to ride on her ship in exchange for forty-three dollars per day. She gave him a pirate pass, in the form of a ring, ensuring that the pirates wouldn't lay a finger on the curious journalist.

Lilius, who had taken many pictures of Lai Sho Sz'en, was fascinated by her. "The entire time I had the feeling of living side by side with a mystery," he wrote of his sojourn with the pirates.

Lai Sho Sz'en was surrounded at all times by her two maid-servants. They delivered her orders to the men in the fleet, as the commander herself never spoke to men. The male crew members were forbidden to enter across the threshold of her cabin, a tiny room that was fashioned after a small temple. It sheltered the portrait of a sea goddess and the relics of her father. To this room she would withdraw, to burn incense and meditate for hours with her two servants.

Lai Scho San. Source: Ulrike Ottinger, *Madame X - eine absolute Herrscherin*, Frankfurt 1979.

Ancestor worship was and continues to be an important custom in China, based on the belief that the spirits of the deceased ancestors protect the still-living members of their family. They give blessings and expect offerings in return. Ancestors who are not honoured by their descendants are forced to wander, starving, and inevitably avenge themselves on the living who have forgotten them. For this reason, Chinese families pay close attention that women are not unfaithful to their men, since an illegitimately begotten son puts the patrilineal family clan in danger. He would honour the "false" ancestors, and thereby conjure up the wrath of the "legitimate" ones.

Ancestor worship could only be practised by male members of a family. Lai Sho Sz'en, by possessing a temple with the relics of her father, clearly felt herself to be above the constraining principles of Confucius.

Lai Sho Sz'en did not spare her hostages. If she did not receive any ransom after a second warning, the prisoners' fingers or ears would be cut off and sent to the obstinate relatives. If she still remained unpaid, the hostage would be killed without ceremony.

The last reported battle of Lai Sho Sz'en involved an assault against a Japanese torpedo squadron during the Chinese-Japanese War. The journalist Robert de la Croix described this one-sided combat:

> On the one side there were Japanese torpedo boats of the modern sort, *Shupukis*, travelling at thirty-four knots and each equipped with six cannons. On the other side were simple ships similar to those that could be found along the Chinese coast all during the last two hundred years: junks and dragon boats with strange sails. The bows rose high out of the water, the sterns were provided with openings through which the cannons

protruded. Some of them could barely remain afloat and others, a little newer, were remnants from the 1904 Russo-Japanese war. There were also German machine guns from 1914; and American revolvers alongside English rifles from 1812. There was even a still-older weapon found, a French piece that was dated to 1798. How did it get to Asia? The pirates themselves knew nothing about its origins. These pirate ships were a swimming museum.[6]

The journalist relates how the junks, filled with torpedo holes, sank to the bottom of the sea, and concludes his report:

The next day the news spread throughout the taverns and game halls of Macau. It was reputed to be a huge disaster. Not only did the entire fleet now lie on the ocean floor, but its captain had gone down with it. Her name, now uttered in the open: Lai Sho Sz'en.

Whether she actually perished in this battle is a matter of controversy. According to other sources the pirate, who tallied more than 7,000 raids in her career, was taken prisoner in 1939 by the International Coast Guard, put before the maritime court in Shanghai, and sentenced to life imprisonment.

Linda

A Present-Day Pirate

hat girl wouldn't like to have a mother who sails the oceans of the world, her children in tow? One who isn't afraid to navigate the dreaded inlets north of Manila, and accepts an invitation to supper from a pirate, who personally peels a banana for each of her children? The five daughters of the French-Tahitian sailor France Guillain had the pleasure of just such an experience when they accompanied their mother on a sailboat around the world. Her adventure is recorded in the book *Les femmes d'abord.*

En route from Hong Kong, she held a southerly course between Taiwan and China, until she reached the small, uncultivated inlets northwest of Luzon, in the Philippines. In China she had been warned that she should under no circumstances stay overnight in this region, and certainly not in one of the coves, because they were teeming with pirates. She had been told that sea robbers traverse the southern Chinese sea in their double pirogues, sinking everything they came across.

Nevertheless, when France arrived late one afternoon before the rugged coast of Luzon, she decided to cast anchor. She reasoned that attempting to navigate the countless reefs at night seemed more dangerous than the prospect of pirates, and steered the ship into a small protected cove. Upon discovering two pirogues on the beach, France was relieved to see that children were playing beside them. "A native family," she thought, hurrying to prepare her boat and go on land with her daughters.

The group on the beach consisted of about thirty people busily preparing their evening meal. Grandparents, parents, and children were sitting on the sand around two large pots. As the newcomers approached, a man stood up and greeted them in English, introducing himself and his wife Linda. The muscular woman, who spoke no English, laughed and motioned for France and her children to join them for the evening meal. Linda took the younger daughters, while France went with the oldest to look for wood together with the rest of the party.

Soon afterwards they were all seated around the fire, eating rice and fish with their fingers. Meanwhile it had become dark. The steep cliffs rose up out of the water and obstructed a view to the open sea. "A real hideout," thought France, remembering the horror stories the American sailors had told her about the Filipino pirates. They would never have dared to venture into this cove.

After the meal, the younger clan members brought out their ukuleles and commenced to play and sing. Linda opened the dance. France, whose mother was from Tahiti, felt at home in their company. "I have the impression of being in Polynesia. They dance the *Tamouré*, in which the words to the song are depicted with graceful gestures, the eyes following attentively. I sing in Tahitian and they accompany me, without any difficulty."[7] They celebrated well into the night.

The inlet later became quiet. The children had fallen asleep on the warm sand. Linda discussed an apparently serious matter with her husband, and France decided to gather up her children and retire to their boat. Before she set out, Linda's husband indicated to her that he had something important he wished to say. He urgently advised her to never again enter into a protected cove such as this one. Why, France wanted to know. On account of pirates? "That's us," answered the Filipino, laughing.

France stared in amazement as the pirate showed her the interior of the larger of the two pirogues: motors, radios, machine guns, and other weapons were piled inside. "The pirates know no pardon, they kill everyone, even children," he explained to the astonished France.

Piracy as a family undertaking apparently still exists today. Linda is both a pirate and a mother. During the day she raids ships, possibly operating a machine gun, and during the evening she cooks rice and fish for her children.

Naturally, France Guillain asked herself why she and her daughters were so cordially entertained by this pirate family. Possibly because she hadn't had the slightest fear upon entering the cove, or maybe simply due to the fact that the sea robbers had looted enough for the day. "I believe a satiated lion wouldn't have attacked me either," she concluded. Did she purchase an item of booty or two? France Guillain's lips remain sealed.

NOTES

1. Marina Warner, *Die Kaiserin auf dem Drachenturm* [The Empress in the Dragon Tower], Würzburg, 1974, p. 100.
2. Gudula Linck, *Frau und Familie in China* [Woman and Family in China], Munich, 1988, p. 47.
3. See Anna Gerstlacker and Margit Miosga, *China der Frauen* [Women's China], Munich, 1990, from p. 44ff.
4. Quoted in Warner, p. 74.
5. Ibid.
6. Quoted according to Anne de Tourville, *Femme de la mer*, Paris, 1958, p. 212.
7. France Guillain, *Les femmes d'abord*, Paris, 1986, p. 136.

ℳEDITERRANEAN SEA

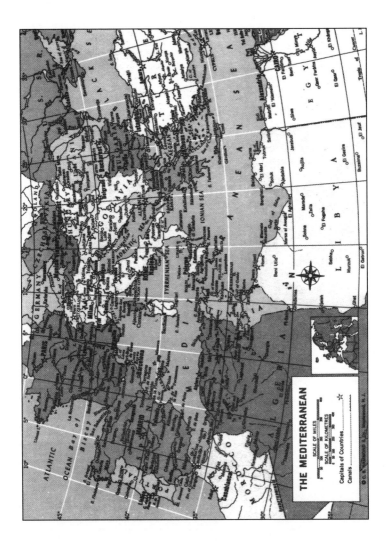

Introduction

From the East Asian seas we cross over the Indian Ocean to the Red Sea. This is where the first historically confirmed ship expedition took place: the journey of the Egyptian Pharaoh Queen Hatshepsut to the land of Punt, in the second millennium B.C. A relief in the columned halls of Hatshepsut's temple at Deir el Bahari, near Thebes, bears witness to the voyage. But was she on a peaceful voyage of discovery, a military campaign, or engaging in piracy? To this day the matter remains unresolved.

The Pharaoh was seeking a supply of incense for her priests and priestesses to burn in the temples. Before Hatshepsut, the Pharaohs were supplied with the pleasant-smelling resin by travellers returning from Punt. Incense was as valuable as the gold, silver, and gems brought to Egypt over the same routes (whether by sea or land can no longer be determined). Punt was the name for the area between the Amhara mountains, the Red Sea, and the Gulf of Aden.

Hatshepsut thought more in economic terms than her predecessors. She didn't just want the resin, but the tree from which it is tapped. She therefore equipped three ships and set off on her way.

The inscriptions in the temple describe the cargo carried in the returning ships.

> The ships were loaded with all the wonders of the country of Punt. With splendid aromatic timbers, great quantities of myrrh and resin, green myrrh trees; with ebony and pure ivory, and gold as yet unshaped from

65

the land of Amu; with eye make-up and baboons, apes and hunting dogs, and leopard furs; with people and their children.

The journey to Punt resulted in an economic boom for Egypt, accompanied by radical changes in society and values, so drastic that they can be compared to the transition from the Middle Ages to Modernity in European history.

Far to the north, in the Black Sea, there were other female seafarers in the prehistoric period: the Amazons. The traditional sources deny that the Amazons had knowledge of navigation or ship-building, but it seems significant that those who did settle built their settlements on coasts near sea routes.

Herodotus (Book IV) tells a curious story about a battle between Greeks and Amazons on the south-western coast of the Black Sea:

> In the war between the Greeks and the Amazons, the Greeks, after the victory at the river Thermodon, sailed off in three ships with as many Amazons on board as they had succeeded in taking alive....Once at sea, the women murdered their captors, but, as they had no knowledge of boats and were unable to handle either rudder or sail or oar, they soon found themselves, when the men were done for, at the mercy of wind and wave, and were blown to Cremni-the Cliffs-in Lake Maiotia [Crimea], a place within the territory of the free Scythians. Here they got ashore and made their way inland to an inhabited part of the country. The first thing they fell in with was a herd of horses grazing;

these they seized, and, mounting on their
backs, rode off in search of loot.

What does this really mean? Somehow the Amazons had
to be driven from the south-western coast diagonally over
the entire Black Sea to the northern coast. This defies all
logic and probability. The Amazons had to know about navigation, and water and wind conditions; otherwise they
would have never got there. Why has such an unlikely report
never been questioned? Apparently the troublesome women
would have been all the more terrifying had they not at least
been said to share the fear of men before water.

Following this little detour into the Black Sea, we now
head for the Mediterranean, searching for Elissa, the first
pirate in the history of sea travel.

Elissa

A Pirate Founds Carthage

Elissa is none other than the Dido set in verse by Vergil, Cato, Naevinus, Ovid, and others. According to their fantasies, she threw herself into the flames of a bonfire. They say she killed herself, mad with unrequited love for the Trojan Aeneas. Now Aeneas happened upon Carthage about seventy years after Elissa had founded the city. Accordingly, Elissa must have been about a hundred years old on the day she jumped into the bonfire out of lovesickness.

To kill oneself out of unrequited love or a murdered husband completely fits the Roman ideal of Woman. At the same time, this story served as a justification for the myth of the eternal Roman-Punic vendetta. But this is also a bit far-fetched, for the enmity between the two cities first arose in the year 265 B.C., during the struggle for dominance over Messina, causing the first Punic War. The founding of Carthage is dated to the ninth century B.C.

Another version holds that Elissa was burned together with her ship, set aflame by the African King Hiarbas, while attempting to escape him and his demands for marriage.

However Elissa may have died, whether of suicide, murder, or natural causes, will not be a subject for further consideration here. Let's just report about her life.

Elissa, the oldest daughter of the Tyrean King Mutto, derived from the clan of Ithoba'al. She was married to a priest named Sicharbas, whose office by no means precluded him from piracy. Elissa was a very active sea robber herself. She lead her own tours of plunder, but the couple threw their booty into a common pot. Piracy was not a dishonourable trade among the Phoenicians, for they were a sea people without resort to agriculture.

As the first born, Elissa had legitimate claim to the throne. But her brother Pygmalion intended to contest that. He tried to turn the friendly tribes neighbouring Phoenicia against Elissa. Wishing to gain control over the profitable piracy enterprise, Pygmalion killed his brother-in-law Sicharbas. But the murder was in vain. The couple's common property was already securely in Elissa's hands. She had dreamed of Sicharbas' murder in advance, but was unable to do anything about it as she was at sea. She therefore warned Sicharbas telepathically, and he brought their robbed sacks of gold and gems to a safe hide-out known only to the two of them.

Returning to land, Elissa found the treasure at the agreed-upon location, but also discovered that Sicharbas was dead, stretched out on a bier in the parental palace. She promptly summoned Jewish interpreters of dreams, and asked to have her dream explained in full detail. These women determined that Elissa could not have prevented Sicharbas's death, for she had unknowingly desired it herself. Her destiny was to strike out on her own. Their prophecy: her brother was determined to kill her and set up a tyranny in Tyros, the capital of Phoenicia.

Elissa was startled, not so much because of the threat of murder, but out of concern for the imminent fate of her country. In keeping with an old tradition, she had planned to introduce a double monarchy.

The dream interpreters shook their heads and declared the queen's plan to be a fallacy. The goddesses and gods, they said, expected Elissa to found a new Phoenician city at another location, for Tyros would soon face great catastrophes.

Elissa followed this instruction and promptly equipped ten ships. Her sister Anna and many priests, senators, and merchants joined her.

Elissa's voyage over the Mediterranean was nothing like Aeneas' confused odyssey. She had a concrete goal. Before she embarked, the African Goddess Tanit spoke to her through her priests, and told Elissa to found a city on a peninsula somewhere to the west. She would know the place was right when she found a horse's skull soon after landing. This is how Quart Hadashit, the "new city" northeast of present-day Tunis, came into being. It went into history as the city of Carthage.

Elissa's journey can also hardly be called an odyssey because at this time the Phoenicians knew much about the entire sea all the way out into the Atlantic proper. They had sailed around the Canary Islands, Madeira, the Azores, and the Scilly Islands. It is thus not surprising that the Phoenicians fleeing from the newly founded tyranny in Tyros were able to find their new city on the Libyan coast.

Nonetheless, Elissa's journey from the Phoenician to the Libyan coast took seven years. What she lived through during this time can be reconstructed through a few archaeological finds and numerous legends.

The first station was Cyprus. The standard history claims that Elissa robbed Cypriot virgins—sometimes said to be twenty-seven in all, sometimes ninety. This was apparently not a robbery, however, but a diplomatic act on the part of the Cypriots. They were intimidated by Pygmalion's intrigues, but feared an attack by Elissa. They were also terrified of inviting enmity from Tyros if they received Elissa peacefully. But they did not want to reject her outright, for they had already received intelligence about her plans to build a new State.

They therefore sent a diplomatic delegation out to the

Phoenician ships, obsequiously issuing floods of friendly
advice for Elissa's further journey. In the process of these
negotiations, the twenty-seven or ninety virgins also came
on board. These are symbolic figures: three times nine as the
exponential holy trinity and magic number; or ninety, a ref-
erence to the ninety clans of Carthage, each of whom claimed
to trace their ancestry back to one of the Cypriot virgins as
tribal mother. At this time it had not been long since the
demise of matrilineal family law. The Syrian Queen Zenobia,
who fought against the Romans around 270 B.C., still
proudly claimed her clan also derived from one of these
tribal mothers, and on many occasions wore Elissa's regalia.

From Cyprus, Elissa undertook the long crossing over to
Sabrata, a city near present-day Tripoli. There was certainly
some privateering on the way. Otherwise the provisions
could have never lasted long enough, especially since the
wandering State had been increased by a few extra citizens.

The Phoenician ships were galleys with sails. No effort of
the oars was required if winds were favourable; only when
the wind died down did the rowers have to put their back
into it. The sails would be cut when raiding, so that the wind
wouldn't hamper the rowers from ramming a booty ship.
There are no reports about how many ships Elissa raided
during her journey of 1,000 to 1,200 nautical miles. At any
rate her stocks were full by the time she debarked in Sabrata.

The people who lived there treated Elissa and her com-
panions to a very friendly welcome. Communication between
them was arduous, however. When Elissa asked the people of
Sabrata to take her to their queen or king, they at first did not
even understand the question. Their language had no words
for such concepts. The people of Sabrata had never conceived
of the idea that one person might rule over them.

The Sabratans invited the newcomers to a ceremony that
they called the "Night of Fleeting Things." The Sabratans

lived in a moon culture, counting time according to moon cycles. Their year had thirteen months with twenty-eight days and nights. There was one additional night, the "Night of Fleeting Things." This night was for changing any laws that had not proven good over the course of the past year, and decrying any losses or injustices that had come about as a result. Anything that had proven good and worthy of retention was praised and extolled.

The ceremony corresponded to the typical tradition of a death night in moon cultures within which a State is forming: the government must resign or be executed. Since there were no rulers in Sabrata, they had to be created just for this one night.

At low tide and waxing moon, an equal number of women and men would go to the coast. Clothed in simple white tunics without weapons or jewellery, they ran into the water, clapping their hands. Criers were chosen by lot. Their task was to proclaim the good and the bad events of the past year. Only men were allowed to do this, however, because women were prohibited from having a memory—an indication that the culture in Sabrata was by no means a female civilisation. "Having no memory" ultimately means being allowed no recognition of one's own history or identity.

Once the criers had ended their stories, the women started creating two gigantic statues out of algae and sand, each about twice the size of a person. Then the men came and decorated the statues with mouth, nose, ears, and eyes. The men and women then formed a circle together around the two monsters, reciting a litany of curses and praises, and demanding new laws. Afterwards any conflicts with neighbouring peoples were reported upon. Other questions, such as whether to build a new temple, were discussed.

As the sun rose once again over the beach and the dunes, the tide came back in. For the duration of one tide cycle,

Sabrata had been governed by a pair of sand and algae statues. For one night these served as rulers, legislators, judges,
scapegoats, and targets for fury. The procedure on this night
was by no means spontaneous, but a fixed and thorough ritual that provided a framework for changes in the law and
regulation of disputes.

The sun announced the so-called "Day of Death." Wailing
and weeping, the Sabratans dug up the remains of their two
rulers of algae and sand. The criers announced that the king
and queen had been buried until the next year. The people
had received new laws, but without the burden of having a
monarch. Perhaps this play encouraged Elissa to think up an
alternative form of government for her own State.

The Sabratans practised agriculture. They offered to teach
the cultivation of crops and care of livestock to Elissa and
her crew—if the Phoenicians would reveal the secrets of
ship-building and sea routes in exchange. The Phoenician
queen was not ready to teach navigation to her hosts, or
betray the routes between Tyros and Utica, or even the safest
corridor to Hadrumentum. This knowledge was, after all, the
basis of her living. Sea travel was her inheritance, piracy her
profession. As the daughter of seafarers, she thanked her
existence to these sciences, viewing them as a secret belonging to her people, indeed the very foundation of Phoenician
power and prosperity. But Elissa did promise to teach ship-
building, how to cut oars and make the pitch that protected
hull and rudder from the water.

The education of the Phoenicians in matters of agriculture and livestock proved to be a flop. The sea people ten-
derly patted the bulls and asked how much milk could be
had from them. They romped playfully about the olive and
fig trees, and constantly fell and injured themselves doing
field work. Their clumsiness inspired great pity among the
Sabratans, much as an albatross that wanders onto the

bridge does among sailors. It seemed impossible for a sea people, whose elements are water and wind, to get accustomed to the earth.

At this point the Sabratans tried theory. They wrote down all the uses and advantages of agriculture, and entitled their work the "Theory of Happiness." The Phoenicians divided the papyrus sheets among one another and read from them as from a work of poetry. About making wine they already knew plenty from their own country. They were surprised to learn that the vines had to be pruned, however. But to them the rest of the methods of cultivation and Sabratan tips on the medicinal uses of plants were more an object of humour than anything else. Phoenician medicinal arts made use of octopus ink, cod-liver oil, whale fat, sea salt, and dried algae. Now here were the Sabratans, recommending onions, garlic, olive oil, grains, raisins, sour milk, thistles, figs, caraway seed-oil, mud baths, yew bark, and pepper. The sea travellers were unable to take this seriously. They amused themselves over the work's naiveté and peasant language.

It was just as difficult to get the landbound Sabratans oriented on sea. Elissa had finally decided to at least teach the Sabratans about the fundamentals of navigation. She had become quite fond of them, and was certain that she would never need fear cunning or betrayal on their part. She took a few Sabratans along on her ship, intending to teach them the rules of coastal sailing. But there soon arose among the land people such a fear of the sea and seasickness that it became impossible to even cast off.

After the sorrowful failure of this attempt of the sea and land people to grow closer together, they bid each other farewell—still in mutual incomprehension, but with heartfelt feeling and respect for one another.

The Sabratans had the following words for Elissa upon her departure: "It is good that land and sea interpenetrate and do not mix. See the tides: are they not like links connecting us? Is it not from the tides that our gods and our rulers come? We should seek no dispute. It is good that land and sea embrace without strangling each other."[1]

Elissa gathered the sheets of the "Theory of Happiness," had them bound in leather, and placed the work with her prayer books. Borne by a favourable wind, Elissa and her following set out from the green coasts of the farmers' country and sailed west, to Hadrumentum.

The harbour of Hadrumentum was barren compared to the rich meadows and fields of Sabrata. Sparse and bleak, surrounded by raw walls, the place looked like a provisional city indeed. The houses were without ornamentation, the people reserved and fearful. Elissa tried to enter into talks with them, but their great mistrust made any communication nearly impossible. This was unjustified, for Elissa had no evil intentions. Land plunder, routine in other sea robber cultures, was simply not part of Phoenician tradition. The Phoenicians knew little of either the arms or the strategies for land combat. They did not consider anything of the sort necessary, for they believed they were the favourites of the gods and needed to fear no enemy. The Phoenicians had no need to haggle over food, either; along the Libyan coast they had encountered plenty of merchant ships. That booty had been more than enough for their needs.

What interested Elissa about the city of Hadrumentum was learning about their customs, traditions, and form of government. She wanted to gather experiences and impressions that might be useful in founding her new city. The well-fortified city walls, she soon discovered, had been built as protection against people like her: seafaring peoples, pirates. The architecture of the city allowed no direct view of the sea; its thick fortifications had no openings. The people of Hadrumentum believed that all misfortune came from the ocean, from the sea's ships, storms, and floods. All blessings came from olive groves and fruit gardens. This is why the city was inaccessible from sea, and open to the land.

The residents of Hadrumentum did not exactly roll out the welcome wagon for Elissa. They threw stones and dirt at the strangers. To them, Elissa was not the respectable regent of a wandering State, but a dangerous queen of the sea, wild and fork-tongued like the sea monsters.

Elissa found the idea of needing protection against the sea nothing less than absurd. "Was the sea not the cradle of the world?" she asked, full of wonder. "And is protection necessary against one's own cradle? The sea is in us, it is like us: passionate and secretive, solemn and turbulent, far from heaven and yet one with it."[2]

At first Elissa was unable to find anything in Hadrumentum that might be of use to her in founding a State. The ugliness of this city, as manifest in the architecture as in the hostile attitude of the population, was as fascinating to her as had been the beauty of Sabratas, with its friendly constructions and open people.

Great anger broke out on the Phoenician ships over the unfriendly behaviour of the people of Hadrumentum. The men of Elissa's crew wanted to attack the city, even if this did contradict the Phoenicians' usual customs. Elissa was unable to calm them down, so she put them off. She promised the men that as soon as she had founded the city of Quart Hadashit, she would raise an infantry and wage war on Hadrumentum. The Phoenician men were thrilled, rummaged about until they found an old war song that they had heard from Assyrian soldiers, and started rehearsing it. The priests vaulted into unctuous speeches about the necessity of punishing ugliness.

The women on board were disgusted with the nonsensical war euphoria. They wanted to discuss things, and showed understanding for the fear the Hadrumentumians felt before the sea and sea travellers. The women advocated leaving the place as quickly as possible and not bothering its residents any further. Elissa shared this opinion. She hoped that the war euphoria against Hadrumentum would pass away during the building of the new city.

But the city of Hadrumentum had taught her one important lesson: a settled people with enemies cannot survive without providing for defence. It could not take to flight, like a sea people, but had to prepare to fight. A high price indeed for being settled. Elissa knew that Phoenicia had enemies. "There are many people who hate the Phoenicians," she thought. "But on the high sea you don't notice that."

Hadrumentum was Elissa's last station before the place where she wanted to found her new State. Once again at sea, a light south wind thrust Elissa's ships towards Utica, as though guided by the hand of Tanit herself. They rounded a tongue of land with a hill covered in aromatic orange, lemon, and fig trees. Beyond that appeared a rocky coast that recalled the cliffs of Phoenicia. The air was damp and warm, but a cool northwest wind made it tolerable. Elissa had arrived at her goal. Here was the place where Quart Hadashit would be built.

Elissa disembarked and explored the area. She was happy about the rich wild growth of pine, oak, and fruit trees, hibiscus and broom. The queen had the oarsmen dig for the horse skull that had to be here, according to the prophecy. But they found only a mouldering cow skull. Elissa was confused. She studied the map again and convinced herself that this had to be the place. Then the virgins brought her the horse skull after all. In the meantime the priests had calculated that Elissa's brother Pygmalion had been in power for exactly seven years to the day. Elissa no longer doubted that this was the right place. But she was disturbed. Why had it been so difficult to find the goddess's sign? The cow skull seemed to indicate coming difficulties.

The land was apparently uninhabited. Even after weeks, the newcomers saw no other people at all. But when Elissa wandered inland she discovered that the hinterlands were inhabited. She saw palms and olive trees among fields of grain and millet stretching over the landscape. It seemed that this was yet another place where the local residents did not feel much connection to the sea.

It turned out that the people who lived here were lead by a chief named Hiarbas. He declared his readiness to negotiate with Elissa. She wanted to buy the uninhabited coast and build her new city there. Elissa had seen enough of the fear the Africans felt before the sea that she was not surprised when the chief refused to come out to the coast with her. She climbed an inland hill together with Hiarbas instead. During the discussion, she learned another reason for the tribe's fear of the coast. Hiarbas related that the land and coast that she wanted to buy had once been inhabited, but the residents were robbed by seafarers. Ever since then, the coast was considered accursed, and no one dared to go there anymore.

Elissa showed her treasures to the chief, offering a substantial sum for the land. Hiarbas took up her offer, but instead of land he gave her a calf's fur. With this gesture he was saying: this is your land, and it is next to mine. He wanted Elissa as his wife. Elissa did not enter into this deal. She interpreted the chief's gesture in her own way. She took the fur, had it cut into razor-thin strips, and used them to outline an area that was large enough to build the fortress of Carthage. The fortress was called the Byrsa, meaning "calf's fur."

Carthage became a republic, with two suffetis (consuls), a council of three hundred, and a court of law. The State, with its division of power, was organised much like the later Rome, and possibly even served as the model for the

Romans. The City-State had armed forces of 240,000 soldiers, 4,000 horses, and 300 elephants.

There is no evidence surviving of Elissa's life after that. An African coin from the time, portraying her with the inscription "Dido" ("she who would not give way"), commemorates the pirate and city founder. In legends dating from later periods Elissa appears again in an amalgamation with the goddess Tanit. But maybe after founding Carthage she just sailed away again in her pirate ship.

We too are again on board, on a course for the Aegean Sea. Sailing by Malta, we swing around the Peloponnesian coast and past all the islands, reaching the Carian coast. We approach the islands Kos and Nisyros, which belonged to the area ruled by Artemisia, the Queen of Halicarnassus. We are in the decade of the seventies, in the fifth century B.C.

Artemisia

Piracy at the Time of the Persian Wars

On the rocky promontory of a steep coast, a woman of about fifty sits in the afternoon sun, weaving a wicker basket. Now and then she holds her breath and squints into the golden light, which is turning the softly rolling clouds to gold. A mischievous and knowing smile lights up her striking face, features tanned by salt and sun. A small boy sits at her feet. He has dug out a bay in the sand and plays with two self-made *triremes* carved from wood. These toys are models of the long, sickle-shaped ships with oars and sails, each with a metal battering ram swung over one side, that for over fifty years have been built for war.

The boy plays sea battle. "Grandmother," he suddenly calls, "tell me again how you commanded in the battle of Salamis." Artemisia, the Queen of Halicarnassus, Kos, and Nisyros, looks up from her wicker basket. It's barely been twenty years since that time. As a wise and energetic regent, she served as an admiral-queen in the Persian fleet. She had been forced to take part in the Persian campaigns because her country had been subdued by the Persians long before. Great King Xerxes, a megalomaniacal tyrant, had trusted her blindly, for he had considered her a loyal ally. Artemisia had detested Persian imperialism, but had been diplomatic enough to hide her opinions. Any open expression of them would have meant a certain death for her. She had instead decided to subvert the rule of the power-obsessed king with her cunning.

Artemisia was not only a queen, she was a pirate. She commanded the most famous sea robber fleet in the Mediterranean, and was known as a brilliant strategist and a courageous warrior.

Piracy was a respectable trade in ancient Greece. Sea robbery was viewed as a craft, pirates as perfectly upright people. This is confirmed not only by Homer, but by the "sea rights" of Mycenean times and an Attic "association law" that protected the rights of pirates, alongside other associations, in the making of cooperative contracts. The pirates on the Carian coast, for example, had made an agreement to dedicate one-tenth of their revenues to Hera, who was still Goddess of the Winds. Even if Zeus was claiming to have transferred the winds to Aeolus' jurisdiction, the pirates continued to pray to Hera for good winds, and got by splendidly.

Great King Xerxes ruled over an empire stretching from the Indus in the east to Egypt in the south, the Caucasus and the Aral Sea in the north, and Asia Minor, Thrace and Macedonia in the west. As the "king of kings" he used brutality and violence to hold all of these countries under his rule, considering it his god-given right. But the Greeks, with their love of freedom and resistance to his supposedly divine ordainment, were causing him plenty of headaches.

Xerxes had been able to subdue the revolt of the Ionian Greeks under his rule in Asia Minor in 490 B.C., but proved unable to restrain their "blasphemous behaviour" against Persian ships (which is how he referred to Greek piracy). Just around the corner, on the Carian coast, Artemisia was also commanding a very active pirate fleet. But the king of kings would have never believed that Artemisia was raiding his ships. Those who knew better kept it to themselves, fearing crucifixion for slander if they so much as piped up. Technically, the Lycian and Carian pirate ships under Artemisia's command belonged to Xerxes' royal fleet. But as always whole squadrons of them went back and forth across the Mediterranean, continuing their honoured tradition of masterful piracy. Artemisia took measures to assure that these skills would not decay, and fell upon plenty of ships belonging to the king's allies.

Xerxes ached to conquer Greece, but there were two large obstacles in his way: the Straits of the Hellespont, which divide Asia from Europe, and the peninsula of Mount Athos, on whose cliffs Persian ships were regularly dashed to pieces. The megalomaniacal Xerxes thought these were challenges from the gods. He believed he could measure well against them, however. He therefore did everything in his power to overcome these natural obstacles by force. The Persian king decided to build a bridge of ships over the Hellespont. And he wanted to bore through Athos, so that his fleet could sail through a canal and elude the treacherous storms that struck when rounding the mountain.

Mount Athos is a high and famous mountain running out into the sea like a giant stone ship. Xerxes approached it with his forces and had a letter read out loud to the holy mountain. "Divine Athos," the letter went, "stretching your summit into the clouds, desist in challenging me, Xerxes, Ruler of the Earth! ... One time you destroyed a Persian fleet, therefore I shall now pierce you through. Bear your punishment patiently, for if you don't, I will have you carried away and scattered as ashes into the sea!"[3] Just to make sure, Xerxes had the letter chiselled into the mountain, presumably so that Athos could not later claim to have not received it.

Many slaves were now brought in from the conquered territories. Driven by the lash of the whip, they had to split Mount Athos. The work was murderous, many lives were lost. At the same time other subjects of the king were building a bridge of ships over the Hellespont. The straits were narrowest between Abydos and Sestos. They anchored ships across the entire width of the straits, binding them to each other with hawsers.

Just as the bridge of ships was reaching completion, with only a piece in the middle missing, a powerful storm broke out. It tore the flaxen ropes and smashed the ships up against the cliffs, until they sank into a raging sea.

Xerxes would not take this sitting down. He decided to punish the sea.

As with Mount Athos, Xerxes sent a herald and a squad of executioners to the beach of Abydos. The king's verdict was delivered: "You salt and bitter water, your master lays this punishment upon you for injuring him, who never injured you. But Xerxes the King will cross you, with or without your permission. No man sacrifices to you, and you deserve the neglect by your acid and muddy waters."[4] The executioners delivered three hundred lashes with iron chains, then branded the water with glowing irons. The soldiers and engineers forced to witness the water's punishment broke out in laughter. That cost them their lives, for Xerxes had no sense of humour. He had them beheaded. New engineers were quickly spirited in to finish the bridge. Xerxes also wished he could punish the wind, but it evaded apprehension.

Xerxes's acts are a vivid example of the fateful destructive rage and senseless hubris of patriarchal heroes, and of the relationship between war and the destruction of nature. After Mount Athos had been split and the new bridge was built, Xerxes was able to invade Greece with a huge army.

There followed the bloodthirsty slaughter at the pass of Thermopylae, which has gone down in history as an example of war's utter senselessness. Only through Ephialtes' betrayal of the Greeks were the Persians finally able to roll over nearly the whole of the country.

The Persians had far less luck at Cape Artemision, where they had 1,230 triremes to the Greeks' 288. But the Persians

could not manoeuvre their large and heavy ships with anything approaching the skill of the Greeks with their smaller
fleet of sleeker ships.

Artemisia's triremes from Halicarnassus, Kos, and Nisyros
were also very sleek and fast. These did not fight against the
Greeks, however, plundering the Persian supply ships instead.
Well-versed in their profession, Artemisia's pirates used fast
oar-strokes to zigzag between the Persian ships, which were
blocking each other and unable to approach the enemy. No
wonder that the Persian fleet was forced to retreat to Salamis.
Nonetheless Xerxes believed Artemisia, who had commanded during the battle, was a heroine. Admittedly he
received no reports about the plunder during the battle.

Artemisia was a woman who was neither intimidated nor
seduced by Xerxes's power. As a queen of Asia Minor, she felt
a self-evident solidarity with the other Greek tribes under
Persian control, and through her behaviour encouraged
them to resist complete subjugation. But the most important
thing was always her own freedom.

In 480 B.C., Greece had largely been conquered by the
Persians, but the Greeks still refused to surrender. The decisive battle came at Salamis.

The Athenian Themistocles sent Xerxes a message that
the Greeks had recognised their own powerlessness, and
intended to take flight. All of the Greek warships were set to
sail. The powerful Persian fleet needed only enter the straits
of Salamis to make easy game of the few Greek ships.
Themistocles' betrayal was a ruse, but Xerxes believed the
advice, recalling his good experiences with Ephialtes' betrayal.
The admiralty of the Persian fleet also considered the matter
credible.

Themistocles then spoke to the council of war, and
Artemisia saw through the plan. An exchange of smiles
between her and Themistocles would have sufficed to confirm

their common interest in halting Persian imperialism. But Artemisia did not look at Themistocles, for she thought his proposal was strategic nonsense for her. Entering the narrow straits, where the Greek ships could quickly sally forth from small bays, attack, and withdraw unharmed, would mean certain defeat for the Persian fleet. On open sea, her own ships could take flight, but in the straits they would also be trapped. By no means did Artemisia want to fight, and not for the Greeks either—whose victory under such conditions was at any rate certain. She was too concerned for the lives of her pirates to expose them to a senseless slaughter.

So Artemisia spoke up in council. "Master, my past services give me the right to advise you now upon the course which I believe to be most to your advantage. It is this: spare your ships and do not fight at sea...Have you not taken Athens, the main objective of the war? Is not the rest of Greece in your power?...If...you now rush into a naval action, my fear is that the defeat of your fleet may involve the army too."[5] The subsequent course of the war proved how right her assessment was.

Herodotus continues:

> Artemisia's friends were dismayed when they heard this speech, and thought that Xerxes would punish her for trying to dissuade him from battle; but others who were jealous of her standing among the most influential persons in the forces were delighted at the prospect of her ruin. However, when the several answers to his question were reported to the king, he was highly pleased by Artemisia's; he had always considered her an admirable person, but now he esteemed her more than ever. Nevertheless

his orders were that the advice of the majority should be followed, for he believed that
in the battles off Euboia [Cape Artemision]
his men had shirked their duty because he
was not himself present—whereas this time
he had made arrangements to watch the
fight with his own eyes.[6]

That very night the Persian fleet advanced to block the
straits of Salamis. Artemisia stood at the stern of her flagship, the *Lykos*, and beseeched Hera for a favourable wind, so
that her flight would be eased and she could return with her
pirates to Halicarnassus unharmed. She instructed her people that they should, once the command to attack was given,
run screaming and crying over the decks and shoot arrows
wildly into the air. No Greek was to be killed or injured.

As the sun rose over Salamis, the battle began. It went
exactly as Artemisia had predicted. In the narrow straits the
Persian fleet blocked itself through its mass. With fast oar
strokes, the Greek ships shot out into the middle of the
nearly immobilised fleet, entered and sank ships or set them
aflame, and then sped back out of range with three, four
strokes.

Artemisia's fleet was at first placed in the middle of the
fray. Then, however, she received orders to bring her fleet in
behind the Ionians, in order to test their loyalty in civil war.
This was just fine by her, for it improved her chances for
flight. Once the fighting in the strait had deteriorated into
complete confusion, she ordered her ships to leave the battle.
The Ionians followed her example. But the ship of the vassal
king Damasithymos blocked her way. With a crash the snout
of the *Lykos* bore into the uncut timber of the Persian
trireme, sinking the ship. Now Artemisia gave an explicit
order to sink all ships blocking her fleet's way to freedom.

The bronze beaks of her ships sank Persians and their allies. The ships from Halicarnassus, Kos, and Nisyros broke through the Persian barrier and sailed into the open sea, followed by the Ionians.

Xerxes had ordered a throne with silver feet set up for him on the mount of Aegalos on the western coast of Pireus. Surrounded by in-laws, nephews, and his closest advisers, he observed the battle. First he directed his attentions at the large Phoenician fleet's desperate manoeuvres, but couldn't figure out what was going on. Much clearer to him was the vigorous sinking of ships pursued by Artemisia. He announced that he recognised the *Lykos*, her flagship, but not the ship it had just sunk. His company also failed to recognise what was really happening, and therefore answered cautiously that Artemisia had sunk an Athenian ship. The king of kings was overjoyed.

By evening the sea battle was over, the Persian fleet defeated. Xerxes retreated with his throne, leaving the fleet behind.

The Athenians had set a high bounty on Artemisia's head, for they thought she was fighting against them. They considered it an exceptional crime that Artemisia, a woman, was fighting against a city dedicated to a goddess. Quite apart from the fact that Artemisia did not actually fight against Athens, the latter accusation was sheer mockery. Athena at the time of the Persian Wars bore no relation to the original, wise old Goddess. She had long been debased to a being birthed from a man's head. The goddesses had all been deposed or coopted by the patriarchy, just as the women of Greece had become slaves of the men.

The bounty was about as irrelevant to Artemisia as the fate of the Persians. As a woman she could not really identify with either people. Her goal in battle was flight, and so she had issued the order: sink everything in our way.

After the battle, Xerxes summoned all of his surviving commanders. The Phoenician admiralty came to justify themselves. Xerxes ordered "their heads to be cut off, to stop them from casting cowardly aspersions upon their betters."[7] He let Artemisia come forward, for he did not know that Damasithymos and many others among his forces had been killed by her hand. Artemisia had in fact risen even higher in his esteem, and he now asked her personally for advice. "My men have turned into women, my women into men," he called to the other commanders.[8] He placed two of his sons in Artemisia's charge, so that she might educate them into true heroes. He sent his favourite eunuchs along, for it was usual that boys were looked after by eunuchs. Artemisia was happy to accept this mission. She was very well aware of how quickly she too might fall into the king of king's disfavour, and in that case it would be good to have the two princes under her roof as possible hostages. This eventuality never came up, however. The clever queen was able to spend many more years engaged in piracy. She was also never again forced to participate in a Persian sea campaign, for Xerxes was murdered soon after these events, and the subsequent tyrants had lost any taste they might have had for sea combat.

Artemisia has put her basket aside, for the sky is getting dark. The queen stands, jumps nimbly off the rock, and bends over the child and his toys. "Let the sail drop before the attack, lest the rowers be hampered when ramming. It often takes several blows to capsize a ship. That requires three strokes of the oar back, then three again forward. You can't have wind in the sail when doing this. That could cut your momentum. In a sea battle the trireme becomes a rowboat. But now it's time to go home. Come, Herodotus!" And Artemisia disappears between the cliffs with her grandson.

We, however, shall now disappear from the Aegean, and take course for the Adriatic in the third century B.C.

Teuta

An Illyrian Queen in the Sea Robber Wars

With an arrogant smile Teuta greets the two Roman emissaries. Coruncanio the Elder and Coruncanio the Younger have been sent by the Roman Senate to the court of the Illyrian Queen, to lodge complaint that Roman merchants on their way to or from Greece are constantly being raided by Illyrian pirate ships. The two brothers courteously request that the queen forbid these evil practices to her subjects in the future. Teuta replies that she is ready to order her own fleet to stop raiding Roman ships immediately. But she has no authority to issue prohibitions to private parties, for sea robbery is an Illyrian right.

This outrages Coruncanio the Younger. "Among the Romans, o Teuta," he cries out, "it is a commendable custom to have those who wrong others be prosecuted by the State, and to place the injured parties under its protection. We will therefore, so god wills, quickly and emphatically force you to improve the laws governing the rights of monarchs against the Illyrian people."[9]

The young Roman has clearly struck the wrong tone. His words so enrage Teuta that she has him murdered. She takes the rest of the Roman delegation hostage.

This is how the scene must have looked, at the court of the Illyrian Queen Teuta in the year 230 B.C., if we want to believe the story as told by the Greek historian Polybios. The image of a moody, terrible and unpredictable Teuta corresponds to the chauvinist image in the Roman propaganda against the monarch, who was blocking Roman imperial expansion.

Teuta's country, Illyria, was on the Dalmatian coast of the Adriatic Sea, just across from Italy. Illyria was the area inhabited by Balkan tribes, reaching from the Adriatic to the Morava River, and from Epirus to the middle Danube. It was by no means a kingdom in the proper sense. Teuta, like the men who sat on the throne before and after her, actually had nothing to govern, for Illyria had neither fixed borders nor uniform laws. Each of the tribes was largely autonomous. As a woman on a king's throne, Teuta was exceptional for her time. The royal succession was male. Teuta had taken over the regency for her stepson Pinnes after her husband succumbed to pneumonia following a banquet.

Teuta, whose dreadfulness is a matter of legend, was a pirate queen. Piracy was a free commercial enterprise recognised in Illyrian law. The inhabitants of Illyria were dependent upon sea robbery. The sparse agricultural yield on the Dalmatian coast was inadequate for their needs. But there were the rich Roman ships, passing just under their noses, loaded with grain and fish on their way to Greece, or carrying Greek slaves on the return trip.

Teuta engaged in plenty of raiding herself. The rob-happy queen had equipped a splendid fleet for this purpose. Recently they had sailed along the Dalmatian coast and into the Ionian Sea, plundering coastal cities of the Peloponnese. On the return journey, they carried out a spectacular attack on the city of Phoinike in Epirus, which would today be located in Albania across from the Greek island of Corfu. Teuta took the city and made herself its queen for a short time. Phoinike was considered the richest city in the region, and Teuta was not shy about plunder.

Constant uprisings against her and her people nonetheless

prompted her to surrender the city of Phoinike for a sum of money. She kept the plunder, too, but released all prisoners and withdrew with her troops. The tours of plunder in Epirus were by no means over, however. Teuta did not restrict herself to coastal cities, but also raided inland localities until the Epirans felt forced to enter into a formal alliance with her, and cede a strip of land as the prize of her victory. During these military actions, she and other Illyrians continued raiding Roman merchant ships.

The Romans soon recognised that this was no longer the sporadic plunder of ships and towns, an old tradition among Illyrian tribes. What Teuta was pursuing was not just piracy, but politics: expansionary politics. The Romans feared that with her new allies in Epirus, the pirate queen would soon gain control over an important sea-merchant route: the Channel of Otranto.

This was why the Roman emissaries were sent to Illyria. Teuta's refusal to compromise with the delegation stems not from the moody whim of a powerful woman, as historians claim, but from the limited power of the throne to control the tribal chiefs, who would have never accepted a ban on private piracy.

The murder of Coruncanio, possibly a fantasy of Roman propaganda, was a welcome justification for a military expedition to Illyria. "So great was the outrage at the woman's wantonness when the news reached Rome that war preparations broke out immediately, legions were mustered, and a fleet was assembled," Polybios reports.[10] The Romans had their pretext for a "just" war against the inconvenient Teuta.

Until then her tours of plunder had been left undisturbed, although reports about her merciless attacks were piling up at the Senate. The Romans had good reason to avoid a war with Illyria, for this would mean war at sea. Sea combat was anathema to Romans, and ship-building was not their forte. They built their ships out of newly-cut timber, so that they were always heavier and slower than their enemies. Someone from Carthage once described Roman navigation skills as follows: "Their steersmen act like blind men and fools. Where there are cliffs, they see harbours, and in every harbour they find cliffs. They do not know how to read either the stars or the sky, and they think the distant growling of an approaching storm is the mooing of a herd of cows being lead to their ship."

That the Romans were lousy sailors in later times as well is confirmed in the Bible. After all, the Apostle Paul's many shipwrecks could not have all been matters of divine providence.

Roman sailors and officers also had little idea of sea combat or techniques of entering ships. In the year 230 B.C., the retractable entering bridge—a practical device that was later hailed as an example of Roman ship-builders' inventiveness—was still in its infancy. The water-shy Romans did not yet have enough practise in its use.

Teuta reacted to the Roman declaration of war by offering to return the hostages. She refused to extradite the murderer of Coruncanio the Younger, however, and otherwise she kept robbing, with no intention of changing Illyrian law to favour Roman merchants.

But she had made so many enemies through her plunder along the Greek coast that the Romans could reckon with Greek support. Various Greek tribes allied with the Romans and recognised Roman rule. This made it possible for the Romans to attack Illyria by land. Arriving by ship, the Roman legions were combined with Greek armies. They defeated a few tribes allied with Teuta, forcing a "protectorate" on them and calling it "pacification." Other tribes prevailed against the Romans and remained allied with Teuta. The year 228 B.C. witnessed a rough struggle for Illyrian autonomy against Roman dominance.

Teuta

Teuta was finally able to hold the Dalmatian coast and her original country as an independent kingdom. In the peace treaty the Romans insisted on a clause prohibiting more than two Illyrian ships at a time from sailing into the Ionian Sea toward Greek coasts.

Whether Teuta held to that is unknown, for the sources say nothing more about her life.

From the Galley:

Grilled Moray

Preservation of food played an important role in ship travel. The salting of meat or use of a salt solution was already known from prehistoric times, and also practised on pirate ships. In ancient times fresh or cooked meat and fruit were preserved in honey. Fried fish was preserved by pouring hot honey on it. Pork or beef rinds would keep especially long when smeared with mustard, vinegar, salt, and honey. Vegetables were sealed in vessels insulated with pitch, and stored in dark and dry spaces.

"Liquamen" or "garum" sauce became famous. The Romans made this from fish leftovers. When the sauce began to stink, it would be reprocessed by shaking it within a vessel smoked in laurels and cypress wood, then salted again and thickened with honey.

Grilled Moray:

Skin the morays (eels). Set the innards aside for liquamen. Roll the morays in salt, pepper, and lemon juice, and brush them with olive oil.

Unfortunately the old sources do not specify grilling time, but we do know that moray must be grilled for at least 25 minutes to become edible.

For the sauce: fry onions in a pan, extinguish with mead. Add damson plums, pepper, lovage (a type of parsley), vinegar, and liquamen. Boil until the sauce thickens.

Grilled Moray

Cooked Moray:

Boil the skinned moray in salted water.

The sauce is prepared from the stock. Thicken with flour and spice with pepper, lovage, wild caraway seeds, celery seeds, coriander, dried peppermint, pine kernels, rue, honey, vinegar, wine, liquamen, and oil.

Fish Fricassee:

500 grams cubed fish (remove bones)
300 grams jellyfish
1/4 litre white wine
1/2 litre meat stock
3 leek stalks
0.1 litre olive oil

Add Liquamen, salt, coriander, pepper, lovage, oregano if desired, and flour for thickening.

After boiling the fish, sauté in a pot with the washed jelly fish and olive oil. Chop the leeks and coriander and add them to the sauté. When everything is tender, pour the white wine over the fricassee and add spices.

Sida Al Hurra

The Arabian Pirate

A strong wind drives us through many centuries, towards the west. There, approaching the end of the fifteenth century A.D., we are caught in the midst of a tumult: Christians battling Muslims.

Moorish Grenada, the last Arabian emirate on European territory, fell in 1492. In the same year that Columbus and his horde first debarked in America, the *Reconquista*, the reconquest of Spain by the Christians, celebrated its triumph. The 100,000 Muslims and 75,000 Jews who had until then lived in a tolerable *convivencia* with the Christians in Spain were now persecuted by the Inquisition, with the goal of establishing a united Europe under the rubric of the "Holy Roman Empire."

The Muslim Moors, who had enriched Spain's culture with their sciences of mathematics, medicine, and philosophy, were resettled in ghettos, enslaved, or driven from the land. The ideology of the *Reconquista*—non-Christians are unbelievers and thus not really people—paved the way for the unscrupulous, bottomless greed that drove Christian seafarers over the Atlantic to plunder the "New World" and exterminate large parts of its population. The riches brought back from the newly "discovered" world to Europe served to finance wars between the emergent nation-states.

The Moorish families who did escape from Spain and the inquisitional terror tried to establish a new existence in North Africa. The pirate bands of Algiers and Tunis—who were to become the fright of Christian seafarers—started forming at the end of the fifteenth century. Sea travel and piracy, two occupations that Europeans had always considered the peoples of "the Orient" incapable of, now became Arabian specialties.

The Christians called the Arabs of North Africa the "Barbary," and told the most incredible tales of their atrocities. Much of this is simply anti-Islamic propaganda. It is unlikely that the Barbary pirates were any more horrible than Christian seafarers. Even when they robbed under orders from the Sultans in Istanbul, the Barbary pirates did not by any means raid merchants out of patriotism. Often enough, they were in fact hired by the European rulers waging war upon each other. France, Holland, and England each hired Arabian pirates to raid their enemies, paying in money and/or nautical and naval equipment.

The Barbary pirates had only one true enemy in the Mediterranean: the Knights of St. John, fanatic Christians who had carried on the holy war against an unbelieving world since the Crusades. This military order of the Christian church never surrendered the fight against Islam. They sailed in stately galleys, tinned up in knightly armour and hefting long, unwieldy swords. They surely had no easy time in battle against the Arabs, who could squat in their comfortable, baggy breeches and effortlessly swing their short, light scimitars.

One of them was called Sida Al Hurra. She was not only a pirate, but served as the regent of the western coast of Morocco for over thirty years.

Muslim historians are curiously silent about Sida Al Hurra. Only in Spanish and Portuguese sources can it be discovered that she played an important role in diplomatic negotiations. "She had the power in Tetuan and all of Morocco, and possessed uncontested authority over the pirates of this region. Her allies included 'Barbarossa,' the famous Turkish corsair Cheireddin [Chair ad-Din] operating out of Algiers," Fatema Mernissi writes.[11]

Sida was from a rich Andalusian family that fled to Morocco after the fall of Granada. She was only a girl at the time she went into North African exile with her family. The Banu Rashid settled in Chechanuen. Sida was married to a man from the neighbouring city of Tetuan. He too belonged to a well-known Andalusian family that had fled the Inquisition. At first the refugees still believed that they might one day return to Spain. A few of them occasionally lead military campaigns against the Spanish.

Had peace still reigned in Andalusia, Sida might have become a genteel lady in some harem. As is almost universally the case in situations of war and crisis, however, the expulsion from Spain had torn many Moorish women from their traditional roles, and involved them in dealing with the political catastrophe. Sida became a pirate. She raided Spanish ships, and in a short time was able to regain the wealth that the Christians had taken from her and her family. At the same time her tours of plunder were a means to set forth the fight against the Christians, whom she and her people now hated.

Although Sida Al Hurra by no means grew up wandering the planks of a ship, she soon proved to be a skilled pirate, and was called "Hakimat Tétouan," the "steerswoman of Tetuan." With her booty and outstanding organisational talent, she contributed greatly to the revival of Tetuan, which had been in ruins when the refugees first arrived. Sida steered the city's fortunes from 1510 to 1542. To Spanish and Portuguese diplomats, she represented a leading sea power, and they had to negotiate with her over questions such as the release of hostages. The title Al Hurra, the Arabian name for a woman who exercises power, was truly hers by right after

1515, when her husband died and she was elected to lead the city government. Later Sida Al Hurra married the King of Morocco, Ahmed al Wattassi.

"She left no doubts that she intended to retain her political influence," Fatema Mernissi writes. "For the wedding the king had to travel from his capital in Fez to Tetuan. It was the only time in the history of Morocco that a king's wedding was held outside the capital."[12]

Madame de Frèsne,

or, How did the Marquess Get on the Pirate Ship?

orne by the thrill of curiosity, the Marquess moved forward through the narrow streets of Genoa. Accompanied by her servant girl, Margot, and her husband, the Marquis de Frèsne, she approached the harbour. It was Sunday. The mild rays of a morning sun did not reach into the narrow passageways. It was as though the houses of Genoa were crowding against each other in fear of the sea's fury. The young Marquess was enchanted by the city. The harbour and its dimly-lit dives had an atmosphere of a big wide world, full of adventure and crime. She loved the smell of fish and sea and rotting wood, the sounds of creaking ropes and waves against the bellies of the ships.

The ships belonged to Christian merchants, Maltese knights, and pirates from the Orient. Like all other people from North Africa, the latter were called the "Barbary" by the locals. The Marquess knew that dark deals were being made in the harbour, that the official distinction between good Christians and evil Muslims did not bespeak reality. Here everyone had something to hide. The Christian seafarers, who spread such horrible stories about the sea-robbing Barbary, had no compunction about cooperating with the pirates if it suited their interests. Today the de Frèsnes had a rendezvous with one of the Barbary.

The noble couple from Paris was in Genoa on business. The Marquis had been invited here by a banker. His wife of only a few months accompanied him on his journey. At a banquet, they had met the Algerian pirate Gendron, who had been invited to report to the bankers and merchants about the latest news from the Barbary. Madame and Monsieur de Frèsne were very impressed by Gendron's tales of adventure, his oriental clothing, and his dagger—the blade inscribed with sayings from the Koran, the handle inlaid with mother of pearl.

Gendron originally came from La Rochelle. He was a renegade, meaning a baptised Christian who had converted to Islam. Quite a few Christians had become renegades at that time, and for many the reasons were more of a political than a religious nature.

Gendron got to talking with the good gentlepeople from Paris, they entered into an acquaintance, and after a few days he invited them to take a stroll and visit his ship. He now welcomed the three guests onto his narrow, three-mast ship, resplendent with rugs, gold inlays, and a giant crimson baldachin—a canopy with a wealth of golden half-moons. Gendron wore baggy breaches and a turban of shiny silk. Everything had the scent of precious perfume. The de Frèsnes and Margot were served a princely meal, accompanied by exotic liqueurs.

Twenty-four hours later, Gendron's ship was on the high seas—together with the Marquess de Frèsne and her servant Margot. The Marquis stood on the coast of Genoa, weeping. What had happened?

"There was certainly a difference," the Marquess de Frèsne writes in her memoirs, "between what my husband and Gendron drank, and that which they offered to us, Margot and myself. For they remained fully in their faculties, while ours became ever less clear. Everything spun about us, and we both soon fell into a deep oblivion for the next twenty-four hours."[13]

When she awoke, the Marquess found herself on the bed in the corsair's cabin. She quickly realised that she was now his captive. Gendron sat next to the bed. He assured her that her husband had rented her to him against a very high reward. As the proof he showed her her own clothes, which the Marquis had supposedly sent to the ship. The Marquess reports that Gendron was very obliging with her, showering her with tender protestations of his love, and consoling her with the assertion that she need not grieve over any scoundrel who would give her away for money—especially since she now had a man who would love and honour her to the end of his days.

The Marquis, however, was running all over the city, piteously claiming that his wife had left him and eloped with the barbarous corsair.

Whom do we want to believe, the man or the woman? Should we, so as to live up to our feminist claims, believe the woman, and assume that the Marquess was the innocent victim of a male intrigue? Not necessarily. Taking the woman's side might sometimes mean believing that a woman can also lie and show cunning. Perhaps this is even a good way to improve her hopeless situation as a woman.

How did the life of a woman like the Marquess de Frèsne look towards the end of the seventeenth century? As the daughter of a family from the gentry, she was supposed to be married to a rich man from the province. But Mademoiselle Tillet felt no desire to spend the rest of her days well-housed in some remote country manor. The only alternative to marriage for a woman of her station would have been a monastery, a possibility that many of her gender preferred. But this was out of the question for someone as curious and hungry for travel as Mademoiselle Tillet. Introduced to the Marquis de Frèsne, she accepted his proposal of marriage. The Marquis, who frequently travelled about Europe on

La Marquise de Frèsne. Source: G.C. de Sandraz, *Mémoires de Madame de la marquise de Frèsne*, Amsterdam, 1714.

business, seemed to her the lesser evil. Either he would travel alone, and she would lead the privileged life of a Marquess; or she would accompany him and see the world. It is nonetheless easy to imagine that a life as a happy spouse among the high society of the early Baroque soon bored the adventurous Marquess. What is the evidence that she did not, having listened to Gendron's adventures with great interest, voluntarily decide to join him, and really live through something?

In the end we cannot possibly decide which of the two was lying. What needs to be kept in mind is that what the husband may have done was by no means forbidden. There was no punishment for selling or renting one's own wife. By comparison, what the wife may have done was a deadly sin. Leaving one's husband was a serious crime subject to the most terrible punishments.

However the Marquess may have got on to the pirate ship, she and Margot stayed on board. The first raid that she witnessed was against a Dutch frigate loaded with cargo from Smyrna. "It is superfluous to describe my state. When one is well-fed, like I had always been in delicious Paris, and then suddenly finds oneself in a hurricane of bullets...It should be obvious that I greatly rued my fate!" wrote the Marquess, who observed the battle from an armchair. "This terrible fight lasted two hours, which seemed to me like centuries. It ended with the death of the Dutch captain, who was killed like his son, who had been truly brave. After their deaths the survivors saw no reason to fight on, and raised the white flag in a sign of surrender. They were taken on to our ship and put in chains, while Gendron brought a part of their cargo onto our ship as well." Afterwards the Marquess congratulated the pirate on his victory. She regretted only that Margot had lost an arm in the shooting.

The next prey were three ships of the Maltesian Knights

of St. John, arch-enemies of the pirates. Here Gendron plundered great wealth. The Marquess de Frèsne derived mounting pleasure from the battles, and especially from the rich prizes. It appears that she herself did not fight as a pirate, but played the role of a goddess of luck observing the battle, spurring the fighters on. Gendron worshipped her madly. He placed his heart and his treasures in her hands.

By the time they reached the coast of Morea, word of the noble pirate bride had already spread. "Some were saying that I was the princess of here and there, and others the princess of this and that," she writes. "A third group thought I had to be the Baroness of Mazarin, for she had left her husband just around this time. But yet others held the opinion I was the Baroness of Chaulnes, without taking regard of my height, my face, or my age, none of which had anything in common with that remarkable woman. But since none of them had ever seen any of those of whom they spoke, it is no great wonder that they mistook me for so many different people."

Apparently the Marquess de Frèsne was not the only woman at this time who preferred the life on a pirate ship to boredom on land. She took over the management of the corsairs' treasure. After a couple of jealous men attempted to snatch her away, Gendron gave her bearer bonds of great value and letters in her name allowing free passage through all states. She was free to go anywhere she desired.

At some point the two decided to marry. With help from a Maltesian knight, they made it to Rome and an audience before Pope Clemens X, where Gendron regretted his crimes, and the Marquess de Frèsne begged that her marriage be annulled. The Pope cashed in a large indulgence and freed Gendron from his sins, but refused to annul the Marquess's marriage before God. At any rate, he praised her for having turned the pirates to the good. What the Pope did not know was that Gendron had already promised her a large part of his fortune. The rest he gave to the monks. They were able to convince the repentant pirate to enter their order. Gendron became a monk.

The Marquess de Frèsne, however, took her share of the booty and disappeared into the depths of history.

NOTES

1. According to Fazwi Mella, *Die Irrfahrt der Königin Elissa* [The Odyssey of Queen Elissa], Frankfurt am Main, 1989, p. 82.
2. Ibid., p. 128.
3. According to Wolfram zu Mondfeld, *Entscheidung bei Salamis* [Decision at Salamis], Würzburg, 1976, p. 26.
4. Herodotus, *The Histories*, VII, 35. Translated by Aubrey de Sélincourt (1954). Penguin Classics: Middlesex, England and New York, 1985, p. 457.
5. Ibid., VIII, 68 (p. 545-6).
6. Ibid., VIII, 69 (p. 546).
7. Ibid., VIII, 90 (p. 553).
8. Ibid., VIII, 88 (p. 553).
9. Polybios, II.
10. Ibid.
11. Fatima Mernissi, *Die Sultanin* [The Sultaness], Darmstadt, 1991, p. 27.
12. Ibid.
13. According to Gérard A. Jaeger, *Les Femmes d'abordage*, Paris, 1965.

$\mathcal{T}$HE ATLANTIC

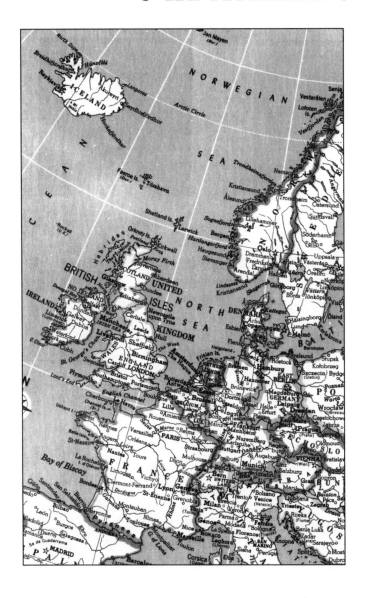

On Dragon Ships

Viking Women

Through the Straits of Gibraltar we reach the Atlantic Ocean, a body criss-crossed by Viking ships from the sixth to the eleventh century A.D. This seafaring folk had reached the coasts of America long before Columbus. Starting in the eighth century, Norman hordes became the terror of the European coasts. They invaded many countries, destroying and plundering, killing men and children, abducting and raping women.

Their most important word was "force." In Thor and his hammer, they honoured a god of patriarchal violence. Destruction and atrocity were embedded in the religious system of the Vikings. But the spiral forms of the prow and the dragon heads on the bows of Viking ships do indicate an older, female civilisation.

The Vikings decorated their ships with rich ornamentation, caring for them as though they were living beings of flesh and blood, like thoroughbred horses that they loved. The terrifying figureheads on the bows, to which they attributed magic powers, were especially important to them. An Icelandic law prohibited ships from sailing in "with open-gobbed monsters or yawning dragon snouts" lest the good-natured land and crop spirits be frightened away. When Vikings approached Iceland with friendly intentions, they would therefore take down their figureheads beforehand.

Insofar as it was available, Viking ships (also called snigs, skeidhs, or dragons) were made of hard oakwood.

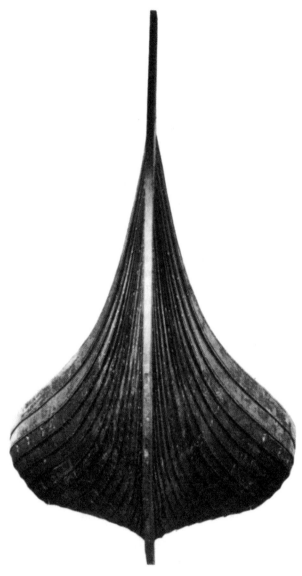

Dragon ship. Source: Wolfram zu Mondfeld, *Wikingfahrt*,
Cologne 1985.

Ornamentations were cut from ashwood, the wood from the tree Iggdrasil—the Tree of Life in which they believed everything in the world had its roots. At the roots, the Norns (Fates) spun the fabric of human lives. These goddesses were honoured long before the phallic Thor and his hammer found entry into Viking culture. With the cult of Thor, the Norns were deformed into *Valkyries*, beings mediating between this world and the world beyond, who gather expired heroes and carry them to Valhalla.

The richest Viking burial site ever discovered, the ship grave of Oseberg, is that of a woman. Archaeologists assume that it belongs to the Norwegian Queen Aasa. Whatever status this woman may have had, she must have been a seafarer with her own ship, for she was buried with it. Person and ship were so closely bound in Viking life that the ships of the dead were either buried along with them, or sent burning out to sea.

Generally, only men sailed on the feared ships that set out to plunder. Women either came along on supporting expeditionary craft, or stayed on land, where they had full authority over family economy. But like everywhere else, there were apparently some women pirates among the Vikings. Best known was the Gothic princess Alvida, also called Alwilda or Altilda.

So jealous was Alvida's father of all her suitors, so the story goes, that he kept her imprisoned in a high tower. The people only ever saw Alvida up in the tower, which was guarded by poisonous snakes. These would slither forth and kill any man tried to enter the tower with their deadly bites. The father proclaimed that anyone who wanted Alvida's hand in marriage would first have to dispatch the snakes. The Danish King Alf killed the snakes and stormed into the tower. But Alvida was already gone. Her freedom-loving and proud mother had helped her escape. She had provided

Alvida with a ship, and Alvida had left the coast unobserved, together with her maids and women of the court, while Alf was still busy squashing the snakes. Alvida and the other women on the ship became pirates. They soon encountered a group of male pirates whose captain had just died, and these promptly made Alvida into their new leader. Meanwhile, a furious Alf sailed out in hot pursuit of his rightfully-won "booty," but failed to find her, for Alvida "had left no prints in the wind," as Gérard Jaeger writes in *Les femmes d'abordage*.

It is said that Alvida was incorrigible and dreadful, that she wanted to be free and alone. All men were her enemies; she desired no lord to determine her fate. Soon enough her piracy was endangering Danish trade, and so King Alf sent out an expedition to stop her. Alvida was tracked down to Finland, surrounded by the Danish fleet, and defeated. The story ends with the marriage of Alf and Alvida, who supposedly became a calm and happy housewife. The pirate women who survived the battle were also said to have married among the Danish victors.

We are ill-advised to take this story literally. Quite apart from the unlikelihood that a woman would marry a man who has just killed her friends and her beloved snakes, or that a successful pirate would turn into a happy housewife, it is actually just as improbable as a story that a woman who spent her life imprisoned would suddenly turn into an excellent sailor. The story can only be interpreted as myth. The tower in the fairy tale of Rapunzel can be seen as a place of shamanic education, while the snakes are a symbol of female wisdom. Since the Vikings often described their ships as snakes, the tower with the snakes may actually represent an education in handling waves and wind.

In German-language tradition, the Alvida legend is turned into a romantic love story. It tells that Alvida loved the Danish prince Alf, who asked her parents for her hand.

The mother refused to grant permission, however, and also made fun of the Danish prince. So enraged was Alvida over her mother's reaction that she left the parental home along with her maids and court women, and they became pirates. When Alf found out, he and his men jumped into a ship and flew off in pursuit. He raided wherever the women raided, hoping to provoke the pirates to turn upon their unwanted competitor.

Bombastically Hans Leip describes how the pirate ships of Alvida and Alf collide, and how the lovers fall into each other's arms:

> Her sword drawn, with her flaming blond shock of hair, Altilda stood at the bow, thirsting to drown her desperation in a bloody struggle worse than all the others. But then Alf sprang onto the point of the bow and—boat-flank already crashing against boat-flank—embraced his lover, and she him, so that after so much trouble and danger they could, after all, despite all mothers and mothers-in-law, plight their common troth.[1]

Here piracy is the masochistic kamikaze run of a woman unhappily in love—apparently the preferred male explanation for female speeders.

Another well-known Viking was Princess Sela, sister to Norwegian King Kolles. Sela, who also lead her own ships, plundered without mercy along Atlantic coasts and sea routes. Her greatest enemy was her brother Kolles. She was more bitterly determined to defeat him than any other opponent. Once she nearly had him. Kolles, himself a pirate, was heading for an attack upon Baron Horwendill of Jutland, on a small island near Norway. Sela was thick on Kolles' heels, but arrived too late. When she reached the scene of the battle, Horwendill had already killed her brother. In the ensuing battle, Sela also met with death.

The Norwegian princess and pirate, Rusla, also had a big conflict with her brother, King Tesondus. "Danish vassal," she called him, for he had lost his crown to the Danish King Omund. Rusla was disgusted at her brother's failure to oppose Omund, and equipped her own fleet to wage war on the Danes. She murdered with vigour, plundering any Danish ships that had the bad luck to appear before her bow. One day she sank her own brother's ship. Tesondus barely managed to swim back to land. He sent warships after his sister, but Rusla eluded apprehension. Still unable to pacify his sister, Tesondus now equipped a huge fleet for a military campaign. In a long and bitter battle, Rusla's ship was finally capsized by that of her brother. But although Rusla had once let her brother swim to safety, he now came up to her in his ship and had her beaten to death with oars.

In comparison to all this sibling rivalry, the Norwegian sisters Russila and Stikla got along splendidly. Together they lead an association of pirates who mostly plagued the Dutch Baron Hirwitto, attacking his ships and his villages. Once again, these acts of plunder by women were attributed to unrequited love. Russila and Stikla, it was said, actually attacked the Dutch man's properties because he had rejected their desires to marry him. Why should women practice piracy for such reasons? We shall assume that the sisters plundered out of greed, desire, or restlessness.

Jeanne de Montfort:

The Flame

A mysterious storm has left us near the south coast of Brittany, where we can see dolmen and menhirs standing among deeply fissured cliffs. There are more of these stone monuments here than anywhere else in the world. Well into the modern period, Brittany was still considered the passageway to the hereafter. To the Celts, it was holy land. This is where we find the Ile de Sein, the aforementioned island of the wind witches. Christian missionaries so feared the wind witches that even as late as in the seventeenth century they still did not dare to set foot on the island. *Sein* means breasts or lap. The Ile de Sein was not the only island around the Breton coast to be inhabited exclusively by women until just a few centuries ago. Another is the Ile d'Ouessant. It is across from the Finistere promontory, the "end of the world." Before undertaking long journeys, seafarers would land at the Ile d'Ouessant to receive a blessing from the women. As for the Belle Ile, the "beautiful island," it is said that it was created from the bloody crown of an elfen queen, back when the elves where driven from the mainland. The famed Druid school is still here, for we are now in the fourteenth century A.D.

In France, the year 1343 is known for the War of the Three Jeannes. Two of these Jeannes—all three of them Bretons—were widely-feared pirates who made life difficult for the French king, fighting relentlessly for the independence of Brittany. The third, Jeanne de Penthievre, was far less touchy about her French neighbours. In fact, she married one of them, Charles de Blois, the nephew of the French king.

Jeanne de Penthievre was the niece of the late Duke of Brittany, who died childless. He would have gladly seen her on his throne, but the Bretons had serious objections to the wife of a Frenchman. Jean de Montfort, the baron's half-brother, therefore contested the succession. According to French law, Jeanne de Penthievre had no claim to the throne, for the "Salian Law" in force there excluded women from the royal succession. But the French were willing to make an exception in this case, and supported Jeanne de Penthievre. After all, France had desired to annex the attractive Duchy of Brittany for quite some time. The marriage of Jeanne de Penthievre and the French de Blois was meant to seal their shared interest in power.

Her enemy, Jean de Montfort, was married to one of the two notorious Jeannes who used all available means to fight French rule in Brittany. Jeanne de Montfort was good friends with Jeanne de Clisson, another pirate woman of the local nobility. Both women were to continue fighting the French crown with unimaginable tenacity long after both of their husbands were dead.

But Jeanne de Penthievre was also not exactly a tender rose. When her husband, the Frenchman, was captured in the war with the English, she personally took over command of the troops for nine years, until the moment she freed him with the words: "My lord, I asked you to defend my inheritance, and not to allow it to be taken from me."

England had taken up the cause of the Bretons in 1339. The Breton War of Succession became a side-show for the Hundred Years War over French succession (ultimately decided with help from a fourth Jeanne, Jeanne d'Arc, the Virgin of Orleans).

Jeanne de Montfort. Source: *Armel de Wismes*. Nantes et le pays
nantais, Paris 1983.

But back to Jeanne number one, Madame de Montfort.
She was already famous and widely admired in Brittany due
to her exploits as a rider and jouster. "She could swing herself
up on any horse with far greater skill than any stable master.
In the midst of a throng of armed men, she would strike

about her like the most courageous of field commanders. She fought on land and water, and knew all about drawing up a plan of battle, holding a position, negotiating with princes, or organising all necessities. She could carry out sieges and overcome sieges, and bear the worst of strains," according to Bertrand d'Argentré, writing in the sixteenth century.[2]

How did it come about that there were so many women in Brittany for whom fighting was a self-evident matter? Presumably our three Jeannes and many other Breton women were trained to fight, in keeping with the Celtic tradition that if the husband falls, the wife must take up his weapons herself. This Celtic custom had already been related by the Roman historian, Tacitus. Just when the Romans thought victory was imminent in their campaign against the Breton tribes, women suddenly arrived at the battlefield and fell upon them with a ferocity even greater than that of the men. Tacitus also describes how Celtic women beat to death any of their men who retreated from battle, even brothers, sons, and other relatives.

The Bretons were generally known for resisting any foreign rule, whether Roman or Germanic. Nor did they want anything to do with the French crown. They wanted the popular Jean de Montfort as their duke. "Madame," he had said to his wife Jeanne, "thou shalt become the Duchess, or I shall lose my life." He lost his life. He was defeated and captured at Nantes, and died shortly thereafter in the Louvre, the notorious Parisian prison, from complications arising from his imprisonment.

Jeanne de Montfort sent her child to safety in England, and from that moment dedicated her life exclusively to the resistance against France. At Hennebont, a town besieged by the enemy, she set fire to the French camp. After this she was called "the Flame." The French won, however, and took her prisoner. The English sent troops to reconquer Hennebont and free "the Flame." Jeanne de Montfort went to England, thanked them for their assistance, and spent the winter with the English king, according to Bertrand d'Argentré. She found an ally in Messire Robert d'Arrois, equipped a fleet with his support, and sailed out to sea.

The king of France spat curses that this Montfort belonged back at the spindle. Jean de Blois armed 4,000 soldiers and lead them on a campaign against "the Flame." Meanwhile, twenty-three French ships waited to ambush Jeanne de Montfort on the passage to Brittany, near the island of Guernsey. They were commanded by Louis of Spain, who had recently allied with France.

Jeanne de Montfort's fleet sailed into the passage and battle broke out. "It was unheard of that so many had ever been under arms, and never had there been such a wild struggle. As for the lady, she was there and stood up to the enemy unbowed, she used the weapons in her fist with greater skill than any of the soldiers," d'Argentré describes the battle with undisguised admiration.

The stories about the outcome of this battle sound quite mysterious. The winds began to howl as evening arrived, and a powerful storm appeared. It drove the ships apart and scattered them in different directions. By the time the storm subsided, the French and Spanish ships were floating in the English Channel, about fifty miles away from the site of the battle. Jeanne de Montfort's ships had gone in the opposite direction, towards the coast of Brittany, and landed at Vanned, where "the Flame" and her people found good accommodations with friends. The chroniclers speak of a "welcome coincidence." What a coincidence! Jeanne de Montfort, who lost four ships and a lot of ammunition in the battle, is suddenly blown from the Channel all the way around to the southern coast of Brittany, and lands just at the spot where friends are waiting to take her in. With help from the elements, she escapes being slaughtered by a far more powerful fleet.

Jeanne de Clisson, according to these stories, also escaped from the fangs of the French by means of a sudden storm, as we shall relate in the next chapter. Where these really coincidences? Or did the priestesses on the Ile de Sein perhaps play a part? Might the two Jeannes have been in control of the wind? Or do we have another case, as with the Amazons, of historians unable to recognise that both women were excellent sailors, and might have succeeded in mounting the waves of the Atlantic and reaching their goal even as the mighty French and Spanish fleets were blown far away?

Jeanne de Clisson:

The Lioness of Brittany

The winter of 1343 is upon the northern coast of Brittany. A tiny lifeboat bobs in the waves some miles from the harbour of Morlaix. Ice-cold winds fill the little sail. A woman and two children sit in the barque. The seven year-old boy holds his younger brother, who lies lifeless, in his arms—white lips, eyes shut. His mother holds the rudder. Her name is Jeanne de Clisson.

"Hold your little brother tight, Olivier," she tells the older boy, "keep him warm. He's sleeping. We're almost there. Soon we'll see the coast of Brittany. It's time. Six days and six nights like this!"

"I'm thirsty. I can't stand this anymore! I can't feel my hands or my ears," the child replies.

"I know, the wind is freezing. But it's leading us to the coast, where we want to be. Look, the waves are smoothing out. We're picking up speed."

"Why didn't we stay in England?" the boy asks.

"That's not possible, you know that, my son. Who else should fight the French, if not us? If not me and my friend Jeanne de Montfort?"

"But Madame de Montfort left her child in England. Why didn't you leave us at the king's court?" the child insists.

"Because I wanted to have you near me. I have no one else. Only you and your brother. Your father is dead. Olivier de Clisson, after whom you too are named. He went to the gallows because he fought for the freedom of Brittany.

Remember, in Nantes, how he was hanged for all to see, outside, in front of the Porte Sauve-Tout? I wiped your tears away, and I told you then: look carefully, and never forget what you see here!"

"Since he died, every day has only been worse and worse."

"Yes, the day of his death changed our lives. For then I determined to continue the fight, the fight for the freedom of Brittany. No Frenchman should come before my eyes without living to regret it!—The wind's getting stronger, I have to cut the sail a bit."

With one hand she lets down the sail and rolls it up. "The Frenchman from the palace next to ours was my first victim. You should have seen how he looked when I drew the blade. Here comes poor Madame de Clisson, the suffering widow, he probably thought when he saw me, riding up with my escort over his drawbridge. And then I stabbed so fast he didn't even have time to scream, and I bet he took that hypocritical smile he wanted to greet me with to his grave. We killed his whole retinue and plundered the palace down to the fixtures."

Little Olivier stares out at the sea.

"Soon I had enough to buy the first ship. I threw my own jewels in the pot. I paid the yard of the fast brigantine with jewel-studded chains. The foresail, the sail, the bow I paid with rings, pearl crosses, and that gold rose I used to wear in my hair for gatherings of fine society. My father gave me that clasp when your brother was born. Do you remember, Olivier?"

"Why did we always have to come along on this ship?"

"You'll understand when you're older. When you are a free Breton, and you can stand on the beautiful rose-coloured cliffs of Perros-Guirrec and look out over the Atlantic, then you will be able to say: we beat the French on this sea! Or in the south, at the banks of the Loire, you'll stand and say with pride: my mother raced with us in her ship up and down the Loire, and attacked all who were with the French! She took us deep into the interior of the country, destroyed barns and chapels, and I was always there with her. She was called the 'Lioness of Brittany.' She stopped Brittany from turning into a French province. And she…"

"What's a French province?" Olivier interrupts.

"If Brittany becomes French, that means that we'll no longer speak our Breton language, that our customs and traditions no longer mean anything, and that the king far away in Paris will rule over us. In the harbours there are French ships, and we must pay taxes so that the king can eat goose liver everyday with golden utensils."

"Food, something to eat, just a little piece of bread…"

Jeanne seems not to hear the child's words. "She took me and my brother on her ship over the English Channel, you'll say when you're older, and they took us into the English court and gave us new ships. She had three ships and plundered without mercy. Commandeering French ships was her daily work, sea combat her profession. You'll tell all that, Olivier, and not a word of it will be exaggerated. And every time, before she left a ship, she made the sign of the cross and cried: Down with France! Death to the Blois!"

The barque now rushes with great speed over the sea.

"The king hasn't a moment of rest anymore. Who would have thought it? The respectable Madame de Clisson, she looked like no butter would melt in her mouth, and now she is a pirate. Like Melusine of legend, who became a dangerous monster: half woman, half reptile… Jeanne de Clisson and Jeanne de Montfort, two women sacking the ships and castles of the French!"

"How much longer is it? I want to go home."

"Home? We have no home anymore. The king has placed a ban upon me. This blackguard invited me to come to Paris.

Should I make the same mistake as your father? They lured him into Paris to celebrate the Peace of Malestroit. And then they arrested him and killed him for a traitor. I'm not crazy. No, I did not go to Paris. That made him furious, the King, and he sent troops to besiege our castle. For days the French stood around the empty castle, armed to the teeth, and never noticed that we were long gone. No, Olivier, we can't return to our castle. It has been surely requisitioned by the French troops. But we'll find somewhere for us. There are people who will help us. I know that. And all will be well. It won't take much longer."

"My brother feels so cold. I'm getting colder and colder."

"Think of something else, Olivier, think of something pretty. Think of the warm cabin on our ship."

Jeanne bends over her children and draws the foresail tighter. "The cosy warm nest on our ship. You remember, the captain's palace we called it, our little house on deck. That was your home after I became a pirate. After every battle I came to you and told you what happened. I took you in my arms, and I was so happy that we were all still alive."

"Then you prayed with us and sang lullabies," the child recalls and starts to hum a song, in a thin voice, to his lifeless brother.

"The last battle, Olivier, it didn't go well for us. You were in the cabin with your brother. The French were after us the whole time, armed to the teeth. We got the idea at some point to board their main ship anyway. We had already come astride the ship, and just then those cowards ran up their foresail to clear off. But their bow was caught in our ship's hawsers, and smashed with full force into the hull. We couldn't manoeuvre anymore. The masts fell over, right on top of the French ship, and with all the lines tangled up, they had a bridge right onto our deck. They poured in. They started a terrible slaughter. Just at that moment a mad storm broke out. Perhaps this was our salvation. For it became so pitch-dark that no one could see how I let down the little boat, lead you and then your brother to it, and climbed in after you. Then we were on the way."

Suddenly she inhales, stares into the southern horizon for a while, and calls out: "Look, that stripe there! It's land, look, we've made it!"

armes de Clisson

Jeanne de Clisson did in fact reach the harbour of Morlaix, on the northern coast of Brittany. With her waning strength she got past the narrow entrance to the harbour. Only a very good sailor could do that, for at that time ships normally entered the harbour of Morlaix, with its powerful tides, only at high tide (today the harbour is shielded by a dam). Entry was made all the more difficult by dangerous cliffs and reefs.

Jeanne de Clisson disembarked. Her younger son was dead. She and Olivier found refuge in a castle in Morlaix belonging to Jeanne de Montfort's estates. The pirate wom-an, who had destroyed fleets and laid waste to whole coun-trysides, retired. She possessed nothing, her estates were all confiscated, and Brittany was bled dry.

In the year 1343 she disappeared altogether, and left the field to her son, who in the meantime was training together with the son of Jeanne de Montfort. But Olivier de Clisson was to later take the side of those whom his mother had so bitterly fought. He became an ally of Charles the Mad, the new king of France. As a memorial to his mother, he founded the Order of the White Ermine.

The "Lioness of Brittany" became the most famous pirate in French history. She appears in all French pirate books. A few, with shudders of admiration, describe her as a wild fury, while others compare her to a sea monster, or attribute mystical powers to her. "The way she stands there with wind-swept hair, she looks like an Amazon from the Iron Age," Françoise d'Eaubonne wrote, "a Celtic woman like Boticea, the queen of the Picts who attacked the Roman fleet. Her eyes shoot blood, and thus Madame appears, with a kilt tied about her waist and an axe in her fist, more like a goddess of death than a spinner and singer of crib songs, risen from the waters to cleave skulls and bore through breasts."[3]

On the Trail of the Folka ten Broke:

The Riddle of Störtebeker's Wife

First Station: Marienhafe

Marienhafe in the late twentieth century. A care-free little town in East Frisia.[4] Red brick houses with snow white window frames stand within carefully-trimmed gardens. The Störtebeker Tea Room, the Störtebeker Boutique, and many little souvenirs in the supposed image of the famous pirate remind us that a long time ago, the world in this town was not as orderly as it seems to be today.

Marion was often here. She has criss-crossed East Frisia in her old VW bus, searching for clues about Störtebeker's wife and other women who were once involved in piracy around these parts. Now we sit in front of the Marienkirche —the Church of the Holy Virgin—and observe the blocky, medieval church tower.

Ulrike: Why do they call that the Störtebekerturm?
Marion: Because it is claimed that Klaus Störtebeker and his pirates often resided in this tower, and there is plenty of evidence for it.
Ulrike: What did they do here? Did they live here in a church tower?
Marion: Yes, they lived in the church tower.
Ulrike: And where did they go to the toilet?
Marion: The situation with sanitary facilities in the old

fortresses—and this church tower is built like a fortress—
was that they just did it out the window. There was no toilet
inside fortresses.

Ulrike: Out of a church tower, too?

Marion: I hardly think it disturbed anyone. People back then
knew that they couldn't just lean against the wall of a fortress
under a window, and there weren't that many people running around this marketplace anyway. This tower was originally built because Marienhafe was supposed to become a
bishopric. But they couldn't find enough people who wanted
to settle here, and so no bishop wanted to come, either. But
this giant church had already been built, and because it was
just standing here, empty, the pirates were able to later use it
as a place to stay.

Ulrike: But there's no sea here. It's fifteen kilometres away.

Marion: Now that's true. But back then, towards the end of
the fourteenth century, the sea was still here, or at any rate
there was a waterway to the sea. There was a harbour [*Hafen*]
here, which is why this burg is, after all, named Marien*hafe*.
But this church tower, right next to the water, wasn't inhabited, and that's how the Likendeeler found a place to stay.

Ulrike: Who were the Likendeeler, anyway?

Marion: Likendeeler were the people who practised piracy
against the Hanseatic League. Well, actually, at first *for* the
Hanseatic League. They had an official written license to raid
ships, issued by the Hanseatic cities of Rostock and Wismar,
for the purpose of supplying Stockholm with the plundered
food. Stockholm was under siege at the time from Queen
Margaret of Sweden. Actually the pirates were at first called
the "Vitalien Brothers." That came from the word victuals,
food, and that was turned into *vitalien*. But they took great
liberties with the whole deal, they didn't care very much
about the political conflict. They just wanted to be pirates,
and they did that with the ships that the Hansa gave them.

Likendeeler was the name they acquired later, because they divided all booty amongst each other equally, never mind if it was the captain or the *smutje*. They called that the *gliken deel* [equal deal] which then became "Likendeel."

Ulrike: What was the significance at that time of the Hansa?

Marion: The Hansa started in the twelfth century as an alliance of rich patricians and merchant-dealers who set around in commercial ships either buying or selling goods. The Hansa was a defensive alliance, an association, that later turned into a formal league of cities.

Ulrike: Why was the Hansa unpopular among the people?

Marion: It was unjust that the sailors, or the people who worked on the ships of the Hansa shuttling around, barely got any wages. They worked under terrible and difficult conditions, under which they were hardly able to feed a family. The pay was just enough for an individual to survive. They lived almost exclusively on the ship, and then under very poor conditions. The Hansa had put all the little shippers and small-time fish traders out of business because they dealt in much larger quantities and could buy and sell at better prices, and that was very bad for the farmers in East Frisia as well. They became even poorer than they already were anyway, because there were hardly any markets left.

Ulrike: And the pirates worked for this Hansa?

Marion: At first, yes. They were given ships by the Hansa. Störtebeker was most likely among those who worked for the Hansa to begin with, but then turned to free piracy and found support by paying for it, or among people who gave his group habitation. Here in Marienhafe, Störtebeker and his people were supported by the ten Broke family.

Ulrike: And why did they help Störtebeker?

Marion: They were peasant chiefs, and always had feuds going with other peasant chiefs.

Ulrike: Who were the peasant chiefs?

Marion: They were the voice of the peasants. At some point they started getting elected.

Ulrike: They were democratically elected, in the Middle Ages?

Marion: That's right. Getting elected would give a family higher status, but after that the right to govern would be inherited within the family. Because these chiefs were very much in conflict with each other, they had a big interest in winning over the Likendeeler to their side, so that they would have reinforcements against the other peasant chiefs. Even little villages would fight against each other. There were perpetual conflicts and wars in East Frisia.

Ulrike: This surprises me. Elsewhere Störtebeker is always portrayed as a big hero who fought for the poor old peasants against the evil Hansa.

Marion: Yes, very many legends and tales grew out of all this. But that was the idea in the first place, because in his speeches he was, of course, always attacking the injustice of the Hansa.

Ulrike: But it's a legend that Störtebeker was a kind of Robin Hood

Marion: Yes, well, a lot of invention was added to the accounts, very often they credited him with very noble qualities. We can't tell whether it was really so. It's naturally possible that he was a Robin Hood, but the historical evidence is lacking. The people, who are always happy to have someone who stands up for them, naturally add some poetry to it and say, "now there was a fellow who had really helped us!" But there's no historical evidence.

Ulrike: What did Störtebeker do concretely as a pirate?

Marion: He raided ships of the Hansa. There is no doubt about that. These were the richest ships anyway, and he did a great deal of damage to the Hansa with his raiding tours. As for the connection to the peasants, it's entirely possible that it was a matter of true solidarity. But he would have urgently needed it anyway, if he was going to have any harbours to land in. He naturally needed people who would support him, who would sell the goods and give him some protection. The peasant chiefs were just the ticket. And again, they were interested in the Likendeeler because this meant support against other peasant chiefs. The peasant chiefs who supported Störtebeker and his people, including the ten Brokes, ended up in major conflict with the Hansa.

Ulrike: This tower here in Marienhafe, did it also belong to the ten Brokes?

Marion: Yes, it belonged to the District of Brookmer Land, that was the ten Broke district. And it was just perfect, because this is a very big, strong, and roomy tower. They would have had very good accommodations in it, and naturally a direct way to the sea and a wonderful view from the top.

Ulrike: And isn't there also a treasure in there or something?

Marion: I don't believe in the treasure, because these treasures, well, they're a strange phenomenon. Some pirate treasure is always being sought. Certainly the pirates took in huge amounts of booty, that's true of all piracy. But they always blew it right away. There was never an organisation that combined such high revenues and such great waste as in piracy. Everything captured was immediately spent and dealt, sold off for a third of the price, or just given away. If they hoarded a treasure, then at most a small chest towards maybe buying a new ship. But I don't think the Likendeeler even did that, because they got their ships by capturing them. They would just switch from their old ship if they had captured a better one.

Ulrike: How great is the chance, since nothing is known about this, of whether there were also women on these ships?

Marion: It's hard to say. If there were women, then they were probably in disguise, in men's clothing. Hans Leip even put a Beguine aboard in his novel *Godekes Knecht* [Godeke's

Vassal]. That's probably Hans Leip's own invention, although he was extremely knowledgeable about history and wrote the best German-language work about piracy. It's not improbable that Beguines or other cloister nuns were on board pirate ships, because as novices they would have gotten lessons in astronomy, which is needed for navigation. Hans Leip worked that into his novel, and had a Beguine do the navigating. It is also known that many wandering Beguines had gotten involved in politics, and specifically that they supported the Likendeeler. From the research on cloisters and Beguine convents, we know that they were often mixed up with political matters, or were perhaps involved in some political movements from the ground up. The cloisters had knowledge, wealth, and a large part of the political power.

Ulrike: What was the status of women in East Frisia in the Middle Ages?

Marion: That's another tough one, because there are as good as zero documents on the matter. One thing is certain: the women here worked at least as hard as the men, and were seen as doing so. They had house rights and key power within the house, and took care of everything organisational.

Ulrike: What does "key power" mean?

Marion: That means power over all spaces within the family property. To decide which room will be open or locked, as well as when and who is allowed to enter, and who not. An old East Frisian woman once told me that the jokes about the imputed stupidity of East Frisians (among majority Germans), have their basis in the fact that the German historians or visitors who came here in the old days to ask the local people about their views and customs only asked men. The men often had no clue, because they were always in the fields or at sea. To these historians the local men appeared very one-dimensional and stupid, but they didn't survey the women—who would have answered differently, because the women really knew their way around in life. But this area has not been researched, and I've often been told that it can't be researched, because in the past women were never considered in any of the written documentation.

Ulrike: That already speaks for itself.

Marion: The status of women in East Frisia nowadays is rather miserable. There isn't a single woman in the emergency medical services, for example, whereas women have been trained for this profession in other German states for quite some time. In 1990, according to the state employment agencies and trade unions, most women employed here are involved in unprotected work situations, meaning no health insurance, no social security. The image of women among East Frisians today is straight out of the nineteenth century. A woman is seen only as a mother and wife, and if she does work on the side, then her insurance comes from the man. So it's no coincidence that the highest proportion of recipients of social assistance in East Frisia are single mothers.

Second Station: The Stone House in Bundehee

Finding the old stone house on the road from Bunde to Bundehee is difficult. We first see it after driving past it three or four times. It's behind a clump of beech and spruce, and from the road the view of it is blocked by an extension dating from the eighteenth century. A neighbouring woman confirms that this was the house of the ten Brokes. The buildings are inhabited, she says, but apparently she wonders why—because the old part with the high rooms, she notes, must be very difficult to heat. It turns out the house is now home to a professor of music and his wife. The travel guide had claimed it was an organ academy.

Marion: This old stone house was supposedly already standing at the time of the Vikings. The iron rings are evidence of this. They supposedly tied their ships here.

Ulrike: But the ten Brokes didn't exist at the time?

Marion: No. The ten Broke family first appears in the *Norden Annals* as a family of chiefs in the year 1309. Their rule was ended in 1427, during a feud among peasant chiefs in which the last ten Broke chief fell. That they did rule is evident in their possession of stone houses. Ordinary peasants were not allowed to build or own stone houses, that was the law. They had to live in loam huts, which were prohibited from being higher than thirteen feet. And back then stone houses were as good as castles. This one here looks like an ordinary and very large house, but the walls are one-meter-fifty thick. All the local farmers could hole up in here whenever they had feuds with other villages or other peasant chiefs.

Ulrike: And this was the house where the legendary Folka ten Broke lived?

Marion: That's not confirmed, because the ten Brokes had several houses and castles.

Ulrike: Why did you pick out this house to visit?

Marion: Because I heard that this house is haunted by a woman. And since I couldn't locate any historical documents on this Folka ten Broke, I thought maybe she's the one haunting the house.

Ulrike: Who was Folka ten Broke, anyway?

Marion: Folka ten Broke, according to legend, was married to Störtebeker. It is said that she hoarded the treasure in Marienhafe, or that she came along on the ship and took part in the plundering. She appears in many legends, theatre pieces, and novels. And the craziest thing about it is that you can't find her in any historical source! She is supposed to be the daughter of Kenno ten Broke, who supposedly had her marry Störtebeker. But she doesn't appear in the family tree.

Kenno had two daughters, and neither of them was named Folka. They were both only three or four years old during Störtebeker's heydays. Nonetheless, it's possible that Kenno did marry Störtebeker to one of his daughters. This would have been a marriage of convenience, anyway.

Ulrike: What would have been the point of it?

Marion: The ten Brokes, as we said, were allied with the Likendeelers. And the bonds of marriage were very important in East Frisia. One couldn't just marry and then disappear. Marriage was more than a sacrament in the Christian sense. A family clan constituted a following that could not be superseded or replaced by any contractual association.

Ulrike: What interest could Störtebeker have had in such a marriage?

Marion: He would receive the right to disembark at any harbour belonging to the ten Brokes' district. Whether there was a castle there or other farmers there, he would have had the right to land regardless, anywhere he liked.

Ulrike: Were child marriages common at that time?

Marion: There were child marriages among the dukedoms and baronies in East Frisia in the seventeenth century, also to solidify alliances. Possibly they were already using children for this in the fourteenth century. But there is no surviving certificate of this marriage. Let's hope it wasn't this way— marriage of convenience or not, Störtebeker—Robin Hood or not, it's unbearable to think about, a marriage between a four year-old child and a grown man.

Ulrike: This Folka ten Broke appears only in oral tradition, not in any documents?

Marion: Exactly. She's not in the family tree. Perhaps she was crossed off. There were cases of women who were crossed off family trees because they had done something that was socially intolerable. We don't have a clue how many women were crossed off, because they are thus forever absent from any historical documentation. They remain only in legends and spook stories.

Ulrike: But there is a Folka who is confirmed in the sources.

Marion: That was Foelkeldis Kampena. She was called "Quade Foelke," because she was the most horrible woman in East Frisia. She was also Kenno ten Broke's mother. He was the one held responsible for bringing the Likendeeler to the East Frisian coast. In reality it had been his mother, however, because at that time, end of the fourteenth century, Kenno was still a minor, and she was ruling in his place. But he never stopped asking for her counsel and obeying her after he became an adult. In the documents Kenno is always the one who appears as the negotiator with the Hansa, but in one document there is a suggestion that he always asked his mother first.

Ulrike: Why was she called the most horrible woman in East Frisia?

Marion: She had done two things so terrible that historians cannot imagine how a woman was capable of such acts. After her husband was strangled, she let two of his enemies starve in a dungeon and had the corpses buried. That was bad, but even worse was the story with her daughter, Ocka ten Broke. She was married to a man with whom she had constant fights, and this man beat her to death.

Ulrike: The daughter?

Marion: The daughter, yes, and then Quade Foelke gathered together her peasants and stormed the castle of her in-laws, where the son had fled to his father. Then she had both, her son-in-law and his father, brought out of the castle and beheaded. That is how she got the name Quade Foelke. Which means evil or bad Foelke, but "quade" can also mean cunning or clever.

Ulrike: What did she have to do with Störtebeker?

Marion: She made the alliance with the pirates. She was the

Quade Foelke. Source: Günter Müller, *Burgen und Schlösser im Raum Oldenburg/Ostfriesland*, Oldenburg 1977.

one responsible for bringing the Likendeeler to East Frisia, and she was probably very cunning. It was clear to her that she had acquired substantial power by attracting the pirates. Piracy after all represented a sea power; you can look at it as you like, but it provided a lot of intimidation and power.

Ulrike: Could it be that in the oral tradition the two women, Quade Foelke and the daughter of Kenno ten Broke, ended up melding into a single woman named Folka ten Broke?

Marion: Yes, that's entirely possible. Quade Foelke had supported the pirates. But for a legend like that, you need a beautiful young woman, a woman who stands by a hero like Störtebeker unconditionally, who supports his great acts. A seasoned woman like Quade Foelke, who had so much dirt to hide, just doesn't fit into such a legend.

Ulrike: And she's the one spooking this place, you think?

Marion: This is a haunted house. They say that at night a woman in a white dress sings Gregorian songs. Well okay, a single woman can't sing a Gregorian song; all of these old Celtic overtone chorales require several women. But we can just fantasise about which of the ten Brokes the ghost might be. Is it the always discreet Folka ten Broke, who only appears in legends and is nowhere confirmed historically? Or is our ghost is standing in for all the discreet women in the history of East Frisia and of piracy?

Third Station: At the Boggy Lake

We go on to a place where Marion had a very interesting encounter in the course of her investigative journeys. Marion parks the van at the edge of a forest. Astounded that the end of the world is so near to *A*, I get out and follow her along a nearly impassable path, grown over with high grass and surrounded by trees, shimmering in the bright evening sky of East Frisia. After about twenty minutes, Marion turns off this path and onto a barely visible track. Two steps further on we can suddenly see a lake, all the more surprising because there was no hint of it from the path. The round body of water lies before us, unmoving, surrounded by reeds and low firs. Insects buzz. Otherwise it is dead calm. We have come to a bog, the name and location of which we shall not betray.

On the Trail of the Folka ten Broke

Ulrike: How do you know about this secret place?

Marion: That was in a bar in *A*, where I heard some dodgy story about this lake. *A* was once along the sea, and this moor was almost the sea, where we now have a lake. About ten years ago they did in fact pull a cog dating from the time of Klaus Störtebeker out of the lake. I didn't really believe all the other things they told me at this bar, such as how you could swim here and feel around on the bottom of the lake (and/or sea) for engravings on slabs dating from that time. But on that evening I didn't really know what else to do with myself. The research hadn't lead to all that much, so I thought, why not go visit this boggy lake? And then here I was, and at first I thought everything was very pretty here, and just walked around the bog. Suddenly there was someone in front of me—one of the fellows from the bar who had told me about the bog. I knew there was no going right or left, that was only bog. The only other possibility was backwards. But suddenly another one of these guys was behind me. So then I reached for my can of mace. But I didn't have to defend myself after all. The two were very peaceful, and apparently were pleased no end that I had in fact come out here.

Later, when I got to talking to them, it turned out that both of these young men were alcoholics. They have hideouts around here. They do burglaries and fish the lake. This is private property. The owner, who apparently has a lot of land around here, releases all kinds of fish into the lake so that he can go fishing on the weekends. That evening we grilled a couple of these fish ourselves. Although I naturally found out nothing more about any pirate women around this area, I at least experienced a fine feeling of piracy among these people. In all there were two women and three men, all more or less with teeth missing, tattoos, rather foolhardy and rather young, all around twenty.

Ulrike: They lived here.

Marion: Yes. They had hideouts here. At night, every second or third night, they would go away and do burglaries. And they lived from the things they stole—not only spirits, though that was the main thing, but also canned goods and such.

Ulrike: Did you sleep here in their hideouts?

Marion: Yes. That first night it all seemed a bit too hairy for me. I went back to my hotel room, and I didn't think I would come back. As nice as it is here, it was all somehow too uncomfortable. But over the course of the next day I decided to come back after all, talked to the group, and decided to sleep here for a night. Then I ended up staying here for three days and three nights. I slept in one of their "storerooms," meaning a little tent that they hid under firs in the bog, where they normally kept canned goods. I spent the three nights in there. During the day we lived from the captured fish and the stolen goods.

Ulrike: How was the atmosphere?

Marion: There was a feeling, though not an explicit feeling, of freedom. I really thought that this was how the pirates must have lived: stolen food, and living by your wits. We would lie under the trees or in the sun and tell stories, whatever. They drank a lot of alcohol, and sent their dog to hunt fish. Then the fish were grilled in the evening around a nice campfire, and so it went into the night. We slept until midday.

Ulrike: Weren't you afraid?

Marion: No. Only once. That was at night, when they had gone off to steal something. I was in my tent with the canned goods. Suddenly I heard cars arriving and apparently also a motorcycle, from the sound of it.

Ulrike: Were you alone?

Marion: Well, I also had Chicco, the German shepherd, who

belonged to these wild people. We were together in the tent, and I suddenly saw big spotlights over the lake, and heard voices. I realised it was the police, and Chicco started to growl. I stroked her to calm her down, which she did, much to my relief. The police lit up the moor and called out. What exactly, I couldn't understand, but it was clear to me that this was a raid. They were very close, something like two meters from our hideout, and struck at the bushes around us with their sticks. But they didn't find the tent under the firs, or us either. After a while they just up and left. And about two hours later, around four in the morning, the gang returned and brought me some things too. I wanted cigarettes, and they had brought a whole bunch of packs. And some warm fresh schnitzel with breadcrumbs. Four in the morning. I never found out where they had been. I only dared ask once, and then I got a strange answer which left no doubt that it was none of my business.

Ulrike: What kind of answer?

Marion: They said that they had fished the schnitzel off a grille, through the chimney. I couldn't imagine this, and it was clear to me that I wasn't supposed to ask again. Same with the cigarettes, though it was pretty obvious that they had broken into a machine. And then I ate this schnitzel in the night, with the dog of course, and stayed here another two, very lovely days.

Ulrike: The two women who were there, what were they like?

Marion: They were young and didn't expect very much from their future. They had seriously decided not to work, and to steal whatever they needed to survive. They were both alcoholics, like the three boys.

Ulrike: Did they tell anything about their lives?

Marion: What they related was not so remarkable in and of itself. They weren't from an orphanage, if that's what you mean, they didn't fit any of the standard clichés. They all had family and said they were still in contact with them. They just had no desire, as the old saying went, to live a bourgeois life.

Ulrike: Would you say that they were the pirate women of today?

Marion: That would seem to be plausible. I don't know how aggressive they might become. One of the girls told me that she had often been in fights earlier on, the one who was missing a couple of teeth. She said she had taken pleasure in starting fights in bars, but those days were over now, and she would rather just lie here in the sun and live the good life. Perhaps that really is the piracy of today. In the past it would have been possible that these were the women you might have met on a pirate ship.

From the Galley:

Labskaus Stew

The most important drink on Viking ships was not, as might be presumed, mead, but beer. Until the complete Christianisation of the people, beer was brewed exclusively by women. Intoxication was a regular part of ritual ceremonies on land, and, much like the worship of the beer goddess Nidaba in ancient Babylon, tantamount to a religious commandment. On board as well, beer had to be in plentiful supply; it went against Freya's will to run out. Only after the introduction of monasteries for males did the art of brewing, over time, become a matter conducted by men.

Round flat loafs baked from barley, water, and salt were the nearly imperishable Viking staple. Since the Vikings knew nothing about yeast or other leavening agents, the bread is presumed to have been barely edible, which is why it was apparently used more for brewing beer (the bread would be placed in water to ferment) than for direct consumption. These loafs were hard as stone, in part because they often contained small particles from the stone mills in which the grain was ground. Archaeologists attribute the poor dental situation among Vikings to traces of stone found in the loaves.

The women on the dragon ships were far more flexible when it came to the uses of milk. Next to butter, cheese, yoghurt and buttermilk, they would make a salted sour milk called Skyr, which kept quite long at sea.

Fish, of which there was no shortage, were fried, spiced, and poured over with beer, simmering in it until ready to eat. Cod, the gills of which were dried out to keep from spoiling, served as a protein supplement to the flat loaves on long voyages. Incredibly, this product was and remains a highly demanded export article.

The pirates of the North Sea at the time of Störtebeker ate a fine-tasting fish stew. Here is a fourteenth-century recipe for serving about thirty pirates:

Ingredients

2.5 kg salted veal
6 kg ship's biscuits
25 onions
20 garlic sprouts
30 herring filets
20 sour pickles
1 kg red beets
.5 kg pork lard for frying

Cook the meat and onions in a big pot until tender, then chop them finely. Crush the biscuits and stir into the stock from the meat. Coarsely chop the garlic sprouts, pickles, herrings, and red beets. Melt the lard in a large pot and add everything. Bring once to a boil, stirring constantly. Spice with pepper.

Lady Killigrew

rossing the Channel, we hold course for England, which was developing into a major colonial power throughout the sixteenth century A.D.

In the previous century, Pope Alexander VI had divided the "New World" among his Catholic favourites. In a papal bull dated to 1493, addressed to the Spanish king, he wrote:

> Viewing the discovery by Columbus of certain remote islands and mainlands, We hereby ordain, of our own free will, and without taking into account your influence or that of any other, and based upon our apostolic power absolute, that all these newly discovered islands and mainlands, insofar as they are not yet ruled by any Christian King, do belong to yourself and your heirs; and We furthermore forbid anyone, under the penalty of excommunication, to travel there and engage in trade without your prior consent.

The pope then drew a line, to the west of the Azores, from the North Pole to the South Pole, and decreed that everything to the west of this line belonged to Spain. Portugal, on the other hand, was to secure the eastern part of the islands and mainlands, which did not yet belong to a Christian king. England and France were left with nothing. As a consequence, they resorted to piracy.

The French king issued letters of marque to seafarers,

permitting them to attack and loot all ships bringing trea-sures from the "New World" to Europe under Spanish or Portuguese flags. These freebooters were called corsairs, an expression that was supposed to sound less criminal than pirates.

Queen Elizabeth I of England also adopted a positive stance to freebooters. Seizing ships with full holds, corsairs kidnapped wealthy Spanish voyagers and put them up for auction in Dover, making about one hundred pounds per head. Speculators would buy the travellers with the intention of releasing them in return for a larger ransom. Pirates with especially successful careers were later even made into nobles, and celebrated as national heroes.

Reacting to complaints by the Spanish, England declared it would put an end to piracy. But for all practical purposes, everyone in authority in England was involved in it. Not only the crown, which took in its percentage of the loot, but the nobility and the navy, as well as civil servants down to the last customs officer in the harbours, all profited greatly from these activities.

Cornwall, the most south-westerly tip of England, was the seat and dominion of the Killigrew family. Outstanding musicians, diplomats, and soldiers came from this respected clan. And pirates. As the English historian Philip Gosse puts it, the Killigrews were members of the "oligarchy of sea-robber capitalists" in the Elizabethan period.

The Killigrews operated from the coast, where they main-tained a sort of family enterprise. Their business did not just encompass the seizing of ships. Hiding and trafficking goods, buying and selling boats, distributing bribes to officials, and paying freelance pirates were all also a part of it. The captain received only one-fifth of the booty. As was usual with such early capitalist enterprises, the largest part of the loot went to the proprietors. But the Killigrews, as owners of the syndicate, were by no means above taking the boarding axe into their own hands, and also participated in raids personally.

By today's standards, Sir John Killigrew was the chief executive officer of the business. As Vice-Admiral of Cornwall, Royal Governor of the neighbouring fortress of Pendennis, and blood relative of the queen's prime minister, he did not necessarily have to fear any obstructions on the part of the law enforcement authorities. His lordship was able to seize ships, smuggle, and traffic without being held answerable for any of these deeds. Sir John's father had already been a pirate by profession, and legend had it that his uncle Peter turned the Irish Sea upside-down in his youth. The Killigrews resided in the beautiful old castle of Arwenack, in a secluded section of Falmouth. Located close to the sea, this estate still exists. Legend has it that there is a secret tunnel to the harbour, over which the pirates were able to bring the booty into the Killigrews' cellar vaults without being seen.

Arwenack Castle was a popular and well-known refuge among pirates. The nice, elderly Lady Elizabeth Killigrew, who was either Sir John's mother or his wife (historians are still disputing this matter) provided food and drink for the crews. Pirates felt themselves safe as part of the Killigrew syndicate. If, as occasionally happened, one of the freebooters was tracked to the area by an English warship, Sir John would take a rowboat and get himself on board the royal vessel. After negotiating with the commanding officer, he would then invite him to his castle for a grand breakfast, and subsequently treat him to a hunting spree in the surrounding forests. With one hundred pounds of hush money in his pockets, the officer would return to his ship—that is, after the pirates had got to safety with their loot.

The Killigrews were, however, able to profit from nepotism and corruption only as long as their victims were not more influential than they. Their pirates' realm could be shaken by tremors on those occasions when they were unlucky enough to come across someone with even better connections to the ruling class.

This happened, for example, when the Earl of Worcester was set upon by pirates between Dover and Boulogne. As envoy to Elizabeth I, he was on his way to bring a golden salver as a present from the queen to the daughter of Charles IX. When the pirates attacked, they were surprised to find the ship being defended. The earl was able to flee with the tray, leaving a mere five hundred pounds to the sea robbers. Soon afterwards, the queen gave orders to conduct a large raid along the Channel coastal regions, in the course of which hundreds of pirates were arrested. Three were executed. Presumably Sir Killigrew and his cronies again managed to regain control of the situation, however, for their activities continued as before.

Another operation by the Killigrew syndicate almost led to an even more disastrous outcome for the pirate clan. It was a deed of great risk, committed by an especially adventurous person.

It was the first day of the year 1582, when a large Hanseatic ship entered the harbour of Falmouth, docking right in front of Arwenack Castle. Two men left the ship. The arrivals had barely touched English soil before a violent rainstorm broke out and caused them to seek refuge in the neighbouring castle. Old Lady Killigrew opened the gate, offered them a seat by the fireplace, and served tea and pastries. In front of the crackling fire, the two men told their story, speaking in Spanish accents. They had left Danzig and had brought their 144-tonne ship into the harbour of Falmouth to wait for the threatening storm to pass. The hospitable lady bade them stay for some days, stressing that Falmouth offered a safe haven. She then recommended that they take up accommodations at a guest house in Penryn. The two Spanish men,

Lady Killigrew

Philip de Orozo and Juan de Charis, thanked the nice elderly lady and left for Penryn. They were not the least bit worried about their ship's safety. For one thing, the Hanseatic League and England were at peace. Even better, their ship was anchored just across from Sir Killigrew's castle, and they knew that he, as a high official of the crown, was responsible for combating the pirate menace.

On January 8, 1582, the storm had gone by. Calm seas mirrored the steel-blue sky over the bay of Arwenack. Sails, sun and the whole area shone. Two Spaniards stood on the quay and glumly looked out to sea. Their ship had disappeared. Where they had left the proud 144-tonne vessel, hungry seagulls were now crowded on the water, and contributed to the general impression of no ship ever having existed there. What had happened?

Hospitable old Lady Killigrew had made an appraisal of the valuable boat and come to the conclusion that she wanted to take it away from the two Spaniards under their very own eyes. The lady had a liking for especially original actions, she loved the thrill of it. Her whole life long she had been a pirate, learning the trade from her father as a child. Even now, topping sixty years, she was still able to seize a boat with a great amount of dexterity and cleverness.

On the night of January 7, she had led her gang to the sea, presumably over the secret tunnel. It was pitch-dark. Even though the storm had passed, the sky had not yet cleared. Lady Killigrew knew that this was just the ideal moment for a seizure, and she was familiar with the particular characteristics of the weather. When they had entered their boats, the pirates rowed to the great ship. The lady steered to the vessel's stern, and after a sailor had fastened it with a rope, the gang climbed up onto the deck. Taking up the positions the lady had determined beforehand, they jumped the guards on a signal. The bodies were flung overboard. Not one member of the Hanseatic ship's crew is supposed to have survived.

With fully-laden boats, the lady and two of her gang returned to the castle, where they dragged the rolls of cloth and kegs into a hiding-place. The other pirates disappeared into the dark with the ship.

The robbed Spaniards filed a lawsuit against the thieves in Falmouth. Naturally, suspicion was sure to fall on Lady Killigrew, because a theft of this audacity could only be attributed to her. And it goes without saying that it was impossible

Lady Killigrew's tombstone.

to prove she had committed the crime. Following endless investigations, the judges declared that they were unable to determine the perpetrators.

Needless to say, Philip de Orozo and Juan de Charis were not very happy with this verdict. They went to London, voicing their complaints at the highest level. As a consequence the case was reopened. Among other peculiarities, it turned out that the judge in Falmouth was a son of Lady Killigrew.

Thus, the thieving old lady had to stand at the bar as a defendant, and at her advanced age. Together with two of her gang, she was sentenced to death. In the last moment, however, old age and nobility saved her from the executioner. Lady Killigrew was granted a pardon by Queen Elizabeth I.

Grace O'Malley

$\mathcal{N}$umerous castles and palaces rise above the rocky Irish coastline. They were once the seat of the Irish family clans, which for centuries not only fought against the English colonial power, but also often engaged in bitter feuds among themselves. One of these strongholds is Howth Castle, a solid structure to the north of Dublin. To this day, a covered table waits for Grace O'Malley, a legendary Irish pirate. Once she had stopped and asked for hospitality on her way back from England. The lord of the castle, however, would not allow her to enter. He was just in the middle of a meal and not willing to be disturbed. Out of revenge, Grace O'Malley kidnapped his son. She only returned him after the lord promised to make Howth Castle more hospitable in the future—and to set the table for her during every meal. The current owners of Howth Castle still keep this promise.

Granuaile, as she was called in her Gaelic mother tongue, was born in 1530 as the only daughter of the O'Malley clan. The O'Malleys were an old family of seafarers, living predominantly on fishing and trading, with a little piracy conducted on the side. They had their family seat on the storm-swept west coast north of Galway. Sea robbery was nothing unusual in Ireland during the sixteenth century. Granuaile discovered her predilection for boats and the sea already as a child, with her father teaching her the trade.

Granuaile was six when King Henry VIII had himself proclaimed "King of Ireland" by the English parliament. His intention was to make Ireland an English colony. Up to that point, only the region around Dublin had been in English hands. Gaelic clans determined the political arena in other parts. Because they were engaged in constant strife, and consequently not in any condition to organise a common front of resistance against England, it was quite easy for the English king to assert his interests in Ireland.

How does one go about converting an independent country into a colony? For starters, Henry VIII offered English titles and privileges to the clan leaders under the condition that they take on English customs and morals. This included introducing the Anglican denomination in Catholic Ireland. The leaders of the O'Malley clan did not accept the offer. In contrast to neighbouring families, the O'Malleys refused to submit to the English for quite a long time.

At sixteen, Granuaile was married to the next-door clan leader Donal O'Flaherty, who was also known as Donal of the Many Battles. He did full honour to his name, and was constantly engaged in all manner of feuds. Granuaile always stood by his side. She also raided ships headed for Galway.

Galway was a major trade centre not just for Ireland, but for the British Isles in general. The principal city was also the seat of English power and administration, and thoroughly at odds with the neighbouring Gaelic clans. "O God, free us from the wild O'Flahertys" was written over Galway's western city gate in large letters.

Neither the O'Flahertys nor the O'Malleys were allowed to run a business in Galway. Exporting wool, the most important product of Gaelic clans, was generally prohibited. This strengthened English traders and helped to keep Ireland dependent on England.

If she wanted to guarantee subsistence for herself and her family, Granuaile had no other choice but to raid ships, or at least extort a large amount of protection from all passing along her strip of the coast. Moreover, this pirate also undertook long voyages to Spain and Portugal, buying wine, spices, glass, iron, silk, and other goods, which she then sold back home. People in Ireland much preferred to buy her merchandise, because Granuaile did not demand customs.

Donal of the Many Battles was killed while defending a fortified island on Lough Corrib, which he had occupied. To the surprise of all involved, Granuaile managed to hold the fortress. She had the lead roof of the stronghold melted down and poured over the heads of the enemies, who promptly fled the island. The building was thereafter called Hen's Castle, because Granuaile had defended it like a hen defends her nest. Granuaile had to run away, however, without time to even survey the land to which she was now entitled. According to Gaelic law, she had the right to claim one-third of her deceased husband's possessions. The daughter of the O'Malleys returned home, and settled down in a fort on an island off County Clare.

Meanwhile, Queen Elisabeth I had come to the throne. She pursued an even more rigorous policy of colonising Ireland. English adventurers fell into Ireland and appropriated land. Believing Irish culture to be backward and inferior, the colonists tried to replace it with English culture. Many habits and moral attitudes dating back to the times before the island became Catholic still prevailed in Ireland in the sixteenth century. For example, women were not worse off than in modern England with respect to their legal status. Under Gaelic law, a woman marrying a man was equal to him in matrimony. The marriage had a provisional status of one year. During this period it was possible for either side to revoke it without needing to state a reason.

In her second marriage, Granuaile made use of this right. She took the powerful clan chief Richard Burke, who was also called Iron Richard, as husband. Several explanations exist for his name. According to some sources, he is supposed to have owned iron mines. According to others, he always wore chain mail—for fear of fire-belching dragons. In any case, Iron Richard was the owner of Rockfleet Castle, a beautiful fort situated at Clew Bay. It remains well-preserved to this day, and has a great four-story square tower with massive, high walls. Granuaile spent most of her life on the fourth floor of this tower. Through the western window, she was able to overlook the whole bay and observe all ships headed for Galway. A small hole is still discernible on the southern side of the thick stone walls that face the sea. Legend has it that a rope ran through this opening, connecting Granuaile's favourite boat to her bedpost. Her fourth child was born on this vessel. She named the child Tibbot-na-Long, Theobald of the ships.

In only a short period, Granuaile had established herself as mistress of Rockfleet Castle. And one day, returning from the warpath, Iron Richard found the gates to his castles shut. Standing up on the battlements, Granuaile shouted down to him: "I dismiss you! Rockfleet Castle is now mine!" As the probationary year was not yet over, Richard Burke, the man of iron, had no choice but to ride away swearing. He never tried to take back his castle.

Legend has it that the local Catholic priest was so aghast on hearing about this Gaelic divorce that he fled from the island. Granuaile had him caught and brought back. She feared people might otherwise believe the devil had settled down there.

The relationship between Granuaile and Iron Richard remained friendly. They continued to fight and plunder side by side.

****

Meanwhile, the colonialists had come up with a new method of getting Ireland under their control. As would be the case ten years later, when the objective was to send

Englishmen and Englishwomen to the newly discovered coastal regions in America, entrepreneurs and other willing people in England were supplied with propaganda material offering them a place to live in Ireland. The arrivals experienced a nasty reception, because it turned out that the land was, contrary to the promises, already inhabited. Bloody disturbances and revolts broke out as a result. The rebellious Irish lost more and more land, which was then given in turn to loyal Englishmen. To this day, Ireland suffers from the consequences of English colonial policy.

Grace O'Malley was a rebel, but she was by no means a patriot, as is often falsely stated. At one point she even gave a promise of loyalty to the queen. One of the few historic sources on Granuaile is a letter by the English governor of Galway, where he describes this event. "In came the most famous living woman captain, Grany Imallye, offering her services together with three galleys and two hundred fighting men, even in Scotland and Ireland, wherever I might order her to go. She brought her husband with her, because she was much more than woman and wife. She was a woman notorious on all the coasts of Ireland."[5]

This stood in sharp contrast to Granuaile's behaviour in other instances. She continued to harass and rob English merchants and land owners. A letter written in 1578 documents how she was caught and taken prisoner in the course of a robbery: "Grany O'Mayle, a woman shamelessly going beyond the part of her womanhood as a great robber, commander-in-chief and leader of sea-bound thieves and murderers, who ravaged the province, was arrested this year by the Earl of Desmond and sent to Lymerick, where she will remain in secure custody."[6] However, Granuaile was released from prison after eighteen months, against a promise to put an end to her activities at sea. She did not keep the promise for a single day.

Grace O'Malley's second husband died in 1583. This time she did not forget to claim all of his possessions, even though as a divorcee she was not entitled to it. After having occupied Rockfleet Castle with her entourage of thieves, she became its mistress.

The English crown had, meanwhile, managed to cement its power in Ireland to the point where the nobility in the province of Connaught were obliged to sign a disadvantageous agreement. In the "Composition of Connaught," the Crown promised not to take away land from the big Irish landowners if they were willing "to pay an annual interest of ten-and-a-quarter shillings for tillable land and to appear in field camps with a predetermined number of men, and furthermore to abolish the Irish legal system and its relevant ruling on the allocation of land and livestock."[7]

All clan chiefs and nobles of the country signed this treaty, including the O'Malleys. There is no personal signature of Granuaile. Her position as clan chief of Rockfleet Castle and the surrounding areas, which she had attained with her husband's death, was contrary to English and Gaelic jurisdiction. No one, however, dared question it.

The queen sent a new governor to Galway, who turned out to be an especially rigid keeper of the legal system dictated by England. Richard Bingham became Granuaile's most bitter enemy. He fought the pirate with merciless determination, calling her a "remarkable traitor and architect of every revolt in the province during the past forty years."

She in turn took revenge on him wherever she could. When she found out that her son Morrough was involved in a conspiracy with the hated Bingham, she attacked his castle, plundering and destroying his property. To top it off, it is said she gave her flabbergasted son two resounding slaps in the face.

In 1593, Granuaile was captured by Bingham's people

and thrown into prison. He confiscated all of her livestock, almost one thousand animals in all. Bingham wanted to have the pirate hanged. Granuaile, however, was set free as hostage in exchange for her son-in-law, Richard Devilsclaw. She came out of prison poor and powerless.

That year Granuaile wrote a letter to England, addressed to the Tudor's clan chief. She begged Elizabeth to grant her protection, and to release her brother and her son Tibbot, whom Bingham had taken into custody. She justified her attacks at sea as necessary, and provoked by the English administration. Queen Elizabeth granted an audience to the pirate.

When Bingham heard about this, he wrote to court:

> Two remarkable traitors have come to England, Sir Morrow Nedoe and Gainy O'Maly. Both have been rebels since their childhood and constantly active. If they now have the possibility of complaining about an officer, or are in any way rewarded by Her Majesty, this will only bring forth more rebels in the end. They may demand compensation for the time they spent in jail, in spite of their many pardons. There is now enough known evidence against them to hang them according to the law.[8]

Numerous legends have grown around the meeting between Granuaile and Elizabeth I. It is said that Granuaile was the only guest ever to have been served a cup of tea by Elizabeth personally. In any case, Granuaile was the only Gaelic woman ever invited to the royal court.

Grace O'Malley is supposed to have worn a yellow skirt and a yellow girdle with the green cape of the clan chiefs

GRANA UILE introduced to QUEEN
Elizabeth.

Grace O'Malley meets Elizabeth I. Source: Anne Chambers,
Granuaille, Dublin 1986.

draped over her shoulders. A long veil covered head and body. She had put up her hair with a silver hair slide. The Gaelic woman went up to the petite queen with large strides and vigorously shook her hand.

Seeing courtiers in constant kow-tow positions was too much for her. Granuaile spat on the ground of the mirrored hall, as she was accustomed to do at home. A woman courtier gave her a silk handkerchief covered with embroidery. Granuaile probably held a handkerchief in her hands for the first time in her life. She heartily cleaned her nose, and threw the handkerchief into the fireplace. When she was told that she might have kept the valuable little cloth, she answered: "In Ireland we always throw away used handkerchiefs."

It is not certain if this oft-recounted scene really happened this way. But there is no doubt that Grace O'Malley made a good impression on the queen. She managed to have her son and her brother set free, and was given a royal charter allowing her to pursue her activities on the sea and on land—but only under the English flag.

NOTES

1. Hans Leip, *Bordbuch des Satans* [Satan's Log], Berlin, 1986, p. 45.
2. Bertrand d'Argentré, *Histoire de la Bretagne* [History of Brittany], p. 410.
3. Francoise d'Eaubonne, *Les grandes Aventurières*, Paris, 1988.
4. East Frisia is the area around the border between the Netherlands and Germany on the North Sea. The local dialect constitutes an independent language.
5. Anne Chambers, *The Life and Times of Grace O'Malley*, Dublin, 1983, p. 85.
6. Ibid.
7. Karl S. Bottigheimer, *Geschichte Irlands* [History of Ireland], Stuttgart,: 1985, p. 79.
8. Chambers, p. 141.

$\mathcal{T}$HE CARIBBEAN

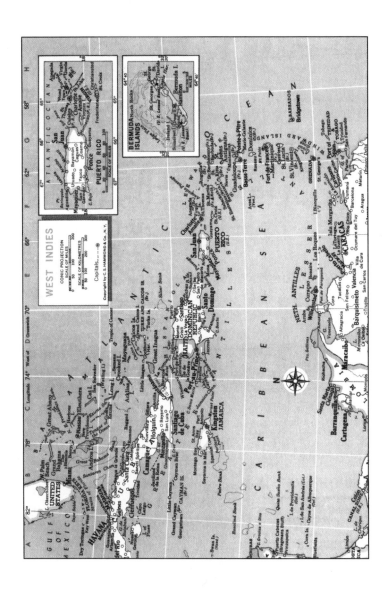

The Golden Age of Piracy

orne on southerly winds, we are swept to the "Virgin Islands." Columbus christened the Islands thus in memory of Saint Ursula and her entourage of virgins, who were, according to legend, murdered by a horde of Huns in Cologne around 452 A.D. On the largest of these islands, Saint Ursula (today known as Santa Cruz), Columbus encountered a seafaring female archer. Columbus' son, Don Fernando, describes the scene in his Columbus biography:

> On Thursday, November 14, 1493, forced ashore on an island by an inclemency of weather, Columbus issued orders to find and bring a native on board, hoping thus to learn his location. Returning to the fleet, the sloop...spotted a canoe bearing four men and a woman. The natives, realising it was useless to attempt an escape, prepared to defend themselves. They quickly pierced two Christians with their arrows, which they strung with great dexterity and strength. The woman shot an arrow that pierced through a shield. The sloop rammed the canoe, however, causing it to capsize, and enabling Columbus' men to seize their captives from the water.

This attack of European invaders upon inhabitants of the "West Indies" (as they mistakenly called the islands, believing

they had succeeded in reaching India) marked the beginning
of a campaign of eradication and pillage that lasted for centuries, the repercussions of which are still felt today.

By the seventeenth century, vast territories of North and
South America had become European colonies. A large part
of the treasures of the newly-discovered world had by then
been plundered by the whites under the slogans "freedom of
trade" and "freedom of the seas." The indigenous peoples
had been pushed almost to extinction, not only because of
the inhumane working conditions in the silver mines and
pearl fisheries where they were forced to work, but also from
exposure to European diseases carried by the invaders. Still,
the demand for labour continued to grow. The colonialists
began abducting people from Africa, bringing them to the
"New World" to sell as slaves for plantations and the newly
developed sugar industry. In the course of this, in the largest
kidnapping operation of all time, twenty million people were
violently uprooted from Africa and sold like animals over a
period of 350 years.

Manufactured products from Europe were carried to the
West African coast and sold in exchange for slaves. The ships
then continued to the West Indies, where their human cargo
was unloaded and traded in turn for pearls, sugar, or money.
Europeans called this variation of their international looting
expeditions the "triangle trade," John Hawkins being the
inventor of this imperialist transaction. His expeditions,
graced with the complete favour and support of Queen
Elizabeth I, disrupted the Portuguese monopoly in Africa
and the Spanish "Las Indias" monopoly. Thus began the "free
contest" of international trading powers. The resulting conditions could not have been more ripe for piracy.

The Caribbean Sea became the focal point of the political
conflict over the settlement of the Americas and the expro-
priation of its resources. The West Indian islands form a

wide span arching from Florida to Venezuela. Whoever could win land here held a key to the Western hemisphere.

As long as the European powers were in conflict over possession of the colonies, piracy played an important political role. The English, French, and Spanish states each issued "letters of marque," commissioning freebooters to rob the ships of their adversaries. These political pirates were not only richly rewarded, but also honoured openly for their services. For many, piracy actually marked the beginning of a career in colonial trade and administration. The famous Henry Morgan, for example, commissioned to loot for the English, later became vice-governor of Jamaica. Less famous sea robbers received coveted posts on the ships of large trading companies. Indeed, a third of the French captains in the East India Company had formerly been pirates. Freebooters even founded their own republic, on Tortuga and in northwestern Haiti. It existed for several decades and was absorbed as a French colony only in 1697, following the Peace of Ryswick.

This peace was made only after the European powers had finally reached an agreement specifying who was entitled to which slice of the colonial pie. From then on piracy came to be regarded as a disturbance to the colonisation process, and was increasingly criminalised and persecuted.

But among sea robbers there were also those who were always under pursuit because they refused to subjugate themselves to rulers—largely people whom we would today describe as "dropouts," who did not want to submit to bourgeois laws, or who had already come into conflict with those laws. These pirates did not view plundering as a means to becoming wealthy. Their goal instead was to attain booty as quickly as possible, at a minimum expense of labour, so as to squander it just as quickly.

This kind of "autonomous" piracy was a monkey wrench thrown into the colonisation process. Its practitioners were unwilling to be registered or corrupted by either money or office. They therefore became the target of international police pursuit. It is certainly no coincidence that it was, for the most part, among these adventurers that we can find the women pirates who are still known to us today.

Buccaneer Jacquotte Delahaye

North of Haiti lies the small island of Tortuga, the Spanish word for turtle. This island and the northwestern portion of Haiti, known as Santo Domingo, once constituted the area of a filibuster republic. The word filibuster evolved from "Flibustier," the name that French pirates gave themselves in mockery of English "freebooters." Having left France for whatever reason, many adventurers and others who remained on the fringes of society found a new homeland in this remote paradise. Here they hoped to realise their dreams of a free life, one without laws and courts. Many of them learned the art of smoking meat from the indigenous peoples. They sold the product to their seafaring customers. They were also known as "buccaneers" because of the special "Boucan" grills upon which they plied their trade.

One day in the 1660s, a Spanish ship dropped anchor off the coast of the filibuster republic. Forty Spanish *lanzeros*, mounted soldiers armed with lances, went ashore to finish off the French who were living there. The Spanish weren't interested in the land, for there was nothing left to plunder. Indeed, they had already seen to it themselves that Haiti and Tortuga had been stripped of their riches in the preceding centuries. After mining all that there was of silver and pearls, having practically wiped out the native people through forced labour, the Spanish had taken their leave of the area. Left behind were only a few cows and pigs that, in the meantime, had propagated to enormous numbers.

At this time the Spanish were concerned only with the few French buccaneers who were increasingly disrupting the long-standing Spanish trade monopoly on meat. Captains and sailors generally preferred to buy meat that had been smoked on the Boucan grill. Not only did it taste better, it also kept longer than the European meat imported by the Spanish—already half rotten upon arrival in the Caribbean. The Spanish, afraid of losing their market, opted for hunting down the buccaneers and thus eliminating their competitors.

The forty mounted Lanzeros combed the bush in search of their prey. Upon the discovery of three human footprints, they picked up the trail and the hunt was on. The three buccaneers—unable to flee because their yelping dogs gave them away—waited with rifles in firing position until their pursuers had surrounded them. One of the three was a woman.

"Turn around immediately," yelled the Lanzeros, "then we'll let you live."

"You'll know the brunt of our rifles first," answered the woman.

"But you are three against forty," replied the Lanzeros.

"Even if I was alone, I wouldn't turn around," she cried, and opened fire.

The woman who lost her life in the ensuing shoot-out was none other than the notorious Jacquotte Delahaye. Little is known about her other than stories such as this one about her death. Having lost her parents in a Spanish massacre, Jacquotte Delahaye was raised by friends of the family. No taller than one meter fifty-six, she was known for her unrestrained courage and desire for freedom. When the corsair Michel de Vasque—of whom it was claimed he could split heads—made a proposal of marriage, Delahaye declined on the following grounds: "I couldn't love a man who commands me—any more than I could love one who lets himself be commanded by me."

She herself commanded about 100 men, with whom she attacked the Fort de la Roche one night in 1656, attempting to win back the filibuster republic that had been in Spanish hands for two years. The strike was a success. The freebooters regained control of their island, and Jacquotte Delahaye was appointed adviser to its governor.

Like most of her fellow islanders, Jacquotte Delahaye was both a buccaneer and a filibuster. In short, this means she hunted, collected, and plundered ships according to the whims of her fancy, or whenever the need arose. A portrait of the wild lives of these "coastal brothers," another name which they gave themselves, was described by the explorer Alexandre Exquemelin, who spent a period of time among them.

> These buccaneers remain in the bush up to two years, after which they travel to Tortuga in order to replenish their supplies of gunpowder, lead slugs, rifles, cloth, and the like. Upon arrival, they squander in one month all that they have earned in the previous two years. The spirits pour like water. Tapping a full cask of wine, they guzzle it down in unbelievably short time. After they have spent everything they have, they live a little while on credit, then return home to the bush where they remain for another year or two.[1]

The life of a buccaneer could in some ways be viewed as anarchistic. Their economic practices were based on subsistence, meaning they took care to provide only for those immediate needs essential to their livelihood. Accumulation, particularly the accumulation of possessions and property, did not interest them in the least. "Why save, when tomorrow we could be dead?" That was their motto. The coastal brothers knew neither family nor homeland. They did not plunder with the intention of amassing infinite wealth, but so as to subsequently squander everything as quickly as possible.

This lifestyle put them at odds with the concept of a capitalist system based upon the accumulation of property and possessions—which was after all the driving force behind the colonisation process. All attempts to capture the buccaneers and to govern them, or even to make stationary settlers out of them, were in vain.

It is for this particular reason that the buccaneers enjoy so much sympathy today. With their spontaneous insubordination and their "Government?—No Thank You!" attitude, along with their contempt for bourgeois values such as thrift, diligence, and moderation, they were not a bad model for an autonomous society. "Peace of the barques—war of the galleons," could have also been their motto.

Various historians tend to idealise the buccaneers, painting a highly stylised portrait of them as forerunners of a socialist society. In doing so they neglect the fact that buccaneers also had slaves and forced labourers, who by no means received better treatment than the slaves of the other invaders. As Alexandre Exquemelin wrote: "The buccaneers' treatment of their slaves is brutal and ruthless. I would rather live three years as a galley slave than spend one year in their service."

Their attitude towards women was also no different from that of the other invaders. For the buccaneers, women were simply goods to be robbed, traded, or shared in "brotherly" fashion. In short, the band of buccaneers were no less racist or sexist than the rest of the world in the eighteenth century.

Jacquotte Delahaye, who enjoyed "equal rights" status among the coastal brothers, was a rare exception. Her position in this men's society had presumably been earned through extraordinary toughness and cleverness.

An Invitation to a Banquet
on the Beach

Buccaneers did not subsist only on their tasty, smoke-cured meat. They liked to throw many feasts, serving fresh pork from the grill in abundant quantities. An detailed description of such a banquet is found in a travel report by Father Labat, dating from 1692.[2]

The buccaneers first fashioned a grating by driving four forked branches, each thick as an arm, into the ground, setting up a rectangular form of approximately five by three feet. Two of the stakes at a time were linked with tie beams, then finger-thick branches with the bark removed would be fastened over them. The grill was stabilised by binding it together with strips of liana.

Other buccaneers would meanwhile dress the pig, seasoning it with salt, lemon juice, and liberal amounts of ground pepper and pimento. Thus prepared, the pig was placed belly-up on the grill, and the fire lit.

While the pig was roasting, further members of the company went to hunt more game. Others busied themselves tying the four corners of Cachibou leaves with thin liana strings, forming receptacles for gravy. This was prepared in the pig's stomach cavity from the roast juices, and spiced with a variety of condiments. Another sauce was made from a mixture of lemon juice, pepper, salt and pimento.

Father Labat continues: "As soon as the roast was thought ready, the hunters were given a signal by firing two rounds in short succession. This is the prescribed procedure, as bells have not yet been introduced in buccaneer societies. When all have returned, the dressed wild birds are either thrown into the stomach cavity, which serves as a pot, or fixed on spits and grilled in front of the fire..."

When the meat was done, everyone would cut off a piece and dip it into the gravy of choice. Bananas were consumed together with the hot and spicy meal, soothing the burning sensation in mouth and throat. To accompany the food, the buccaneers drank wine and sugar cane liquor.

Freebooter Anne Dieu-le-veut

A certain Bertrand d'Ogeron became the ruler of the filibuster republic starting in 1664. He had very good connections to France, and intended to make law-abiding settlers out of the filibusters and buccaneers. The uncivilised whites were expected to marry and metamorphose into caring providers of families. To accomplish this, however, d'Ogeron needed women—white women. This in turn lead to the rise of a prospering trade in girls between France and Tortuga. It was a profitable business for both private parties and the French West Indies Company. They brought poor women who saw no future in their home country to the "New World." But only a tiny minority of them ever thought of inducing freebooters to settle down, and even less of marrying one. Most of them quickly left again, and only a few joined the buccaneers. One of these was Anne Dieu-le-veut.

The Breton woman married filibuster Pierre Le Long, founder of Port François on Haiti. He died soon after their marriage. One day, Dieu-le-veut heard word that the well-known pirate Laurent de Graffe had spoken disparagingly of her. She went to see him, intending to clarify the affair. Laurent de Graffe was lying in bed inside his sparsely furnished hut, sleeping off a hangover.

"Get up," screamed the woman standing at his doorstep, hefting a pistol in her hand.

Still sleepy and blinking, Laurent commenced in gathering his wits.

"Get up!" Anne Dieu-le-veut underlined her command

with a severe blow to the nape of de Graffe's neck. "Or my voice will be the last you hear, and this bed your final resting place!" With a reflex action the pirate went for the boarding sword at his belt, without which he never went to bed. Quick as lightning Anne fired a round to dissuade him, and then commenced to perforate his leather treasure chest with bullets.

It finally began to dawn on the pirate just what Anne was talking about, and he said: "By the devil's horns, I've spoken badly of you. If you insist, I readily agree to excuse myself in public. But I will not aim at a woman. I do not fight with women."

"Do whatever you will," answered Anne. "I will leave now. I shall return as soon as the sun has reached the buffalo path. It is entirely up to you to defend yourself. I'm going to draw."

Anne Dieu-le-veut did in fact come back. If we are to believe Alexandre Exquemelin, Laurent de Graffe was so gallant in excusing himself that she married him on the spot. Exquemelin's explanation of Anne's decision: "The captain was a very good-looking man. He was quite tall, had a beautiful face, golden hair, and a Spanish beard that suited him best of all men in the world."

What exactly made the republic of freebooters or filibusters different from other colonies? After all, it was also a State-like entity with a governor and laws. Freebooters from Tortuga and Haiti plundered the new territories and foreign ships as readily as the others. However, they did not do it for their country, but rather entirely for themselves. Filibusters were generally not in the least interested in their victims' nationality or current political relevance. This was why their actions were branded as criminal acts of violence. Plundering for one's own needs was piracy, strictly outlawed in Europe. Robbery in the name of a European nation was called seizure, and sanctioned as political action.

Even though most inhabitants of the sea robbers' republic were from France, the French king refused to take responsibility for their misdeeds. His response to complaints was to declare that he had no land on Tortuga or Haiti, and collected no taxes there.

The laws regulating the filibusters' lives on their ships almost amounted to grassroots democracy—certainly in contrast to ships of the navy or merchant marines, where a captain wielded absolute power over his crew and had the right to command torture and executions. Freebooters had already achieved something quite close to our modern ideals of worker participation. The captain was elected on the basis of majority decisions, and could be voted out at any time. Only in battle did he act as supreme commander. Apart from this, he hardly had special rights. All crew members received the same food, and booty was divided according to set rules, with special premiums granted to those who first sighted the seized boat, as well as those first to board it.

The filibusters' health care and insurance system was unique for its time. Whoever suffered an injury in battle received compensation. Sailors on navy and merchant marine vessels could only dream of social security like this. All the same, those pirate historians of our own time who would like to portray the filibuster republic as the precursor of a social State, or even of a communist society with equal distribution of all goods, greatly exaggerate the case. Records from the time demonstrate that the society of filibusters was by no means as classless or as lacking in racial discrimination as is often maintained today. Alexandre Exquemelin's description of the filibusters' laws is most revealing in this respect:

> If a man is wounded or has lost an extremity, he will receive the following compensation: For the right arm, 600 pesetas or six

slaves; for the left arm, 500 pesetas or five
slaves. For a lost right leg, he will obtain 500
pesetas or five slaves; for the left leg, 400
pesetas or four slaves. For a disabled eye, the
same amount is due as for a lost finger,
namely 100 pesetas or one slave...Thereafter
the rest is divided evenly between the crew.
The captain is given four to six parts for his
ship, and a further two parts for himself.
Ship's boys are rewarded with half a part.
Members who have not yet participated in a
raid, or who have proven unfit, have a part
deducted, which is then distributed among
the others.

The aforementioned optimist historians enjoy mention-
ing this filibuster law, but tend to omit the part about the
slaves. This does not fit into the romantic image of the noble
sea pirate. Furthermore, as the allotment of booty according
to the motto of "higher gain for higher risk" demonstrates,
even filibusters were not entirely free of the fundamental
capitalist principle of performance-related remuneration.

Following her marriage, Anne Dieu-le-veut accompanied
her husband Laurent de Graffe on all raids. She did not participate in the fighting, however. She was regarded as a lucky
charm, and indeed from the moment she joined the boat's
crew all of their attacks met with great success. She only participated in a battle herself on the occasion of her husband's
death.

In the course of an exchange with a Spanish ship, Laurent
de Graffe was hit by a cannonball and torn into two right in
front of the crew's eyes. The men were thunderstruck. For a
moment no one thought of continuing the battle. But Anne
Dieu-le-veut promptly took over the command and ordered

various manoeuvres. Just as the Spaniards were on the verge of boarding the ship, she turned its powder-laden flanks towards them. Anne Dieu-le-veut led the crew with such cleverness that she soon managed to reverse the situation from defence to attack. Within a short time the filibusters' boarding hooks buried themselves into the wood of the Spanish vessel.

Nonetheless the Spaniards, being superior in numbers, emerged victorious after a protracted battle. Anne was wounded and taken prisoner. It is not known what became of her. What seems to be clear is that she had a daughter, who was also an adventurer, and by no means endowed with an overly tender character. Her reaction to a proposal seems to have also been to challenge the man to a duel.

History books tell the rest about the freebooters' republic on Tortuga and Santo Domingo. It was taken over by the French crown as a colony, and declared one officially following the Peace of Ryswick in 1697.

For this reason we will now set sail for new shores. A ship with polished cannons and well-dressed people is waiting in a bay near Corvocco on the Lesser Antilles. A beautiful figure, dressed in velvet and adorned with diamonds, is on the bridge. We will leave the Caribbean together with Bartholomew Roberts. Vessels of the British Royal Navy are hard on her heels. Since the Treaty of Ryswick, piracy has finally been completely outlawed. It marks the start of an internationally-coordinated (wo)man-hunt for all pirates. Sailing north, we cross the tropic of Cancer, and are soon off the fog-shrouded banks along the coast of Newfoundland.

Sea Princess Bartholomew Roberts

Was "the Most Sucessful Pirate" a Woman?

oberts sailed into the harbour of Trepassy, Newfoundland, in true pirate manner, black flag waving in the wind, drums beating, trumpets blaring. On the main mast hung a flag showing a death's head and a grappling knife. A second flag showed the Union Jack. Although his sloop was armed with a mere ten cannon, she inspired great dismay in the hearts of all the crews and the land-dwellers alike. Twenty-two ships were already docked in the harbour, but all of the crews abandoned them immediately in the very moment they became aware that the pirates were coming. Cowardly they flew to land when they saw how boldly and courageously he appeared, in the fashion that was his wont. But he preferred inspiring terror to killing.[3]

****

Was Bartholomew Roberts, "the most successful pirate of his times," a woman? "Much of the evidence supports the idea, whereas nothing disputes it," the pirate historian Wolfram zu Mondfeld wrote.

There is no definitive proof. The body of Bartholomew Roberts, which would have revealed the truth of the matter, was thrown overboard by her crew, still fully clothed, immediately after her death in battle. This was her express desire, which she had often repeated. The request may well be a clue as to the true sex of Bartholomew Roberts. Quite a few

women went to sea dressed as men in the seventeenth century, and were often only exposed as such after death (see the
chapter on Anne Bonny).

It was not only her legendary success that earned
Bartholomew Roberts fame as a pirate captain—she commandeered more than 400 ships—but also her exceptional
cleverness. A journalist described her:

> He is tall and thin, with a well-chiselled face
> and dark hair. Even in battle he wears
> damask, satin, brocades and silk with rich
> gold braiding over a red skirt cut in the fash-
> ion of the highest British officers. On a
> heavy chain of six gold braids he wears a
> large, diamond-studded cross around his
> neck; it came from the Sagrada Familia and
> was intended as a present to the King of
> Portugal. The grips of his pistols are also
> inlaid with jewels. His hats are decorated
> with the rare and highly coveted blood-red
> feathers of the bird of paradise.

Many of Roberts' contemporaries assumed, or perhaps
even knew for a fact, that the good-looking, intelligent
pirate was actually a woman. Numerous subtle references in
the statements by her crew members at their trial in Cape
Corso Castle also suggest as much. The pictures that show
Bartholomew Roberts with a thick moustache are products
of fantasy. The only authentic depiction shows a slender,
beardless person with a grim look, fashionable knickers, and
thigh muscles like Martina Navratilova.

Little is known about her origins. Bartholomew Roberts
came from Wales. She hired on with an English slave ship in
1719, working as the third mate. What she did before this is

unknown. Reports about her education and high manners lead to the presumption that she had known better times than those on the slave ship—marked by hard labour, poor nutrition, stinking accommodations and physical punishments. The *Princess*, so the ship was called, had a licence from the Royal Africa Company to transport slaves from West Africa to the "New World." After the end of the first Spanish War of Succession, in the year 1713, countless English seafarers started pursuing this lucrative commerce. A special clause in the 1713 Peace of Utrecht gave England exclusive rights to sell "black ivory," as the black slaves were called, within the Spanish colonies. The Royal Africa Company received the monopoly for this trade by royal decree. It was not the first time that the British crown profited from the slave trade.

When the *Princess* was stopped by pirates off the coast of Guinea and robbed without putting up a fight, Bartholomew Roberts and thirty-four other crew members determined on the spot that they would join them. "In an honest Service, there is thin Commons, low Wages, and hard Labour; in this, Plenty and Satiety, Pleasure and Ease, Liberty and Power; and who would not ballance Creditor on this Side, when all the Hazard that is run for it, at worst, is only a sower Look or two at choaking. No, a merry Life and a short one shall be my Motto."

This quote is taken from Daniel Defoe, author of the novel *Robinson Crusoe*. Five years after his best-seller appeared, Defoe published a journalistic work under the pseudonym Charles Johnson, titled *A General History of the Robberies and Murders of the Most Notorious Pyrates, Vol. I & II* (1724-28).[4] The writer knew all about the pirate scene. Presumably he was present at a few tours of plunder himself. Bartholomew Roberts is the figure about whom Defoe reports most extensively.

Bartholomew Roberts

Bartholomew Roberts. Source: Wolfram zu Mondfeld,
Das Piratenbuch, Güterloh 1976.

A mere six weeks after defecting to the pirates, Black Barty—as Roberts was called due to her dark complexion—was elected captain. She described herself and her crew as "sealords." She did not curse, smoke, or drink alcohol, all of which was very exotic for a pirate's life. She preferred to retire to her nobly-furnished captain's quarters and drink fruit juices, which at the time were more expensive than alcohol, or partake of tea from a silver service.

Against the usual custom on pirate ships, Bartholomew

Roberts kept the captain's quarters for herself alone. Everyone in the crew respected her wish to sleep and eat by herself. The noble pirate assigned great value to cleanliness and order on board. She demanded of her crew that they polish their weapons, pistols and knives until they gleamed. Fights were prohibited on or below deck, as were games of cards or dice for money. The pirates were to "keep their Piece, Pistols, and Cutlass clean, and fit for service," according to one of the articles that Black Barty wrote in her delicate handwriting.

These articles regulated life on board. Much like the laws of the filibusters, they guaranteed the same voting rights for everyone, nearly equal shares of the booty—only captain and quartermaster received double shares—and punished betrayal and theft among the crew. The original of this book of laws no longer exists. It was apparently thrown overboard just before falling into the hands of the authorities. Daniel Defoe recited a few of the articles, such as the following: "No Boy or Woman to be allowed amongst them. If any Man were found seducing any of the latter Sex, and carried her to Sea, disguised, he was to suffer Death."

Is it likely that a woman, who herself lived on a ship disguised as a man, had drawn up such a law? The article is directed against women (and boys!) who come on board as lovers of a crew member. Bartholomew Roberts wanted no disguised women as sailor's lovers.

This was the rule not only among pirates generally, but on all ships at that time: women were not allowed on board, for fear of conflicts and jealousies among the men.

But Bartholomew Roberts' regulation differs from the official legal verdicts on a key point: while she threatened any man who smuggled a woman on board with penalty of death, it was otherwise the women who were condemned to die when discovered. As the surviving court decisions demonstrate, the harshest punishments were reserved for those women who dressed as men in order to live the life of a man. Those who were only following their lovers were usually let off with a milder sentence (see the chapter on Anne Bonny).

Anyone joining Black Barty's crew for the first time had to swear on the Bible that he—or she—would adhere to the articles. Roberts was known for only allowing those on board who voluntarily took the oath. Later put before the judges in Cape Corso Castle, some of the accused asserted that they were forced to take the oath, but these were protective claims. Far more likely is that they would have torn each other apart for the honour of sailing under the command of the success-ful "King of the Pyrates."

Bartholomew Roberts always spoke a refined language, regardless of whether the issue at hand was blackmail, the planning of a raid, or the ransoming of hostages. "Exchange is not robbery," she would declare whenever she had acquir-ed a new, fully-loaded ship, leaving her old ship to the rob-bed parties.

With care and precision, she wrote receipts for the benefit of landbound insurance companies. The captain of a French ship received the following document: "This is to certify whom it may, or doth Concern, that we GENTLEMEN OF FORTUNE, have receiv'd eight Pounds of Gold-Dust, for the Ransom of *Hardey*, Captain Dittwitt Commander, so that we Discharge the said Ship, Witness our Hands, this 13th of Jan. 1721-2. Batt. Roberts."[5]

Bartholomew Roberts had a great talent for leadership. Her method is comparable to what is called "soft management" in modern corporations. She was popular among her people and considerate, but knew to keep herself apart. When she noticed that a few envious parties seemed to be plotting a conspiracy against her, she made them into her personal staff. Most of all she provided top performance: in questions of strategy and navigation as well as in those of shooting and stabbing.

At least in comparison to her fellow male pirates, Bartholomew Roberts was relatively restrained in employing violence. Force is admittedly the basis for a tour of plunder, for a raid cannot succeed without a genuine threat. But meaningless slaughters, such as those carried out by the English national heroes Francis Drake and Henry Morgan, were just not her thing. She concentrated on how best to strike fear into her victims. This was usually enough to achieve the desired objective: money, jewellery, weapons, sugar, furs, fabrics, grains, veal, rum. Black Barty and her crew were absolutely merciless with these goods, however. Daniel Defoe describes a typical attack.

> They tore up the Hatches and entered the Hold like a parcel of Furies, and with Axes and Cutlashes, cut and broke open all the Bales, Cases, and Boxes, they could lay their Hands on; and when any Goods came upon Deck, that they did not like to carry aboard, instead of tossing them into the Hold again, threw them over-board into the Sea; all this was done with incessant cursing and swearing, more like Fiends than Men.

The writer seems to have been more aghast at these acts of plunder than at the fact, incidentally mentioned, that the pirates threatened the commandeered ship's passengers with death. But what was human life worth at the time? The lives of blacks were weighed in sugar, the lives of Indians were traded by colonialists for gold, silver and pearls. And Bartholomew Roberts and her crew valued their own lives only as long they could lead them as they wished: "A merry Life and a short one shall be my Motto."

The noble pirate loved the fine arts. Her ship's orchestra

had the function of inspiring terror by making horrible noises during battle, but were also required to play Bach or Händel during more relaxed hours. "The musicians were allowed to rest on the Sabbath, but not, unless they received special permission, on the other six days and nights."

Black Barty was also very open and creative with respect to the visual arts. On several occasions she had a new pirate flag designed to replace the perpetually fixed stare of the death's head. The designs became ever more refined and different. The skull with a grappling knife was followed by a creation with the form of Bartholomew Roberts herself, holding a flaming sword in one hand and an hourglass in the other, standing on a skull beneath each foot. The two skulls were labelled ABH and AMH. That stood for "A Barbadian's Head" and "A Martinician's Head." Bartholomew Roberts had declared Barbados and Martinique to be her greatest enemies.

Another flag showed Bartholomew Roberts shaking hands with Death in the form of a skeleton. The two hold up an hourglass with a bleeding heart below. In its other hand the skeleton holds an arrow, pointing down to hell.

These symbols give an inkling of how Bartholomew Roberts and her crew viewed their relationship to death. Death was always present. By not fearing it, they made it into their ally. "They are like mad Men that cast Fire-Brands, Arrows, and Death, and say, are not we in Sport?" Daniel Defoe wrote. They "told Captain Cary, That they should accept no Act of Grace; that the K— and P——t might be damned with their Acts of G—— for them, neither would they go to Hope-Point, to be hang'd up a Sun drying, as Kidd's, and Braddish's Company were; but that if they should ever be overpower'd, they would set Fire to the Powder, with a Pistol, and go all merrily to Hell together."

Bartholomew Roberts's crew never lost their gallows humour—even when they were chained to each other on board a ship of the Royal Navy after the death of their leader, sailing towards certain death by hanging. When everything was taken from them, they joked that they should at least be left with half a penny to pay old Charon for the trip over the Styx. "And at their thin Commons, they would observe, that they fell away to fast, that they should not have Weight left to hang them," Defoe writes. When one of the prisoners became fearful after all, and started reading the Bible, the pirate Sutton asked him "what he proposed by so much Noise and Devotion? 'Heaven,' says the other, 'I hope.' 'Heaven, you fool,' says Sutton, 'did you ever hear of any Pyrates going thither? Give me H-ll, it's a merrier Place; I'll give Roberts a Salute of thirteen Guns at Entrance.'"

Despite their excellent relations with the Devil and in Hell, the pirates nevertheless held a certain respect for clergymen. Much like the legal plunderers of the "New World," they were especially accommodating in their treatment of preachers. Daniel Defoe reports that on one raid a priest fell into Bartholomew Roberts's hands. A few crew members wanted to hire him on as ship's chaplain. They offered him good money to stay with them. His task would have been to regularly prepare punch and lead prayers. When the priest gratefully rejected the offer, they let him go. "In fine, they kept nothing which belonged to the Church, except three Prayer-Books and a Bottle-Screw, which as I was inform'd by one of the Pyrates himself, they said they had Occasion for, for their own Use," Defoe wrote.

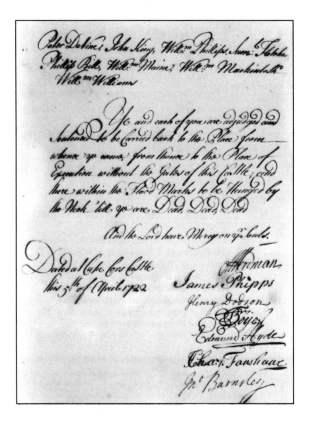

A death sentence passed against 19 of Roberts' crew at Cape Coast in 1722.

For three years Bartholomew Roberts lead successful raids throughout the Atlantic, evading pursuit by the ships of the Royal Navy. In the spring of 1722, however, the warship *Swallow* caught up with the pirates off the southwest coast of Africa. A volley of grapeshot from the guns of the English ship ended Roberts' life. "He settled himself on the Tackles of a Gun, which one Stephensen, from the Helm, observing, ran to his Assistance," Defoe writes. "But when he found his Mistake, and that his Captain was certainly dead, he gushed into tears, and wished the next Shot might be his Lot. They presently threw him over-board, with his Arms, and Ornaments on, according to the repeated Request, he had made in his Life-time."

Bartholomew Roberts at Whydah on the Guinea Coast of Africa in 1722 with two of his ships. Also depicted are 11 ships held ransom for safe passage.

From the Galley:

Piquant Shark Schnitzel

Spices played an important role in seafaring from the very beginning, and that was just as much the case in piracy. Since they had to be acquired from faraway countries, spices were so valuable in the Middle Ages that they even served as a means of exchange. As early as 550 A.D. the Persians, who had occupied the East African island of Zanzibar and the South Chinese city Canton, introduced a pepper tariff. Rich merchants had to pay their passage in pepper. Hence the expression "sacks of pepper."

Thanks to pepper tariffs, the trading crossroads at Baghdad bloomed into all the urban splendour of the fairy tales from "A Thousand and One Nights." In the late Middle Ages, one pound of saffron could be traded for a horse, a pound of ginger for a sheep, and two pounds of muscat nuts for a cow. Spices served as a form of currency into the modern period, and remained prohibitively expensive right up until 1800.

It was greed for gold and spices that caused the Spanish Queen Isabella to hire Columbus to seek a sea route to India. If the Earth did turn out to be a flat disk, then the mad seafarer—who foolishly hoped for the hand of the queen's daughter, Johanna—could go and fall off the edge of the world and into Hell, for all the queen cared. As we know Columbus did return, perhaps not with the hoped-for cinnamon and carnations from India, but at any rate with chilli peppers, pimento and potatoes from America. The merchant ships carrying spices on all seas were a favourite target of plunder for pirates.

Piquant Shark Schnitzel

Brush shark-meat filets with ample lemon juice. Spice with pepper, salt, pimento and cardamom, and fry briefly. How briefly? A wise old pirate maxim recommends holding the shark steak in the right hand and the fire tongue in the left; show a burning coal to the steak, and serve promptly.

Anyone who wants to actually try out this recipe should perhaps use eel instead of shark, since many shark species are now increasingly endangered.

Anne Bonny

We have now returned to more southerly climes. The Bahamas lie before us. Happening upon them in his ill-fated search for India, Columbus positively swooned about their divine beauty. He was taken aback by the scent of unknown flowers and plants, fish "in the most beautiful colours of the world, blue, yellow, red, and in all other colours, and others painted a thousand hues, and so splendid that no one can resist admiring them," flocks of parrots "that darkened the sun."

Of the Arawaks who lived there, Columbus wrote to his King: "Moving people, without guile, without desire for anything. I am convinced, as I assure your Majesty, that in the whole world there is no better people or country. They love their neighbours as themselves, and have the sweetest language in the world, are very gentle and smile constantly." His conclusion: "If your Majesty so desires, they could all be transported to Castile, or imprisoned upon the island itself. Fifty men would be enough to guard over them and force them to do all that is desired of them." Twenty-five years later, this highly praised people had been exterminated. Forty thousand Arawaks were brought to Haiti by the whites, and set to work in the silver mines at the lash of the whip. Most of them died after just a few months.

We are but a few miles from New Providence, an island in the Bahamas, in the second decade of the eighteenth century. A French merchant ship, loaded with valuable fabrics, is on its way west. The captain is worried, for there are said to be over a thousand pirates in the area. The many natural harbours are overflowing with sailing ships flying the Jolly Roger.

The Bahamas seem almost to have been created with piracy in mind. Anyone with a relatively small ship and a knowledge of the archipelago with all of its jagged, difficult-to-round islands, clearly has an advantage over stately merchant ships. Nassau, the capital of the Bahamas on New Providence, is not only considered a stronghold of pirates, but also of homosexuals. That too sets the captain's heart beating.

Suddenly a ship appears by the light of the moon. Sail and deck are drenched in blood. The figure of a woman stands at the bow. In her hand she holds a grappling hook dripping blood, and uses it to strike repeatedly at a human form. The ghostly ship quickly approaches the merchant brigantine. The merchant crew is frozen with terror. Without putting up any fight, they surrender their cargo to the attackers.

The idea for this scenario was Anne Bonny's. During the action she stood at the bow and struck at a stuffed mannequin with her hook. Previously she had drowned the puppet, hook, and ship in turtle's blood. She planned the attack together with her friend, Pierre Vane, a homosexual hairdresser from New Providence. He was not yet a pirate by profession, but after hearing of the French ship and its load of valuable fabrics, he could not resist the temptation. He had a great passion for designing intricate dresses from silks and satins.

Anne Bonny planned her attacks with cunning and fantasy. The horrible shows she staged spared her plenty of battles. This does not mean that Anne Bonny was any less brutal on occasion than her male colleagues. As the expert, Daniel Defoe, wrote:

> She was of a fierce and couragious Temper,
> wherefore, when she lay under Condemna-
> tion, several Stories were reported of her,

> much to her Disadvantage, as that she had
> kill'd an English Servant-Maid, once in her
> Passion with a Case-Knife, while she look'd
> after her Father's House; but upon further
> Enquiry, I found this Story to be groundless:
> It was certain she was so Robust, that once,
> when a young Fellow would have lain with
> her, against her Will, she beat him so, that he
> lay ill of it a considerable Time.

Daniel Defoe's report on the *Robberies and Murders of the Most Notorious Pyrates* is the most extensive and nearly only source on Anne Bonny and Mary Read (see next chapter). Nearly all other writers of sea-robber history—from Philip Gosse in his *Who's Who of Pirates* to Hans Leip, author of *Klabauterflagge* [The Kobold Flag]—have copied or rewritten Defoe's account, at least as far as Anne Bonny and Mary Read are concerned. It is remarkable that their contemporary, Defoe, viewed both women entirely as practitioners of their profession, and described their boldness and bravura with great admiration, even though the general contempt for women was especially pronounced in the eighteenth century. After all, the official persecution of witches had only just ended. By contrast, the later authors increasingly disqualified the two women as mere "pirate lovers" or even prostitutes.

With painstaking research and ample fantasy—what would pirate stories be without fantasy?—the American feminist, Susan Baker, turned the histories distorted through men's eyes on their head. Her book, *Women Remembered*,[5] contradicts the traditional version that Anne Bonny first came on board a pirate ship as the lover of the notorious pirate and "lady's man" Calico Jack. Jack Rackham was not a "lady's man" and not even a pirate yet when he himself first came to New Providence as a captain's lover. His nickname,

Calico, derived from the sturdy calico-cotton pants he wore, of which it was claimed that if never washed they ended up bullet-proof. Without Anne Bonny, Calico would have never become a captain. After a mutiny that was presumably started by Anne, an election for captain was held. Pierre Vane and Jack each received ten votes, Anne six. She added her votes to Calico's. He became the captain, with Anne as second-in-command. But apparently she was the real leader. She evicted Calico from the captain's quarters and resided in them alone.

The eyewitness testimony at the pirate trials, recorded by Daniel Defoe, made it clear who really wore the calico slacks on board: "Just as we had already received permission to continue sailing, the notorious Captain Rackham first appeared on deck. In his colourful suit he did in fact cut a heroic appearance, but he looked as though he had just crawled out of bed. He had puffy eyes and his voice sounded blurred. When his notorious companion told him to get out of the way, he promptly retired."

Anne Bonny was powerfully built. She wore her red hair openly—sometimes under a floppy hat—and broadly-cut satin pants designed and sewed by Pierre Vane. Supposedly she fought barechested. Opinions are divided about her looks. The actress, racing-car driver and pilot Jill St. John, who played a woman pirate in a film, once said that "No one should get the idea that I am supposed to be playing this Anne Bonny in *The Pirates of the King*. She was six foot two, weighed two hundred pounds, and had a face that could stop a sundial."

No one would have ever dared make such a pronouncement in Anne Bonny's presence, lest they suffer a fate like the one-eared sailor who got in her way upon her arrival in New Providence, stupidly insulting her as she came on land. Anne pulled her pistol and shot the sailor's other ear off.

Anne was born in Ireland as the illegitimate daughter of

Anne Bonny from an early edition of Defoe

an advocate and his servant maid. The advocate was married. His mother sided with his wife, and refused to forgive him his "mistake," and so he disowned Anne. Anne grew up with her mother.

"It lasted nearly five Years," Daniel Defoe reports, but "at this Time, having a great Affection for the Girl he had by his Maid, he had a Mind to take it Home, to live with him; but as all the Town knew it to be a Girl, the better to disguise the Matter from them, as well as from his Wife, he had it put in Breeches, as a Boy, pretending it was a Relation's Child he was to breed up to be his Clerk."

At some point the deception was uncovered. Anne's father moved in with her mother, the maid, and lived openly in this disreputable relationship. A "wild marriage" with a child at the end of the seventeenth century was a scandal. The advocate lost his clients and decided to emigrate. As a white man, he thought he could live a life full of privileges in the West Indian colonies. And there he could pretend he had a "proper" family, and would need have no worries about taking care of his daughter. There was an acute shortage of white women in the colonies, and he would surely be able to find a profitable marriage for her.

Indeed, there were few women among the colonialists. In the eyes of the European rulers, this was the reason that white men were entering into long-term relationships with black women, and it conflicted with their racist ideals. It was acceptable as long as a white men raped his slaves, or at worst punished them, because he had "disgraced himself before God and shamed all Christians by dirtying his body and lying with a Negro woman." But to live together with a black woman, or to have a child with her, was forbidden. In the French areas, for example, a white man who had a child with a black woman was required to pay a penalty of 2,000 pounds of sugar. The woman would be sent to a special "home," and could not be bailed out at any price.

Concern for the preservation of the white race finally prompted the governments and trade companies to organise a kind of trade in girls and women overseas. The Dutch East India Company paid a reward to every family going to Batavia who took at least two daughters of eight years or older along. There were additional payments for "respectable young maidens" brought along from orphanages. This group of girls was under the governor's direct guardianship. They were only allowed to marry company employees or free citizens—and that only with the governor's permission.

Anne did not require the governor's approval, only her father's. After growing up in Carolina, she wanted to marry. But she fell in love with the first no-account sailor who came along, spoiling her father's plans to marry her off at a profit. Anne married James Bonny, at which point her father again disowned her. She burned down his plantation in revenge, and fled with her husband to New Providence.

"Blessed with fresh water, turtles and wild boars, New Providence was a pirate's paradise, a harbour for the down-trodden from the New and Old Worlds," Susan Baker writes. She describes the situation of women in the West Indian colonies using examples from among the friends that Anne made there. One of them was Meg, lover to the pirate Captain Jennings. She had met him as a fugitive after stabbing her drunken husband—a crime considered worse than any other form of murder. "Master murder," as it was called, had in the past even been termed "God murder."

Women were forced to acquire a man as protection, for a woman who belonged to no man effectively belonged to all of them. Married women were in every sense their husband's property; husbands could sell or kill their wives with impunity. This was the fate of one-eyed Hawkins, who had been auctioned publicly by her husband. For the crime of absconding from her second owner, Hawkins was captured and sent as a slave in chains to Virginia. She again succeeded in escaping, this time to New Providence. Beth was another fugitive. As a midwife she had been held responsible for death of a child during a caesarean section.

All the same, these women were privileged compared to the majority of women in the West Indian colonies: the black and Indian slaves. There are no heroic stories to tell about them. Except for a "free" mulatto called Zola, mentioned by Susan Baker, black women are not to be found in the history of woman pirates. Of their lives we know only that like their men, they had to work as slaves and were treated by the white rulers as sexual objects, or as birthing machines for making new slaves. According to the situation on the market, they would sometimes be prevented from having children, and sometimes forced to have them. There were times when it was more affordable to "buy than to breed," according to a contemporary writing about the situation at Cuban plantations: "The expenses are so substantial that the Negro born on the plantation costs more by the time he is finally able to work than another of the same age purchased on the open market." A few decades later, when it had become more difficult to capture blacks in Africa, sixteen-year old slave women were forced to become mothers, and agricultural associations felt no shame in labelling seventeen-year old girls who had already borne several children "good breeders," as though they were cattle or swine.

Back in the harbour of New Providence. It is a humid and moonless night. At dawn, the royal amnesty announced by incoming Governor Woodes Rogers is scheduled to take effect. The measure is intended to put an end to the pirate menace. All who give up piracy are supposed to be pardoned, while the gallows await the rest. The governor has received word of a rumour that one crew does not want to take his offer, and intends to flee instead. Accordingly, Woodes has blockaded the harbour, and now arrays his fleet for battle.

Suddenly a small ship goes into motion and heads straight for Rogers' fleet. The governor orders his men to fire. The ship bursts into flame, and with a roar it shoots off a hail of fireballs onto the fleet. Too late, Rogers realises that no one is on the ship, that it was doused in oil and set floating towards his fleet. His volley has set the oil aflame, and acts as a fuse for the cannon, which have been filled with cannonballs and highly-combustible gunpowder. At any moment the fire might reach the gunpowder hold and blow up the ship, taking Rogers' fleet with it. His ships turn and take flight.

In the confusion of the explosion, another small ship gets past the blockade, Anne Bonny on deck. Supposedly she waves to Woodes Rogers, "as delicate as a fine lady setting off on a long sea journey."

She had thought up the plan with her usual cunning and turn for the theatrical. She had determined to accept no amnesty, to continue making the seas unsafe together with Calico Jack and Pierre Vane. The amnesty would not have applied in Anne's case, anyway, for in the meantime she had left her husband, and was sought for the attempted murder of her father; two crimes that weighed more heavily than mere piracy, crimes for which there was no pardon.

At some point James Bonny, Anne's abandoned husband, showed up again to reassert his privileges. By this time she had met the English woman Mary Read, and the two had become inseparable. James Bonny kidnapped Anne and brought her, naked and bound, before the governor. James insisted that Anne be kept bound, for he feared "that this diabolical cat will kill me on the spot." Bonny proposed a divorce through sale. The crew of her ship agreed, and wanted to buy Anne's freedom. But she refused, calling out that she did not want "to be bought and sold like a pig or a cow." The governor let Anne Bonny free on the condition that she return to her lord and master, but he had already fled in fear of his life. Anne and Mary took up his trail. He eluded them, but in revenge they burned his turtle dealership to the ground.

Anne Bonny was very economical in her use of violence. When it was unavoidable she did resort to force, and then without any scruple. But whenever possible she instead employed cunning, treachery, and a good measure of theatre.

A certain "lady's touch" was granted to her tours of plunder. Once she used a trick very much in keeping with the standard image of "the weapons of a woman." The object of her desire was the *Royal Queen*, a beautifully equipped and fast sloop that belonged to her former lover, Chidley Bayard. But at this point he had been after her head for some time, and had even entered into a business relationship with James Bonny. All the more reason for Anne to think up a revenge. The luxurious ship—decorated with mahogany panelling and gold and silver inlays in the cabins, and equipped with twenty cannon—was commanded by a certain Hudson, who was very proud of his own reputation as a lady's man.

Anne accepted Hudson's invitation onto the luxurious boat, but only under the condition that his crew go beneath deck, so that her "good reputation" would be preserved. Alone with Hudson in the captain's quarters, she mixed a sleeping potion into his wine. The lady's man fell asleep, and there were no more obstacles to Anne's inspection of the deck. The next day, Lady Anne had left the ship, and the clueless Hudson set out to sea. When he was attacked a few hours later, he discovered to his surprise that his brand new cannons did not fire; the firing pins had been drowned in water. The *Royal Queen* was taken by Anne Bonny and her crew without a fight. There was only one casualty: Captain Hudson. His murderer: Mary Read.

Mary Read

Mary Read grew up in England. Like Anne Bonny, she was brought up as a boy. Her mother, who was married to a seaman, had first borne a son. Her husband disappeared soon thereafter for unknown reasons; perhaps he suffered a shipwreck. "Nevertheless," Daniel Defoe reports, "the Mother, who was young and airy, met with an Accident, which has often happen'd to Women who are young, and do not take a great deal of Care; which was, she soon proved with Child again, without a Husband to Father it, but how, or by whom, none but herself could tell."

This was a rather precarious situation for a single woman in England at the end of the seventeenth century. As a sailor's widow, she hardly had the money to feed herself or her child. She was dependent upon support from her family. Having a child out of wedlock now threatened to ruin her reputation and lose her the favour of her relatives. In an effort to cover up the pregnancy, the widow without means moved to the country. A few months after the birth of the daughter, the son died. Mary's mother then had the idea of pretending that the girl was actually the legitimate son. She started dressing Mary in boys' clothing and soon thereafter returned to London, where the mother of the deceased sailor lived. The sailor's mother paid for the care of her presumed grandson. Once Mary was old enough, her mother let her in on the ruse, and the girl went on living as a boy. But when Mary was thirteen, the grandmother died. Mary and her mother thus lost their only source of income. Therefore Mary kept wearing boys' clothing and went to work. First she served as a lackey to a French lady, then she hired on with a warship.

Mary had learned an important lesson: if you have no money, it's far better to be a man.

Daniel Defoe's report is full of admiration for Mary's bravery and skill in battle, and points out that she had actually earned an officer's rank. But that accrued only to people with money.

Mary fell in love with one of her comrades in arms, revealed her true sex, and married him. The two opened an inn in Breda. The bar, "Three Horseshoes," became a favourite haunt for many officers. But the Peace of Ryswick, in 1697, marked an end to their career in catering. The officers no longer came to Breda and Mary's husband died soon thereafter. Mary took her men's clothing out of mothballs and joined the infantry. Since, in times of peace, nothing much was happening over there either, she left the military and hired on with a merchant ship on a course for the West Indies.

Women who decided to live as men were not unusual in Mary's time. In their book, *Frauen in Männerkleidern* [Women Dressed as Men], Rudolf Dekker and Lotte van de Pol document 120 cases that they discovered, just in the Netherlands, in the period between 1550 and 1839. Considering that these were only the cases that were discovered and brought before court, and of which the records still survive, we can only guess at how many crossdressing women lived as men and successfully avoided discovery.

There were plenty of reasons to attempt such a switch. In the eighteenth century women had no opportunity to determine their own lives. A woman who married did little more than change her effective owner from her father to her husband, who could do with her as he pleased. Women could not move freely without male "protection," and so it became a custom that a woman who desired to travel alone disguised herself as a man. A few took a liking to the privileges they

Mary Read depicted in Gosse's *Who's Who of Pirates*.

enjoyed as men, and kept the men's clothing. Such women sought professions as manual labourers, soldiers, or sailors. A few even married other women. That the majority of women who are known to us as transvestites were involved at sea or in the military may well be attributable to the fact that these are the areas where a woman was most likely to be discovered.

Dekker and Pol describe how difficult it was to hide one's sex on a ship. There was as good as no privacy on board. Several persons would sleep together in narrow quarters, and there was no certainty of not being seen when going to the toilet. Washing and changing did not pose too much of a risk, as this was actually infrequent behaviour given the ideas at that time about hygiene. But discovery could cost the woman her life. As it says in the Bible: "A woman shall not wear anything that pertains to a man, nor shall a man put on a woman's garment; for whoever does these things is an abomination to the *Lord* your God" (Deuteronomy 22:5, King James Revised). Reason enough, in the view of the authorities, to level the death penalty for transvestites.

In 1643, King Charles I of England decreed the following law: "No woman shall falsify her sex by wearing a man's clothing. She subjects herself thusly to the strictest penalty that the Law or Our wrath may ordain."

By hiring onto a ship Mary Read was thus risking her life. What alternatives did she have? How else could she have made her living? Men without means always had the possibility of at least getting by as soldiers or sailors. This option did not exist for women who were too young, or too strong, to qualify for poor relief. "Prostitution was the last resort in difficult times for many women from the lower classes," Dekker and Pol write. "Girls who became prostitutes came from the same classes and age groups, and often had the same background of poverty and uprootedness, as the women who disguised themselves as men...The decision to switch genders out of desperation represented a simultaneous rejection of prostitution as an alternative."[6]

Life as a man certainly did not mean a life full of freedom and self-determination, at any rate not among the poor populations to which Mary Read belonged. The life as a sailor on a merchant ship was hard. It represented the heaviest possible labour for poor wages, and the worst possible accommodations and board within a system in which corporeal punishments and tortures were the rule. While passengers, ship chaplains, and captains sweetened their long passages with feasts and drinking orgies, the food for ship workers was so meagre that many succumbed to scurvy and other diseases of malnutrition.

In his travelogue, Jean-Baptiste Labat, a French Jesuit father, describes at length the feasting on his passage to Martinique. Every day there were Irish steaks, fresh mutton and veal, or fricasseed young chickens—and fresh salad. "Perhaps it seems amazing that salad was served every day, but we had a good store of red beets, portulac, cress, pickled cucumbers, and two large boxes full of endives, which were kept under armed guard day and night for fear that rats or sailors might do harm," the missionary relates.[7]

In this report, Labat also describes the punishments meted out to troublesome crew members. A sailor who showed up late to his watch was tied to a cannon and lashed fifty times with short hawsers. A soldier had to run the gauntlet for cursing. "I do not believe that he will have any desire to curse on a further journey, for all those who were appointed to punish him did their best to fulfil their duty," the father comments.

The number of crew members who died in passage was great. Not only did countless captured blacks die under the inhuman conditions of their imprisonment on slave ships;

many slave-ship crew members also succumbed to their routine working conditions.

It is safe to assume that Mary Read was pleased when the ship on which she laboured was commandeered by pirates. She was the only crew member taken along by them. At any rate, there was more justice on pirate ships than on naval or merchant vessels. And so Mary Read came to New Providence, where she joined the clique around green-eyed Anne Bonny.

After Anne Bonny was pardoned by the governor, she and her crew accepted the King's Amnesty. For a time they lived in Cuba, where Anne and Calico Jack raised a child together. But eventually they grew restless. When they heard that Woodes Rogers was equipping freebooters against the Spanish, they went to New Providence to register with the governor. In contrast to piracy, freebooting was permitted, for here the commandeering was done in the interest of power.

Rogers' fleet had hardly set sail before the crews, which mostly consisted of former pirates, began to mutiny. The commanders appointed by the colonial authorities were deposed, the British flag pulled down from the mast, and the Jolly Roger raised. Mary Read had instigated the mutiny.

The woman pirate was less reckless and impulsive than her friend Anne Bonny, who was some years her junior. Many authors praise her virtue and sense of justice. "She was proud and bold by nature, but sensitive to the most tender feelings and mildest stirrings. Her behaviour was determined by the principles of virtue, but all the same she was violent in her attacks," according to *The Pirate's Own Book*.

Like Anne Bonny, while on board the pirate ship Mary Read dressed like a woman. Only in battle did both women prefer trousers. But ever since the time when they had been discovered together in bed—this incident is worth its own chapter—their sex was known to all.

How is it possible that two women on a ship were not

only tolerated but accepted as leaders at a time when women were otherwise hated and despised? Presumably because they were very good. Much as women who undertake male-dominated professions today, whether as manual labourers or executives, always have to perform better than their male colleagues, it is likely that the two women pirates carried out their own jobs with exceptional competence.

Anne Bonny clearly had a gift for management. "She had the stuff of a leader, and could have spurred us on to do battle with the whole world," the pirate John Harper said about her during a trial. Mary Read had excellent navigational skills— quite apart from her invincibility in duels. Both women knew too well how to gain respect among their male colleagues. And that was only possible through violence. Anne Bonny took pains to maintain her rough image, for example by severely beating one fellow who annoyed her with a chair, or by relieving her fencing master of his buttons during a duel, one by one, with the point of her dagger.

There are stories about Mary Read as well, of how she would challenge opponents to duels and kill them without remorse. One source diverges from Daniel Defoe's report. In her book, *Storia della Pirateria del mondo*, Anna Franchi writes of a conflict between Mary Read and a helmsman, a man who knew, as did the rest of the pirates, that Mary was a woman, although at the time she was still dressing as a man. The helmsman refused to obey Mary's orders, and slapped her in the face. She promptly challenged him to a duel. In keeping with the usual law on pirate ships, she asked for permission to duel with him at the next landing. Once on land, the helmsman wanted to back out, but Mary insisted on restoring her honour. His gun did not fire. "Mary, now certain of her life, approached him, opened her shirt, showed him her pale breasts, and said: 'You wretch, you knew I was a

woman and yet you dared to strike me. This woman shall
now kill you, to make an example for all who would dare to
insult her.' And she blew out his brains."

Daniel Defoe tells the story rather differently. In his version, Mary intentionally set off the dispute so as to save the
life of a young sailmaker who was her lover. The sailmaker
was the one actually headed for a duel with the helmsman.
Mary therefore provoked the helmsman herself, intending
to render him harmless. "It was true, she had fought before,
when she had been insulted by some of those Fellows, but
now it was altogether in her Lover's Cause, she stood as it
were betwixt him and Death, as if she could not live without
him." Here Defoe's imagination seems to have been given
wings by the wish that even a woman as brutal as Mary

Read could not live without a man she loves, and would sac-
rifice herself for him.

Mary Read's understanding of herself as a pirate was
indeed rather brutal. When she was asked by a prisoner what
she thought about the death penalty for pirates, she answered:

> That if it were put to the Choice of the
> Pyrates, they would not have the Punish-
> ment less than Death, the Fear of which,
> kept some dastardy rogues honest; that
> many of those who are now cheating the
> Widows and Orphans, and oppressing their
> poor Neighbours, who have no Money to
> obtain Justice, would then rob at Sea, and
> the Ocean would be crowded with Rogues,
> like the Land, and no Merchant would ven-
> ture out; so that the Trade, in a little Time,
> would not be worth following.

Mary Read and Anne Bonny went on a mutual tour of
plunder for three years, until their capture by the Royal
Navy. The last battle was hopeless, as the whole crew was
completely drunk except for the two women. Only they and
one man remained on deck, to put up a ferocious and bitter
struggle. Mary Read called out to her drunken comrades,
trying to get them up on deck. When no one appeared she
was so enraged that she shot at the pirates through the hatch,
and killed one of them.

Her trial was held in Sante Jago de la Vega. Anne Bonny
and Mary Read were both pardoned because they claimed
they were pregnant. Presumably this was a lie, but it saved
them from the gallows. The doctor who diagnosed them had
been saved by the two women from the rack of a slave ship
barely a year earlier.

Stamp depicting Anne Bonny and Mary Read.
Source: *Geschichte mit Pfiff*, 5/85.

Calico Jack was hanged. When Anne was allowed to see him one last time, shortly before his execution, she consoled him with the words that she was sorry to see him there. But if he had only fought like a man, she added, he would not now be waiting to be hanged like a dog.

There are no reliable accounts of what became of the two women. Mary Read seems to have died in prison. Anne Bonny escaped, and for many years was wanted, against a high reward, for arson, attempted murder, conspiracy against the crown, and the freeing of slaves on ships.

She could hardly depend on any help from her father, as can be gleaned from a book from the year 1775:

> Her Father was known to a great many
> Gentlemen, Planters of Jamaica, who had
> dealt with him, and among whom he had a
> good Reputation; and some of them, who
> had been in Carolina, remember'd to have
> seen her in his House; wherefore they were
> inclined to shew her Favour, but the Action
> of leaving her Husband was an ugly Circum-
> stance against her.

ℒove Among Woman Pirates

Two women explode the societally-imposed limits on their existence as women in the eighteenth century, and set off into the world of the adventurers. As pirates they fight, commandeer, and command together, and let no man tell them what to do. Anne Bonny and Mary Read lived in a world where homosexuality among men was no secret. Were they lesbians? Did they perhaps even have a lesbian relationship? Posing this question is a self-evident matter today. The contemporaries of the two pirate women, however, were apparently very remote from even being able to imagine the possibility.

It is historically confirmed that Anne was in love with Mary. Daniel Defoe reports of this. But he assumes that Anne—who, like Mary, first appeared in male clothing—was deceived by Mary's disguise, and desired Mary's alter ego, "Marc Read," a new addition to the crew. This is how Defoe describes how the two women got together:

> Ann Bonny took her for a handsome young Fellow, and for some Reasons best known to herself, first discovered her Sex to Mary Read; Mary Read knowing what she would be at, and being very sensible of her own Incapacity that Way, was forced to come to a right Understanding with her, and so to the great Disappointment of Ann Bonny, she let her know she was a Woman also; but this Intimacy so disturb'd Captain Rackham,

> who was the Lover and Gallant of Ann
> Bonny, that he grew furiously jealous, so
> that he told Anne Bonny, he would cut her
> new Lover's Throat, therefore, to quiet him,
> she let him into the Secret also.

It was apparently inconceivable to Defoe that there could be anything like desire among women. According to his logic, Anne would of necessity be disappointed, and Rackham reassured, upon learning of the attractive sailor's true sex. Defoe certainly knew how many male homosexuals there were among the pirates; but love between women exceeded the horizons of an eighteenth-century male's phallocentric powers of imagination.

That this has barely changed, down to this day, can be observed by the naiveté with which the pirate storytellers of our own century describe the attraction between Anne and Mary. A few have shaped the evidence into a racy bed episode fitting the voyeuristic requirements of male-oriented reading. One author, quoted but not named by Susan Baker, relates how Rackham, raging with jealousy, storms into the cabin, hoping to catch Anne *in flagranti*. "For a moment he lost his composure altogether, seeing, as though in mockery of all true lovers with whom he might have found her, that the form stretched out upon the bed was a woman in man's clothing."

Susan Baker is convinced that Anne and Mary were lesbians and loved each other. Her essay on the two is stamped with all the enthusiasm of the contemporary women's movement, breaking centuries of silence about lesbian identities and searching for instances of women loving women throughout history. How could lesbian love be lived out at the time of Anne Bonny and Mary Read? There are as good as no sources on this; little was written on sexuality at the time, nearly nothing on homosexuality, and even less on female homosexuality.

Dekker and Pol report that homosexuality was an absolute taboo in the seventeenth and eighteenth centuries. Sodomy, as love among men was called at that time, and tribaldry, the term for love among women, were both punishable by death. Homosexuality was not yet considered a pathological predisposition as it was in the nineteenth century, but an individual crime that any person was theoretically capable of committing, if they were despicable enough.

The homosexual "crimes" reported from Anne's and Mary's time were mostly committed by men, an indication that lesbian love was especially taboo. The few cases of lesbian love that were brought before court, and therefore became known, were of relationships in which one of the two women had disguised herself as a man. Dekker and Pol conclude from this that sexuality was only conceivable as a relationship between a man and a woman, even in the minds of women.

> In a few cases the disguise has to be considered a kind of aid towards creating the necessary psychic leeway for a woman desiring to court another woman. In the seventeenth and eighteenth centuries, lesbian feelings caused problems with gender identity. A woman who fell in love with a woman could no longer simply feel she was a woman—for, the argument went, anyone with such feelings had to actually be a man.[9]

Why should women have felt or thought that way? Perhaps the reality of the situation was exactly the reverse. Perhaps they thought: "If I love a woman and want to survive in this society, then one of us will have to pretend she is a man."

Anne Bonny and Mary Read. Source: Department of Rare Books,
New York Public Library.

Love relationships among women where one of them did not play a man were not even perceived as such. It barely posed a threat to the men of the eighteenth century when a woman in women's clothing loved a woman in women's clothing. On the contrary, as Lilian Fadermann concludes in *Köstlicher als die Liebe der Männer* [More Delicious than the Love of Men]—a study of romantic and passionate relationships between upper-class women in previous centuries—men often had no objections to such relationships. Fathers were reassured that the "honour" of their daughters, meaning their highly valued "virginity," was not endangered. A husband did not need fear that another man was "putting the horns" on him, meaning that his wife might bear the child of another man as his heir. The female friends were not seen as competitors. They could not endanger a marriage, for women were economically dependent on their men.

But when women dressed as men, when they had the temerity to claim the privileges of a man, to live independently or freely choose a profession—insofar as class differences allowed—then lesbian love became punishable. Of course, transvestites were persecuted even when no love relationship with a woman could be demonstrated.

Dekker and Pol point out that milder punishments were always meted out to transvestites who disguised themselves as men out of love for a *man*, for example, in order to accompany a lover on his ship. The strictest punishments were reserved for women in male clothing who had a love relationship with a *woman*, or even married a woman, which was not uncommon. Most of the latter who were discovered were burned at the stake or hanged.

In the end, we will never exactly know about the relationship between Anne Bonny and Mary Read. Did they have a love affair? Did they love yet other women who were also on board disguised as men? What, after all, is the evidence that the "young Fellow, of a most ingageing Behaviour," who met and loved Mary Read, according to Daniel Defoe, was not himself a woman in disguise?

Normally the discovery of a disguised woman on board represented the end of her career as a sailor or pirate. This was not the case with Anne Bonny or Mary Read. They remained respected leaders on their pirate ship without needing to deny their female identity. Hans Leip is amazed about this, and is able to identify only two possible explanations: "Thus both were common property. Or we might presume that Rackham's crew consisted of a bunch of hopeless introverts."

Who knows? Perhaps these "introverts" were actually a bunch of women in disguise.

NOTES

1. cf. Alexandre Exquemelin, *Das Piratenbuch von 1678* [The Pirates Own Book of 1678], Stuttgart, 1983, p. 99.

2. cf. Jean-Baptiste Labat, *Voyage aux iles de l'Amérique (Antilles), 1693-1705,* Paris, 1979. (Here cited from German version, *Sklavenbericht. Abenteuerliche Jahre in der Karibik 1690-1705*, Stuttgart, 1984.)

3. Stanley Richards, *Black Barth*, Carmathenshire, 1966, p. 41.

4. Daniel Defoe (Captain Charles Johnson), *A General History of the Robberies and Murders of the Most Notorious Pyrates, Vol. I & II*, London, 1724-28.

5. Ibid.

6. Rudolf Dekker and Lotte van de Pol, *Frauen in Männerkleidern* [Women Dressed as Men], Berlin, 1990, p. 95.

7. *The Pirates own Book*, London, 1834, p. 389.

8. Anna Franchi, *Storia della Pirateria del Mondo*, Milan 1952.

9. Dekker and Pol, p. 75.

Glossary

Barque: fourteenth-century term for a ship without a bridge, meaning an open boat without structures built on it and equipped with oars or a sail.

Bow: front part of a ship.

Bridge: structure on a ship serving as command and navigation centre.

Brigantine: two-mast sailing ship with square sails.

Cog: bulbous ship, a development from the Viking drake, with very high bow and prow. Cogs were the first ship models fully covered by an attached and flat deck. They had one mast with a square sail.

Convivencia: Spanish term for living together peacefully.

Cut sail: to "reef" a large sail, meaning either tying or rolling it up so as to reduce wind contact surface.

Double pirogue: two pirogues tied to each other.

Drake (dragon ship): also called drakkare, the large classical Viking ships equipped with dragon's heads and at least thirty banks of rowers. These ships were broader and more manoeuvrable, and had higher walls than the smaller Viking warships (snigs and skeidhs).

Flagship: fleet commander's ship, flies a flag.

Foresheet: the line that holds the foresail.

Foresail: sail in front of the mast.

Frigate (ital. *Fregatte*): earlier warship with three masts and square sails.

Galley: ancient warship with oars.

Governor: chief executive of a colony, representative of the crown.

Grappling knife: two-edged, often curved dagger.

Junk: General term for Chinese ships, typically characterised by a high prow and sails, the latter reinforced and divided into sections by bamboo sticks. These ships may have up to five masts.

Mandarin: powerful Chinese (imperial) bureaucrat or governor.

Pirogue: very long and narrow ship with both sail and oars. Pirogues are mostly built from a single tree.

Prize: the booty from a tour of plunder. That may include the whole ship as well as the cargo.

Prow: rear end of a ship.

Quartermaster: sailor who steers a ship.

Skeidh: "ships of the line" in Nordic war fleets—usually 25-bankers with the same speed and agility as a snig, but with a higher prow and better equipment.

Sloop: fast ship with many sails on a single mast; constructed as a battleship.

Snig: narrow and very agile ship with about twenty double oars and a crew of up to 100.

Smutje: kitchen boy on board a ship.

Steven: strong wood outlining the ship's front and rear.

Tamouré: Polynesian dance.

Trireme: narrow boat in ancient times. Triremes were up to fifty meters long and usually had three decks for the rowers, hence the term "trireme."

Ukulele: four-stringed instrument, much smaller than a normal guitar.

Bibliography

Aeschylus. *The Persians.*

Alioth, Gabrielle. "An allen Küsten berüchtigt" [Notorious on all coasts]. In: *Emma* 8/86, Cologne.

D'Argentre, Bertrand. *Histoire de la Bretagne.* Paris 1588.

Baker, Susan. "Anne Bonny and Mary Read." In: Nancy Myron and Charlotte Bauch (eds.) *Women Remembered. A Collection of Biographies.* [Berlin: *Erinnerungen an Frauen*, 1977].

Bardelle, Frank. *Freibeuter in der karibischen See. Zur Entstehung und geselchaftlichen Transformation einer historischen "Randbewegung"* [Freebooters in the Caribbean: On the rise and societal transformation of a historical "marginal movement"]. Münster 1986.

Bottigheimer, Karl S. *Geschichte Irlands* [History of Ireland]. Stuttgart 1985.

Carter Hughson, Shirley. *The Carolina Pirates and Colonial Commerce 1670-1740.* New York and London 1973.

Chambers, Anne. *The Life and Times of Grace O'Malley 1530-1603.* Dublin 1983.

D'Eaubonne, Francoise. *Les grandes Aventuerières.* Paris 1988.

Defoe, Daniel (Captain Charles Johnson). *A General History of the Robberies and Murders of the Most Notorious Pyrates, Vol. I & II.* London: Rivington Woodward, 1724-28. [Frankfurt: *Umfassende Geschichte der Räubereien und Mordtaten der berüchtigten Piraten*, 1982.]

Dekker, Rudolf and Van de Pol, Lotte. *Frauen in Männerkleidern* [Women in Men's clothing]. Berlin 1990.

Delumeau, Jean. *Angst im Abendland* [Fear in the Occident]. Reinbek 1985.

————. *Der Aufbau der Kolonialreiche* [Creation of the Colonial Empires]. Munich 1987.

Dervenn, Claude. *Hommes et cités de Bretagne*. Paris 1965.

Diesner, Hans Joachim. *Kriege des Altertums* [Wars of Antiquity]. Berlin 1985.

Eberhard, Wolfram, *Chinas Geschichte* [History of China]. Bern 1948.

Exquemelin, Alexandre. *Das Piratenbuch von 1678. Die amerikanischen Seeräuber* [The Pirates own Book of 1678. The American Sea Robbers]. Stuttgart 1990.

Fadermann, Lilian. *Köstlicher als die Liebe der Männer* [More Delicious than the Love of Men]. Zurich 1990.

Fielding, Xan. *Das Buch der Winde* [Book of the Winds]. 1988.

Fox, Grace. *British Admirals and Chinese Pirates 1832-1869*. London 1940.

Frain, Irène. *Quand les Bretons peuplaient les mers*, Paris 1988.

Franchi, Anna. *Storia della Pirateria del mondo*. Vol. I &II. Milan 1952.

Franke, Herbert, and Rolf Trauzettel. *Das Chinesische Kaiserreich* [The Chinese Empire]. Frankfurt 1968.

Gerstlacher, Anna and Margit Miosga. *China der Frauen* [Women's China]. Munich 1990.

Gosse, Philip. *The Pirate's Who's Who*. London 1924.

————. *The History of Piracy*. London 1954.

Grant, John. *Der Mythos der Wikinger* [Myth of the Vikings]. Hamburg 1991.

————. *Guide de la France mystèrieuse*. Paris 1964.

Guillain, France. *Les femmes d'àbord*. Paris 1986.

Heims, P. G. *Seespuk* [Surf]. Munich 1965.

Herm, Gerhard. *Die Phönizier* [The Phoenicians]. Reinbek 1987.

Bibliography

Herodotus. *The Histories.* Translated by Aubrey de Sélincourt (1954). Middlesex and New York 1985.

Höckmann, Olaf. *Antike Seefahrt* [Seefaring in Antiquity]. Munich 1985.

Jaeger, Gérard. *Les femmes d'àbordage.* Paris 1965.

———. "Karibik und Bahamas." *Merian* 10/XXV. Hamburg.

Keller, Catherine. *From a Broken Web.* [Stuttgart: *Der Ichwahn,* 1989].

Krum, Werner. *Florida.* Munich 1987.

Labat, Jean-Baptiste. *Voyage aux iles de l'Amerique (Antilles) 1690-1705.* Paris 1979.

Leip, Hans. *Bordbuch des Satans* [Satan's Log]. Vol. I & II. Berlin 1986.

Linck, Gudula. *Frau und Familie in China* [Woman and Family in China]. Munich 1988.

Mellah, Fawzi. *Die Irrfahrt der Königin Elissa, Gründerin Karthagos.*

Mernissi, Fatima. *Die Sultanin* [The Sultaness]. Darmstadt 1991.

Mies, Maria. *Patriarchat und Kapital* [Patriarchy and Capital]. Zurich 1988.

Mondfeld, Wolfram zu. *Piratenbuch.* Gütersloh 1976.

———. *Entscheidung bei Salamis* [Decision at Salamis]. Würzburg 1976.

———. *Das Piratenkochbuch* [The Pirates' Cookbook]. Herford 1988.

Neumann, Erich. *Ursprungsgeschichte des Bewußtseins* [Origins of Consciousness]. Frankfurt 1986.

Pauly-Wissowa. *Realenzyklopädie der klassischen Altertumswissenschaften* [Encyclopedia of Classical Sciences of Antiquity]. Stuttgart 1893.

The Pirates own Book. London 1834.

Polybius. *Histories.* Scientia 1974.

Pörtner, Rudolf. *Die Wikingersaga* [The Viking Saga]. Düsseldorf 1971.

Ranke-Graves, Robert. *Greek Mythology* [Reinbek: *Griechische Mythologie*, 1986].

Richards, Stanley. *Black Barth, Lllandybie*. Carmarthenshire 1977.

———. *Richtig reisen. Bahamas* [Travelling Well in the Bahamas]. Cologne 1983.

Ricoeur, Paul. *Symbolik des Bösen* [Symbolism of Evil]. Freiburg 1988.

Samuel, Pierre. *Amazonen, Kriegerinnen, Kraftfrauen.* [Amazons, Warrior Women, Muscle Women]. Duisburg 1985.

Schmidt, Vera. *Aufgabe und Einfluß der europäischen Berater in China. Gustav Detering (1842-1913) im Dienste Li Hung-changs* [European Advisers in China, their Missions and Influence: Gustav Detering in Li Hung-Chang's service].

Sitwell, Edith. *Piracy and Piety* [Frankfurt: *Piraterie und Pietät*, 1991.]

Soko, Hans. *Unter der Flagge mit dem Totenkopf* [Under the Flag with the Skull]. Herford 1972.

Stein, Paul. *Zur Geschichte der Piraterie im Altertum* [Towards a History of Piracy in Antiquity]. Bernburg: 1894.

Stone, Merlin. *When God Was a Woman* [Munich: *Als Gott eine Frau wa*, 1986].

Terhart, Franjo. *Ich—Grace O'Malley* [I: Grace O'Malley]. Recklinghausen 1991.

Tourville, Anne de. *Femmes de la mer*, Paris 1958.

Walker, Barbara, *Secrets of the Tarot* [Südergellersen: *Geheimnisse des Tarot*, 1985].

Warner, Marina. *Die Kaiserin auf dem Drachenthron* [The Empress on the Dragon Throne]. Würzburg 1974.

Bibliography

Wimmer, Wolfgang. *Die Sklaven* [The Slaves]. Reinbek 1979.

——. *Wirtschaft und Handel der Kolonialreiche* [Economy and Trade in the Colonial Empires]. Munich 1988.

Ziebarth, Erich. "Beiträge zur Geschichte des Seeraubs und Seehandels im alten Griechenland" [On the History of Sea Robbery and Sea Trade in Ancient Greece]. *Abhandlungen zur Auslandskunde* Vol. 30. Hamburg University, Hamburg, 1929.

LIFE UNDER THE DEATH'S HEAD:

ANARCHISM AND PIRACY

Introduction

ea robbers have been robbing since the dawn of sea travel, just as thieves have been stealing since the advent of private property. But only a small proportion of sea robbers are truly pirates. Piracy is a form of life. It has its own conditions, its own rules and ways of thought. Pirates, men and women, answer to no one except for the crew of the ship in which they are sailing at the moment, and only after joining it of their own free will. Pirates have themselves, their group, their ship, perhaps a couple of retreats, and nothing else. They obey nothing and no one, have no nation to defend, no leader, no God, no government, no State. "They did not serve in an orderly militia, they fought neither for King nor Country, nor any abstract cause."[1] Stirner's maxim applies: "No cause, no so-called 'highest interest of humanity,' no 'holy thing' is so worthy that you should serve it, or attend to it for its own sake."[2] Pirates are "anarchists and nihilists. They robbed and murdered in territorial and nonterritorial waters alike. When forcing entry they showed no concern whatsoever for either the nationality or the proprietors of the ships they commandeered."[3]

According to this understanding, and in contradiction to what is normally claimed, the following are *not* pirates:

Vikings were invading warriors plundering on the high seas and in coastal regions.

Traditional *Chinese sea robbers*, men and women, were actually criminal syndicates operating on the sea.

Sea robbers of Brittany, who were sea robbers in every sense of the word, were not pirates however, but mostly peasants.

Most importantly, *filibusters* were by no stretch of the imagination pirates. They were unofficial English or French imperialist war fleets, plundering and murdering in the name of, and with support from, their kings and queens. "They legalised their privateering by being in possession of official written permission to privateer, issued in each case by their monarch." To describe a Francis Drake or a Henry Morgan[4] as a pirate is thus tantamount to a form of "blasphemy." That many filibusters did end up becoming real pirates does not change that.

But among sea robbers there were also those who were always under pursuit because they refused to subjugate themselves to rulers—largely people whom we would today describe as "dropouts," who did not want to submit to bourgeois laws, or who had already come into direct conflict with those laws...This kind of "autonomous" piracy was a monkey wrench thrown into the colonisation process. Its practitioners were unwilling to be registered, or corrupted by either money or office. They therefore became the target of international police pursuit.[5]

And they are our subject here. True piracy represents only a small part of the history of sea robbery. Geographically concentrated in the Caribbean (and a little bit around Madagascar and African coastal zones) and historically spanning just 30 years—the period from around 1690 to around 1720—the "Golden Age" of piracy is in fact the only time when it ever really existed. It certainly merits closer study and examination than it has received until now.

Definition of Terms

Freedom

Unemployment, subjugation and exploitation, threat of punishment, lust for adventure, boredom... Many reasons are given for why so many men and a few women ran off to live as pirates late in the seventeenth century. "For those seeking individuality, wealth, and flight from oppression, life on board a pirate ship offered incomparable possibilities."[6]

What do all of these reasons have in common? Breaking out of structured obedience, pre-set orders and moral unities; escape from assigned roles, authoritarian hierarchies, and a perpetually expanding apparatus of control and supervision; in short, flight from everything that reeks of an increasingly powerful bourgeois society. Instead, there is a plunge into a world of unpredictability, danger, excitement, excessive living, fast death; of "war, adventure, hunt, dance, fighting games, and everything that strong, free, cheerful action implies."[7] A world of fluctuation (sometimes on this ship, sometimes on that; sometimes this tour of plunder, sometimes that; sometimes these rules, sometimes those). A world within which the individual always remains singular, however, always one's own person, only connecting with others in order to be stronger and have fun, and disconnecting when that is no longer the case. For "ego knows no commandment of 'loyalty, dependency, and so on.' Ego allows everything, including apostasy, defection."[8]

Accordingly it has been observed that: "Pirate crews have a very high turnover."[9] "They [the pirates] were a fluctuating pack in every way, constantly in motion, changing in number or composition from one month to the next. Nothing and no one, neither ship nor captain, or any matter bound to them, obligated obedience."[10] Those who flee the State discover they have joined a molecular world.

Becoming *molecular* (as opposed to molar) is a fundamental principle of pirate life.

The escaped slave, the unemployed manual labourer, the murderess in flight, the lunger without means, and the jaded daughter "of a better family"—all receive the same rights under piracy. "No social distinctions or particular classes could be found within their society. Everyone sailed as an equal on the ship."[11] Especially remarkable are the opportunities that arose in the pirate world for women: "Pirate women were considered especially dangerous, and accepted as leaders at a time when women on land had long been robbed of rights and dignity."[12] Each pirate developed his or her own kind of pirate life, determined by one's self and no other.

> He [the pirate] was considered world enemy number one, to be hunted and killed at anyone's whim. He never sailed in the service of a king, possessed no written license that "legalised" his privateering, and sailed nearly exclusively under a "Jolly Roger" the black sea robber's flag. He had no home, the sea was his only residence. He was considered a stranger and an outcast from society. He had no family in the usual sense, and no children except for those outside marriage. His daily concerns consisted in privateering, robbing, and occasionally killing. Every day he had to be prepared to die.[13]

The pirate thus becomes Max Stirner's "ego"—which bears no relation to bourgeois reactive 'indivi-*Dualism*'—but which destroys the preordained self, and makes concrete and constantly changing subjectifications into the active basis of life. "The ego is one born free, free from the start;...[He] is originally free, because he recognises no power other than his own; he requires no liberation, because from the start he rejects everything except himself, because he values nothing more highly than himself, aims for nothing higher; in short, because he acts from himself."[14] What is true of the ego could also be set up as the defining characteristic of the pirate: "I am my self only when not ruled by sensory nature, or in any way by another (God, people, authority, law, State, church, etc.), but by my self alone."[15]

Of all the reasons we might count among those to become a pirate, there is only one true explanation for choosing the life of the pirate as described herein. In the origins of piracy we see nothing at work other than the unbound desire for singularity and independence. Without the least concern for abstract and thus empty and completely used-up bourgeois ideals of "individualism" and "freedom," pirates show what it means to live in a permanently actualising process of individualisation and liberation. "The pride in being a sea robber was felt equally by every member of the pirate community. They considered themselves the only ones in the world who were not subjugated to any statist force."[16]

Space

A substantive prerequisite for the departure into freedom, with which piracy begins, is the appearance of a space that promises and allows the development of freedom. In the seventeenth century, European space was already very strongly curtailed. The vagabonds of the Middle Ages could no longer vagabond, because no place was left for them to wander about. Just when space on land was becoming more and more scarce, the smooth, still nearly-uncontrolled space of the sea opened up for escape. The sea was not yet divided and controlled, but offered a space of freedom, a space of potential diversity as the precondition for the fluctuations indispensable to pirate life. "Not only does anything populating a smooth space represent a diversity that changes its essence whenever it divides (like tribes in the desert; the distances change constantly, the clans are in perpetual metamorphosis). The smooth space itself (desert, steppe, sea, or eternal ice) is also a diversity of this kind: ametric, acentered, undesigned."[17]

The pirate ship sailing alone on open sea was completely unobserved. No one knew where it was. No aircraft, no radar, no high-tech navigation system, no controlled ship travel. The sea was indeed a smooth space at the time the pirates set out to make themselves "lords of the sea." Some go as far as to claim: "The sea is perhaps the most significant of smooth spaces, the hydraulic model par excellence."[18]

We see that the question of the possibilities in piracy is mostly a question of space. If smooth spaces disappear, if all spaces are carved up, then piracy is finished. Indetectibility, like molecularity, is inseparable from piracy.

Around 1700 it was possible to achieve such indetectibility in the reaches of the Atlantic. And pirates were in fact imperceptible: "Hidden among the islands of the Caribbean or exposed to the tides within the river mouths of the Carolinas, the pirates nearly always spied out their prey before they themselves were discovered."[19] And even when a pirate ship was sighted, it was not normally recognised as such, for the Jolly Roger would be pulled down in advance and replaced with some commercial flag. Only in the last moment before the direct encounter, before the attack, were the pirates suddenly recognisable as pirates: the Jolly Roger would run back up the mast.

Today all of that is but a dream. High-level technology makes any form of imperceptibility impossible. "Of all smooth spaces the sea was the first that had to be enclosed, transformed into a dependency of the land with set paths, constant directions, relative movements, and a complete anti-hydraulics of canals and diversions."[20] "The enclosure of the sea occurs…through navigation on the high seas."[21] The pirates require their space. When there is no space within which we can move unobserved, then there is no more piracy—and no more freedom, "for we have then lost the place of freedom: space."[22]

Nomads

Pirates settled on the smooth space of the sea, just as nomads do in that of the desert. They divided themselves over it without dividing it up. They slid about unobserved, always following the winds. They never came to rest, sometimes sailing completely new routes, sometimes well-known ones. They appeared from nowhere and disappeared back into it. The only landmarks were the many islands of the Caribbean, where they occasionally landed to sell booty, restock the ship, play cards and love women or men. On the sea everything was open—no centres, no outlines, no predetermined paths. "In this sense nomads [pirates] have neither bases, nor paths, nor land."[23] Thus, of pirates it might be said: "The only thing that they had in common was the sea. For this reason, if pirates on the open sea were called by another ship going past, and asked who they were and where they came from, the traditional pirate answer was, 'from the sea.'"[24]

At the time of piracy the Caribbean was a desert of water with small islands as the only landmarks, counterparts to the oases in deserts of sand. It was in the pirates' interest that this space stay the same, remain a smooth space and allow their unpredictable gliding, keep their imperceptibility safe. It was thus unavoidable that "the Caribbean waters practically became a pirate sea."[25] Just as it is not only the desert that makes the nomads, but the nomads who also make the desert, so too is it not only the sea that makes the pirates, but the pirates who make the sea as sea (meaning as a smooth space)—and block its development into state-controlled, waterbound property. "Through a series of local actions with variable orientation and direction, [nomads] add desert to the desert"[26] and, as pirates, sea to the sea.

Pirates are the nomads of the sea. According to Deleuze, the key question today is: "Who are our contemporary nomads?" If this is so, we must also ask who the pirates of today might be.

Activity

There are few people in whom we can see Nietzsche's theory of "energy" or "force" [Kraft] at work as well as with pirates.

Active energy is primarily concerned with itself. Affirming life and itself, and driven by the will to power understood as a life-affirming principle, active energy perpetually struggles towards its full development. It is driven to its last limits, to the complete exhaustion of its resources.

Reactive energy is rather different, for it is driven by a will to power reduced to a will to nothing. Its only concern is limitation and destruction of all energies. No affirmation anymore; only negation and hatred of life. The reactive force wants nothing less than to block the development of other forces, to restrict them, ultimately to make them just as reactive. Reactive force thus voluntarily denies its own possibilities for activity, and constantly restricts itself: ascetic ideal in all its variations.

Statist societies (and most of all the bourgeois) stand for reactive life in its purest form. People trimmed down to their role in a rising bourgeois world, with its cleanliness, refinement, order, and discipline; people forced to correspond to it so as not to be declared delinquent, and hence more or less free game; such people have no choice but to suppress activity and affirmation of life.

Piracy allows renewed development of active energy. We have seen how the departure into freedom is tantamount to departure into a life that begins anew, and knows nothing of rules that provoke reactivity. Class society, hierarchy, oppression, exploitation, national chauvinism, breeding and order—all the conditions of rule that people could not escape in eighteenth century Europe—are merely laughed off and ridiculed in the Pirate Caribbean. For pirates, the point is to live life to the full, guided by molecular production of desire and not by any rigid social institutions. Freedom is unthinkable without the activity of forces, and vice-versa.

Dreadfulness is admittedly still present, and there is no doubt that many pirates were often dreadful. But does that change the fact that under piracy, activity, affirmation of life, and the free play of all energies replace a rigid, reactive societal order? Certainly not. In the pirate's defence we must first of all admit that not every reactive energy can be extinguished so quickly, and the danger always lurks that reactivity can be tickled back to the surface. (Ignoring for a moment, by the way, that pirates were practically innocent lambs in comparison to most captains and officers of national ships of war and commerce). Secondly, the active life does not stand in opposition to dreadfulness as such, but only to reactive life.

Pirates—who appeared, were viewed, and were battled as the "enemies of the world"—could not avoid answering their enemies with acts of cruelty. The pirates' enemies had allowed pirates no life in Europe—or anywhere else. Recall that many pirates were escaped slaves from Africa and Asia. Naturally, these enemies reacted when pirate men and women attempted to find a different way to an active life. Pirates were left with no alternative than to live through robbery.

Raiding and plundering mercantile ships, and sometimes even war ships, was necessary; primarily in order to secure the requirements of life, but also as a representation of the engagement in a struggle made necessary through the pirates' situation as "free enemies of the world." Raiding was a matter of self-defence against those who ultimately only possessed that which they had beaten out of pirates and their like. (There were even pirates who described themselves as socialists, and justified their actions accordingly, like the famous Charles Bellamy.[28]) Beyond this, colonialism's attempt to establish itself in the Caribbean posed the greatest threat to the pirates, and in this sense the mercantile nations were imperialist enemies, and had to be fought. Just as much as pirates needed merchant ships and the Caribbean markets to make a living, they also needed their smooth space. It had to be defended against colonialist enclosure. An existential prerequisite for pirates was that in order to pursue commerce, the rich were forced to bring their wealth over a smooth space—at least for a short time outside state-guaranteed security. Sea routes had to stay unsafe. Otherwise, as proved to be the case, piracy could not survive.

In any case, the greatest part of pirate atrocity sprang out of this double necessity to actively destroy the authoritarian enemy, who, from Europe, attempted to take control of all things and all spaces on Earth. No wonder that according to Defoe, the pirate captain Charles Bellamy once fell upon the captain of a commandeered merchant ship, who stubbornly refused to join the pirate band, and yelled at him:

> Damn ye, you are a sneaking Puppy, and so
> are all those who will submit to be governed
> by Laws which rich Men have made for their

own Security, for the cowardly Whelps have
not the Courage otherwise to defend what
they get by their Knavery; but damn ye altogether: Damn them for a Pack of crafty Ras-
cals, and you, who serve them, for a Parcel of
hen-hearted Numbskuls. They villify us, the
Scoundrels do, when there is only this
Difference, they rob the Poor under the
Cover of Law, forsooth, and we plunder the
Rich under the Protection of our own Courage; had you not better make One of us,
than sneak after the A----s of those Villains
for Employment?[29]

The dreadfulness of activity lies in the lustful destruction
of life-negating forces. It is "destruction become active, aggres-
sion bound tightly with affirmation"[30] "That is 'decisive in a
Dionysian philosophy': the moment when negation expresses
an affirmation of life, destroys reactive forces, and returns to
activity its full rights. Where the negative, like thunder and
lightning, becomes a power for affirmation."[31] Compared to
the "active dreadfulness" of pirates, the traditional, "reactively
dreadful" attitudes—contempt for women, hatred of
Aboriginal peoples, slavery—were barely to be found among
them, and were often opposed directly. Women were often
fully accepted, Aboriginal peoples were left mostly in peace,
and some captains like Mission[32] would immediately liber-
ate all slaves found on commandeered ships.

Responsibility

If it is asserted here that pirates fled from the order and
discipline of statist society so as to live in active self-determination, then by no means does that mean that this life was
entirely without rules. On the contrary, pirates show us that

the twaddle about non-bourgeois lifestyles being totally open and without principles comes entirely from the comfortable, opportunistic-conservative niche that some people might occupy in any economically-oriented society. The development into an active form of life has nothing to do with this vulgar conception of societal laissez faire. The pirate form of life, taken seriously, naturally had its principles and rules, to which individuals felt an obligation. The decisive difference from statist discipline and duty lay in the conscious decision to take on that obligation. The principles are taken to heart, and one feels responsible to follow them or not to follow them. What is piratical "order"? Individual responsibility instead of statist-societal expectations; responsibility instead of duty.

The various pirate groups each had their rules, decided upon by all of their members. Whoever didn't want these rules sought out a different group.[33] Never was the abstract Rousseauian idea of a social contract as concrete as on a pirate ship: "Whoever joined a pirate crew had to add his signature to the pirate articles or pirate rules, and swear upon a bible or a boarding axe to follow them."[34]

As long as an individual belonged to a group, the rules of the group were self-evidently his or her own, and were followed as a responsibility. Those who no longer belonged to the group would leave, exiting the contract. The rapid changes among pirate groups have already been mentioned.

The specific situation of the Caribbean pirates admittedly had the consequence that some principles were practically universal among them. Such principles seem to be unavoidable when a form of life has to develop and defend itself against a permanent threat: solidarity, honesty, determination, severity, mutual support, and so on. According to group and ship, variations on these principles became the guidelines of pirate life.

Most decisive and significant about these practices is that when the rules were agreed upon, anyone who was there, was there. Anyone who wasn't, wasn't. The idea of an absolutely perfect common entity was thus left to rot back at the European home ports.

The rules of pirate clans spring from nothing less than a serious attempt to find a form of life that can fulfil the piratical desire for freedom. It was thus observed that: "one of the most conspicuous characteristics of pirate life was the nearly complete lack of the characteristic signs of normal society, which pirates held in contempt: concentration of authority, class distinctions, the lack of a say in important matters."[35] The rules of a pirate ship are considered carefully, and are in no way arbitrary. They serve a form of life determined to set no limits upon the active play of forces and their intensity, or upon the desire for freedom. The common life of pirates is the best-confirmed case of a society that merely looks to the production of desire, and requires no further justification.

And precisely because the pirates were concerned with a serious form of life beyond any moral legitimations, they were very much aware of the differences between themselves and others, and did the only right thing in such a situation. They emphasised that difference, they declared themselves the enemies of the world. They clamped down on the capitalist apparatus of accumulation. The pirate clans were clear about their rules; they lived up to principles that were honest, serious, and well-considered, and therefore worthy of defence to the death. Those who had different rules but active principles (such as other pirates or "honest" church people) were respected, and left alone. Those who showed hostility as reactive forces were fought, and no quarter was given. The pirates did not fall into the trap of the repressive tolerance granted by rulers. They knew what it meant to preserve a difference from authoritarian power.

On the one hand: determined responsibility, strict anti-authoritarianism, and non-abstract ideals; thus unconditional solidarity, honest social security, and non-bourgeois, amoral honour within the clan. "Within every crew of a sea robber ship, mutual aid was the highest commandment. If a sea robber visibly let down a colleague who was in danger, he was condemned as a common criminal by his peers."[36]

> Among themselves, on board their ships and in their retreats, they were passionate advocates of a primitive kind of democracy, with great respect for justice and the rights of the individual, and a corresponding resistance to tyranny and abuse of power. As raw and violent as they often were, they could be extraordinarily generous to those whom they liked or trusted, and inundated with jewels and Arabian gold the dealers of brandy and the willing girls who gave wings and made sweet their journeys over the broad seas. Ship comrades who lost an eye or a limb in the sea robber battles were allowed to stay on board as long as they liked. Many a wooden leg sounded on pirate decks, and its possessor would earn a half share of the booty as a ship's cook, regardless of whether he knew anything of cooking or not.[37]

On the other hand: no mercy and no restraint against the authoritarian enemy. Friedrich Nietzsche had not failed to notice this curious characteristic of active groups.

> [W]hoever learned the "good" only as an enemy learned nothing other than "evil

enemies."...With each other they prove so inventive in regard, self-control, tenderness, loyalty, pride, and friendship....The same people, when dealing with the outside— there where the strange, where strangeness begins—behave no better than predators uncaged. There they enjoy freedom from all social constraint, they...revert to the inno- cence of a predatory conscience, become happy monsters that might depart from a horrifying sequence of murder, arson, rape, and torture with high spirits and spiritual calm.[38]

A motif of outsiderness without compromises, one that runs from vagabonds, robbers, and pirates, through syndi- calist wage workers and guerrilleros, to modern youth gangs and heroes of Italian Westerns. And fascinates still, because it keeps alive the idea of a life lived in freedom, a life not incor- porated into statist machinery.

Body

Over the course of the classical period (seventeenth, eigh- teenth century) the body was discovered as an object and target of power. It is easy to find signs for the great attention that the body received at that time, directed at the body as an object of manipulation, forming, and dress; an object that obeys, answers, is conditioned, and whose powers multi- ply...A "political anatomy" that is also a "mechanics of power" is on the rise. It defines how one can bring the bodies of others under control, not only to make them do what is demanded, but also to have them work in the manner desired: with predetermined techniques, rapidity, and effec- tiveness. In this fashion, discipline fabricates submissive and practised bodies, obedient and quick to learn.[39]

Because of this development in the "European body" it is worthwhile to observe the bodies of pirates, who were able to escape this discipline. In piracy, the body participates entirely in the process of molecularity. The body is not subjected to supervision, nor is its physicality either devalued or aestheticised (the two go hand in hand). It's not just that a pirate ship (in complete contrast to the armies of European nation-states) included a variety of bodily forms going about tasks according to their means, but also that physical energies and techniques remained in direct and concrete relation to piratical thinking, and always constituted key elements in pirate life.

A successful pirate crew had to be strong, mobile, and fast in body as in mind; one demanded the other. Intellect alone was as insufficient as mere unbridled strength. The artificial division between intellect and body was never completed, and there was no division between intellectual and manual work. There was no captain who did not fight, and no simple pirate who did not have to constantly keep his responsibility for the whole crew in mind. Everyone had to defend oneself on his or her own power. Each had to use his or her own head to make important decisions for themselves or their group. The great dependencies created through the radical division of intellectual and manual work (a separation that at the same time always requires elites and hierarchies) were strictly avoided, and with them the loss of important mental faculties. "The human intellect is empowered to understand very much, and all the more empowered if the body engages in a greater variety of activities."[40]

It hardly needs to be mentioned that the reputation of the pirates as savages was related to their completely uncivilised, barbaric relation to their bodies: naked torsos, long and unwashed hair, ragged beards, scars, burns, uninhibited munching and guzzling, rough motion. The pirates were far removed from any cult of the body. If a pirate lost his ability to fight in the course of battle, he would take some task on deck and be cared for by his fellow pirates, without in any way damaging the fundamental and concrete unity of thinking and manual activity. "With respect to taking care of the sick and disabled, they were far ahead of the 'Europeans' of that time. The 'health and disability fund' was financed in that everyone assigned a certain proportion of their booty to that purpose."[41]

Each individual body as a different quantum of energy, without any physical ideal; the importance of physical performance for each individual pirate, but without any absolute standard; the indivisibility of the body from all other activities; self-defence against domestication of physical powers; direct presence of the whole body in life on deck; an unmediated relation to the body, allowing comprehension of what material really means. That is the body of the pirate.

Death

The pirates' often cynical-seeming contempt for death already had the rest of the world puzzled even while they were still alive. Death accompanied pirates wherever they went, and seemed to worry only a few. "Driven by force of superior arms into a corner on the quarter-deck, or standing on the scaffold before a great chattering crowd, still they often went into death with imperturbable composure and mocking humour."[42]

There are some beautiful stories about piratical contempt for death:

> Bartholomew Roberts's crew never lost their gallows humour—even when, after the death of their leader,[43] they were chained to

each other on board a ship of the Royal
Navy, sailing towards certain death by hanging. When everything was taken from them,
they joked that they should at least be left
with half a penny to pay old Charon for the
trip over the Styx. Of their meagre meals,
they observed that they were losing so much
weight that in the end they would no longer
weigh enough for hanging. When one of the
prisoners indeed became fearful after all,
and started reading the Bible, another asked
him what his intentions were. "Heaven,"
answered the first. "Heaven, you fool," was
the reply. "Have you ever heard of a pirate
who went there? Give me Hell, it's more of a
feast. I'm firing a thirteen gun salute for
Roberts as soon as I get there!"[44]

Such attitudes were completely incomprehensible to a
great many, but actually very easy to explain.

The life of revolt lead by the pirates originates in the
determination to "really live, or die trying." Graffiti in Belfast
still asks today: "Is there a life before death?" The pirate
would answer: "Only if you get one for yourself—like I did!"
Pirates bade farewell from Christian ideals of preserving life
at any price, for they started thinking about the quality of
that life. The pirate wants to live to the full, intensely...or not
at all. Bartholomew Roberts, according to Defoe, summed
up the pirate view in pointed fashion: "In an honest Service,
there is thin Commons, low Wages, and hard Labour; in this,
Plenty and Satiety, Pleasure and Ease, Liberty and Power;
and who would not ballance Creditor on this Side, when all
the Hazard that is run for it, at worst, is only a sower Look or
two at choaking. No, a merry Life and a short one shall be

my Motto."⁴⁵ "Live fast, die young"—who would deny that here an alternative understanding of life and death is being expressed, robbing death of its incredible terror?

The pirate's concern is not mere individual biological survival—as has been developed into an ideal—but everything that makes life lively: freedom, activity, intensity... and that means danger, too. And precisely because of danger, the fear of death disappears, since "death was not opposed to life, but was a moment of life."⁴⁶ Pirates acted like the

Captain Kidd, hanged then displayed in a gibbet in sight of passing vessels on Tilbury Point.

Japanese samurai who "defused death through its constant presence, so that he could go into battle without trembling."[47] Logically the death cult that was thus cultivated strengthened the pirates. Of course it filled their enemies with fear. "Death was a constant presence. In that they did not fear it, they made it into their ally."[48] That admittedly functioned well: "Intimidation through threat of violence [was] a basic weapon."[49]

After she was condemned to death, the pirate Mary Read[50] made it clear that this understanding of life and associated contempt for death represented the defining aspect of piracy, and that the combination of bourgeois life and Christian death would, of necessity, destroy the piratical form of life. "As to hanging, the thought is no great Hardship, for were it not for that, every cowardly Fellow would turn Pyrate, and so infest the Seas, that Men of Courage must starve."[51] Accordingly, the pirate ideal was by no means heaven, but it "arose from a saying of that time: When a pirate sleeps, then he doesn't dream that he has died and gone to heaven, but that he has returned to New Providence."[52] Historians explain why: "Aside from the law of the jungle and the grappling knife, there were no laws on Nassau. In countless taverns, practically the only fixed constructions, the pirates would drink and fight until they fell over. They lay down with prostitutes in tents made of torn sails, or lost a fortune at gambling, knowing they could easily replace this through another tour of plunder."[53]

We might call the pirate's concern the "dignity of life." This was why individual death could be dismissed. Perhaps the enthusiasm for this dignity of life is the only element in which the pirate suppresses his individuality, but doing so precisely in order to preserve it down to the last consequence. Death cannot injure the dignity of life. Only subjugation can do that, and that is the true death of a pirate.

Christianity

Christianity was definitely a factor with pirates. Many a captured man of religion could reckon with mercy. The preferred reading on board was the Bible. There were more than a few enthusiastic ship preachers, such as the famous Caraccioli,[54] who extolled the justice of the pirate cause: "[Caraccioli] stepped up before the crew and explained to them that they were 'not sea robbers, but men who consciously defended the freedoms granted to people by God. Our cause,' Caraccioli continued, 'is just and noble, it is a matter of freedom.'"[55]

At the same time, pirates represented the anti-Christians to Christian Europe. The famous Captain Blackbeard[56]—the most piratical of pirates—was even considered the "Devil in the form of a man." Admittedly, these descriptions were not only the result of the church's practice of portraying all who did not submit to it as the spawn of hell. Pirates themselves worked to acquire this reputation. As much as they paid due to certain preachers, they held no respect at all for the occidental Christian civilisation and its representatives, Christian colonial rulers, church commandments, or clerical rules of life. Many laughed at the idea of heaven, and answered: "Heaven, you idiot? Have you ever heard of a pirate that went there?"[57] Christian rituals were tantamount to torture. Christian ideals of the modest, ascetic life, in consciousness of duty and fear of God, were exactly what pirates wanted to escape, and declared their enemy.

Blackbeard was very proud of his reputation as "the Devil Himself" and took great lengths to maintain it.

> Before going into battle, he would stick burning fuses under his hat. These were long, slow-burning hemp strings that had been dipped in saltpetre and calcium. The

effect was frightening. Clouds of smoke surrounded his face with the wild eyes and lousy hair, so that to his victims he really did look like the Devil personified. His resemblance to a kind of evil sea-robber ghost was completed through a bandoleer with three pairs of pistols, always loaded, powdered and cocked, and through the additional pistols, daggers and grappling knives that he routinely carried with him.[58]

It may sound like a paradox, but pirate Christianity was thoroughly pagan. Like everything else about pirates, pagan myths, deities, and principles fit into their tribal form of life. Their absoluteness never exceeded a particular limit. Everything was subject to permanent revision,[59] and gods and rules were regularly switched according to circumstances—in the same way that some Germanic tribes would disavail themselves of their war god if they lost too many battles, and adopt a better one.[60] It is revealing "how the heathens honoured their Gods. They made arrangements with them through sacrifices, promises, and ruses; through dubious agreements that gave pretext to suspicious rituals, all full of humour and full of fear."[61]

Pirate Christianity was correspondingly diverse, in every sense. Not only did the significance of Christianity differ from ship to ship. It also appeared everywhere in a different guise. It was constantly mixed together with the most divergent of other religious perspectives: African tribal rites, voodoo (influences of the escaped African slaves upon pirate communities) or so-called cosmopolitan convictions. For this reason it is probably true "that nomads [pirates] offer no favourable terrain for religion. A warrior is always sinning against priests or God."[62] Accordingly, Christianity was not

Captain Blackbeard, or Edward Teach. Source: The National
Maritime Museum

the one religion of pirates, but took on particular and always different forms, and fulfilled greatly divergent functions, within the constant individual and collective development of pirate life. Christianity often appeared in piratical initiation rites, was a preferred object of visionary and fantastic thinking, and, as we heard above, was occasionally employed to legitimate pirate action. Christian thoughts were fluctuating points in the lively play of pirate life, admittedly without becoming superfluous or any the less serious.[63]

Pirates, detached from the forced Christian pseudo-tradition back home and coming together with people from many different countries ("on every pirate ship one meets a potpourri of nationalities"[64]), used those fragments of Christianity from which they could not or would not depart as building blocks, and created their own pirate myths, their own pirate faith. Perhaps this was a strongly satanic faith, but on some level it remained very Christian; without bearing relation however to the absolutist Christian ideology of rule that brought so much more terror and destruction to the world than pirates ever did. "Catholics, Protestants, Presbyterians and Orthodox were very neighbourly with each other on pirate ships, quite in contrast to the strictly confessional Europe of that time. The absence of religious strife within pirate society was one of the basic prerequisites of its survival."[65]

Pirates succeeded in molecularising Christianity by paganising it. They took it down from its position of power, transformed it radically in the process of making it into a concrete part of their form of life, and created their own tradition. This tradition fed upon all that they did not want to surrender from Christianity, as well as their own new experiences as pirates. It developed in keeping with pirate ideals and principles: "Nomads [pirates] have a vague, literally vagabond 'monotheism' that serves them well, along with their wandering fires. There is a sense of the absolute among nomads [pirates], but it is in a unique fashion atheist."[66] That is the "heathen commandment" of the pirates.

Jolly Roger

The pirate flag, the Jolly Roger, varies. But the pattern is always the same: a black field with a skeleton or skull, promising no mercy. The pirate flag is the true symbol of pirates, whatever the fascinating bandannas, earrings, grappling knives, parrots, or peg legs.

It is almost as though the Jolly Roger expresses everything that piracy has to offer—pirates, pirate ships, pirate treasures... In short, everything that is piracy culminates in the flag. Indeed, as minimalist as the flag's design might be, we always have the black of death—of Satan, destruction, chaos and anarchy— and sometimes the red of the blood that must flow in war. There is always death grinning, throwing everyone into terror and only allowing the pirates to smile. And there are always knives, sabres, or hourglasses, unmistakably signalling a stubborn relentlessness and determination.

Examples of Flags. On the right, Walter Kennedy. On the left, Blackbeard.

This is no official national or mercantile flag, announcing affiliation to an honest trade or a civilised State. Only darkness and death without compromise fly this mast: everything that pirates have in store for their enemies. They need no God who grants permission for their violence, no government to legitimate them. They need no pretty flag to portray their moral integrity. What does it mean that they do not need it? They reject hypocritical and authoritarian twaddle about morality and moral justifications; they mock and trample upon that. They restrict themselves to a simple announcement: "We are the enemies of the world, because that is the only way for us to live, so watch out!" Their own production of desire is enough knowledge about how to live. They have overcome the drivel about divine commandments and duties to the State—*ni dieu, ni maitre*! So why have a flag as the practically holy symbol of some morally perfect identity, to be defended with pride? As their sign of recognition, the pirates offer only a torn rag with a death's head.

This death's head is inseparable from piracy. We have seen that pirates are the nomads of the sea. They change ships, groups, possessions, rules, hideaways, territories, routes, places to rob. Only one thing is the same wherever pirates appear: the black flag, with Death laughing. The Jolly Roger makes it clear wherein the true expressive power of a graphic symbol lies: in the concrete reterritorialisations that occur on the body represented by the sign.

Piracy is finally a permanent deterritorialisation, and pirates as seabound nomads are "a deterritorialisation vector."[68] Harbours are left behind, seas crossed; even ships are changed from time to time. Hence the release from all duties, terrestrial or divine, and the enthusiasm for the deterritorialising values of individuality, freedom, and responsibility, for euphoria of any kind, for the fantastic in its boldest forms. But deterritorialisation cannot be viewed apart from constant reterritorialisation, for "deterritorialisation is for its part inseparable from associated reterritorialisations."[69] The excitement and attraction grow precisely out of this permanent interplay between de- and reterritorialisation; where it is not of concern to block deterritorialisation through the reterritorialisation it implies, but where reterritorialisation must simply occur in its sequence, as a supplement. Only that this reterritorialisation does not endanger the deterritorialisation process, therefore it can—and only then—be greeted.

The Jolly Roger is one of these welcome reterritorialisations. It is nothing by which pirates swear, or to which they must profess loyalty. Hence it is not a despotic symbol of the sort that constricts all lines of liberation (like a national flag, a dress insignia, a corporate symbol, or a family coat of arms). The Jolly Roger is the picture that occurs to pirates, entirely without ideological colour, as an expression of their radical form of life. It is the field over which the pirates' deterritorialising lines criss-cross, repeatedly. We might steal a formulation from Deleuze and Guattari, and assert that the Jolly Roger "as a fiery, eccentric or intensive flashpoint, finds itself outside territory, and only exists in the movement of deterritorialisation."[70] The latter seems to be undeniable: the idea of a Jolly Roger flying on the flagpole of a government building should startle us. Its only place is wherever the currents of deterritorialisation carry it: on a motorbiker's jacket, as a tattoo, or—still the best idea—high on a ship's mast.

It is no exaggeration that a Jolly Roger is largely what makes the pirate a pirate. As the material announcement and confirmation of the existence of a piratical form of life, it never lets the pirate forget why he or she is a pirate sailing under this flag.

The pirate flag teaches us that the perfection of expression in a graphic symbol lies in the unmediated nature of the reterritorialisation implied.

Captain

Pierre Clastres defines primitive societies as those without power in the sense of institutionalised authority. This is especially visible in the role of the aboriginal chief, who must take over various tasks for the tribe without being empowered to issue commands—without being a ruler. The latter is impossible, because a primitive group is marked through "a radical rejection of authority, an absolute negation of power."[71] Among aboriginal peoples, for example, the chief must fulfil the following three tasks:

1. hold speeches so that the principles of the tribe are not forgotten;
2. constantly give gifts to members of the tribe (which is why he is the only one allowed to produce more, and to keep a limited store of his production);
3. mediate conflicts.

He must do so not as a judge issuing verdicts, but by appealing to the parties in a conflict to avoid endangering the solidarity of the tribe through their disputes.

Only in the case of war is the chief allowed to give orders. He gains and maintains acceptance only when he constantly proves anew that he can fulfil all of his roles (that he is a good speaker, a courageous warrior, and so on), and without ever presuming that he could rule over the tribe. Prestige and his own unpretentiousness are the only things upon which the chief can depend. Should he lose these strengths, his time as chief is over, and the tribe seeks a new one. The primitive societies of such chiefs were, according to Clastres, societies without States—meaning without power, without subjugation or exploitation. There are ultimately only two societal types: "There are the primitive societies, or societies without States, and there are societies with States."[72] If the chief can suddenly command "on his own authority," if he is obeyed without question, then there is institutionalised authority: power, State, subjugation, exploitation.

But what does this all have to do with pirates? Pirate society was also a society without a State, and without power. It could never have been anything else, because "a hatred of authority of any kind was an essential characteristic of every true sea robber."[73] It is remarked appropriately that "pirate society [was] a guild without ideological ambitions."[74] A theory of the pirate captain, analogue to Clastres' description of the aboriginal chief, should serve to clarify this relation.

Much like this chief, with minor differences, the pirate captain fulfills three tasks for the crew:

The captain first of all serves as an orientation for all pirates in the crew. Sometimes not even speaking a common language, they see their similarities in their captain. It is not so much the force of the word that the captain employs (as in the case of the chief) but his or her direct relation to the pirates on the one hand, and to that which is expressed in the Jolly Roger on the other. The captain is a personified reinforcement of the flag, a guarantee of direct connection to the (timeless) springs of piracy, an assurance of solidarity. Again, not through the word, but through the embodiment of the principles united in the Jolly Roger. In a minor variation on Clastres we might write: "Metaphors of the pirate crew, image of their myth—that is the pirate captain."[75]

Second, the captain fulfills the necessary function of one who gives the crew something when it wants something. The captain is assigned a special portion of the booty, but only so that each pirate has someone from whom he or she can at any time take a desired object. The captain is thus not richer than the other pirates—he is merely the keeper of their stockroom. One of the most celebrated pirate captains, Bartholomew Roberts, was permitted, according to Defoe, to "Use the great Cabbin, and sometimes [the crew] Vote him small parcels of Plate and China; but then every Man as the Humour takes him, will use the Plate and China, intrude into his Apartment, swear at him, seize a Part of his Victuals and Drink, if they like it, without his offering to find Fault or Contest it."[76]

Third, the captain must make sure that conflicts are immediately regulated, so as to prevent trouble for the ship. He does not deliver a verdict, however, but appeals to the parties in conflict to regulate the problem. Either the argument is put aside, or one of the parties decides to leave the ship; or the pirates agree to a violent resolution (usually consummated on land), the results of which are accepted without appeal.

The captain's role is to fulfil these tasks for the group. They do not signify either power or profit for the captain. "They only permit him to be Captain," Defoe wrote, "on Condition that they may be Captain over him."[77] In keeping with Clastres, this relation of crew and captain is much the same in other stateless societies: "The chief must serve the society, while the society itself—the true location of power—exercises its authority as such upon the chief."[78] Among the pirates it was therefore clear that: "privileges were considered a first step towards autocracy, and treated accordingly. The pirate captain therefore possessed no form of constitutional authority, and had no claim to special privileges."[79]

The Pirates Striking Off the Arm of Captain Babcock.
Source: The National Marine Museum.

256

Orders can be issued only in battle or during raids. "Only in battle was the pirate captain obeyed."[80] Therefore only those who prove themselves clever, strong, and brave in battle can become captain; only those who do so repeatedly can remain captain. "It was self-evident that pirates sought out a captain who seemed especially appropriate for the post— 'someone superior in knowledge and boldness,' as Defoe observes, 'they call that pistol-ready.'"[81] Once the battle is over, so is any notion of command. "We know that preparing and carrying out a military expedition provides the only opportunity in which a chief [or the pirate captain] can exercise a minimum of authority, which again is based entirely upon his technical competence as a warrior. After the battle, regardless of its outcome, the war chief once again becomes a chief without power. In no way does the prestige following victory transform into authority."[82] Again, whoever tries to go for more will be deposed. A few of the especially great pirate captains therefore met with a sad fate:

> One day Low[83] nonetheless had the temerity to kill his quartermaster, with whom he had had a dispute, while the man slept. Because his crew found this injustice intolerable, they abandoned Low with a bit of gunpowder and food on an uninviting portion of the Cuban coast, leaving him to his fate. Low was found by an English warship and deported to Martinique. There he was recognised by several of the ship owners he had swindled, put before a court, and hanged.[84]

Just as the aboriginal tribe only accepts its chief as long as he remains true to the society, the pirate group accepts its captain only if he represents true piracy; meaning that he fulfills his tasks, proves himself repeatedly in battle, and does not try to rule. He can only depend, we shall now repeat, "on the prestige that the society bestows upon him."[85] Put differently, "the power of the chief [pirate captain] is dependent upon the good will of the group."[86] There is no doubt that pirate society is a stateless society. According to Clastres, it is therefore a society without power. A theory of the pirate captain confirms this. Clastres states that the end of powerlessness and statelessness arrives when "the chief favours the chief"[87] and gets away with it. Is it really a coincidence that the last great pirate captains—Blackbeard and Bartholomew Roberts—were precisely those who played the boss, and became the first to succeed at it?[88]

Organisation

A society without power has corresponding organisational and constitutive forms.

First, it is divided into small groups. We saw above that pirates are always in the midst of crew changes. Clastres again confirms that this defines a stateless life without authority. "In the world of the savage we do in fact observe an extraordinary fragmentation into 'nations' and tribes, societies in local groups. These are always taking great pains to preserve their autonomy within the whole."[89] Further: "The atomisation of the tribal universe is an effective means of blocking the creation of socio-political wholes that integrate local groups; but beyond that, it also prevents the rise of a State, which in its essence is a unifying factor."[90] The particular organisation of each local group is in any case egalitarian, defined by general participation. "But in the heat of battle important decisions were generally made through hand signals."[91]

As we have seen, among pirates there is an idea of basic rules for living together based on social consensus. And the captain's lack of authority leads to shared decision making, as confirmed in all reports. Plans were made together, problems discussed in common, decisions reached cooperatively. "Every important decision, such as whether to privateer a ship or determine an area of operations, was discussed in a full assembly on board and reached through a majority resolution. Every crew member had one vote in the matter, whether captain, ship's mate, or simple sailor."[92]

Perhaps the captain, generally considered experienced and clever, had more proposals and ideas than others. Nonetheless he or she would have been completely unable to force his or her will upon the crew—neither a plan nor a resolution. The captain had to consider the common will, even if it could be influenced. In fact the captain had to adopt the common will so as to avoid becoming unpopular. "The chief is more like a leader or a star than a man of power, and is always in danger of no longer being recognised by the tribe, and abandoned."[93] It is no different with the pirate captain.

Certainly there were no formal democratic voting procedures on pirate ships, but lively arguments instead, ultimately allowing only two possible outcomes: consensus, or dissolution of the group. "If a large minority was of a different opinion, it would leave the ship and take off on its own."[94] The free determination of the individual, taken as a fundamental principle from the very beginnings of piracy, was untouchable, "for the individual is the relentless enemy of every generality, every band, meaning every binding tie."[95] Self-determination could not be violated without causing general dismay among the pirates, who would see therein an attack upon the foundation of their life.[96]

To the pirates, anything less than the living determination of their common life, without deadening abstractions and formalisms, was inconceivable. Law was in the heart, not in a book. Decisions arose from a common grappling among individuals, not elite government debates. Life was organised on the daily basis of its conditions, instead of according to predetermined duties. That was the common life of the pirates.

Anything else was little more than a subject of mockery. One of their favourite pastimes was to stage European court procedures, revealing them in all their silliness. Daniel Defoe reports how one such theatre piece ended:

> (Finally the judge asked in a loud voice if supper was ready).
> Prosecutor: "Certainly, my lord."
> Judge: "Then hear me, you Scoundrel over there in the Court's Dock. Hear Me, you there, hear Me. You must do Penance for three reasons: first, because it would be improper for Me to sit here as a Judge and not have Anyone hanged. Second, You must hang because You have a Face for the Gallows. And third, You must hang because I am hungry. For know, You there, it is a Custom that should the Judge's Supper be ready before the Trial is over, the Prisoner self-evidently must be hanged. That is the Law, you Rogue. Take Him away!"[97]

We see that a serious shared struggle over decisions, common principles, and appropriate organisational forms fit well with pirate individualism, and with desire and satirical lightness within a living and free community.

Capital

Pierre Clastres argues that while primitive economy can be described as "subsistence economy" so as to differentiate it from modern economy in State societies, it should by no means be conceived of as an economy of scarcity, of just enough for survival. Instead we must understand primitive economy as performing the minimum labour for satisfying elementary needs, without interest beyond that in capital accumulation or acquisition of possessions—for true pleasure consists in leisure. Aside from a couple of months a year, there was hardly a primitive tribe where more than four or five hours were worked a day.[98] As we have seen, the chief, as the only one to produce more and keep a store of goods, also has no property. The chief is merely responsible for creating a larder available to everyone.

It is not technical imperfection that prevents accumulation, but "the refusal of an unnecessary surplus, the will to adapt productive activity to the satisfaction of needs. And nothing more."[99] "That means that as soon as energetic needs are globally satisfied, nothing can persuade the primitive society to want to produce more, meaning to invest its time in a work without a goal, when this time is available instead to leisure, war, games, or celebration."[100] The assertion follows that "so-called primitive societies are not societies of scarcity or subsistence (for want of work), but on the contrary societies of free activity and smooth space, which have no need for a factor of labour because they do not amass goods."[101] Hoarded property can only appear when there is power, meaning when someone can command others to work for him. Hoarded property is thus always private, and creates a society hierarchised through relations of property—a society in which working and acquiring property become categorical imperatives.

Primitive society produces no surplus because everything produced beyond the securing of food, clothing and housing is of no use. Arts and crafts, such as the making of baskets, beautiful clothing, masks and so on, are mostly a matter of leisure. Instead of producing far too much, one prefers to do that which creates pleasure: "hunting, fishing; feasts, drinking sessions;…satisfaction of their passionate love for war."[102] For egalitarian reasons, it is made impossible that one should stand above the rest of the tribe by amassing goods. It is also completely useless, for "what would be the use in a primitive society of being rich among the poor?"[103] The situation is clear: "In the economic activity of a primitive society, of a society without a State, there is nothing that allows the introduction of a difference between rich and poor, for no one here feels the peculiar desire to produce more, to possess more, to seem to be more than one's neighbour. Everyone is equally capable of satisfying material needs, and the exchange of goods and services among them persistently inhibits any private accumulation of goods. The development of a desire for property, which is ultimately a desire for power, is thus rendered impossible."[104] When overproduction was unavoidable there were feasts, like the potlatches held by tribes like the Kwakuitl in North America, where the whole excess was eliminated. Whatever the tribe could use directly was used immediately; everything else was put aside as an unnecessary burden. The relationship to power among pirates, who are also a stateless society, is astonishingly similar.

The captain, like the chief, had the function of keeping a larder. What did the rest of the pirates do with their shares of the booty? The answer is simple. As soon as they were on land, they acquired everything they needed for survival in the next weeks. The rest was used to eat, drink, pay whores and play cards for a few days, until there was nothing left. Then it was time to set sail again. "The sea robbers nearly always gave away their…money on land as quickly as they had got it. Among sea robbers money reached the highest speed of circulation ever recorded in the whole of economic history."[105]

The potlatch finds its counterpart in the much-celebrated buried treasure: "In contrast to merchants, they [the pirates] assigned no special value to money. Many a pirate hid his robbed jewels, gold coins, and other gems on uninhabited and inhospitable islands. Thus one or another pirate treasure is surely still buried in the sand of some Caribbean island, or on Madagascar."[106] A pirate never withdrew with the booty to safety to begin a "new life." "Most pirates died at sea, and the sea became their grave."[107] The rest were hanged on "execution deck." The tours of plunder were a necessary and beloved part of their way of life, receiving the greatest attention from all sides. But they never served the acquisition of wealth. "Their concern was not to plunder in order to become rich. Their goal instead was to gain booty as quickly as possible with the least possible effort, so as to fritter it away just as quickly."[108] Exactly herein lies the distinction between true

A group of pirates burying their treasure on Barron Island.

pirates and all other sea robbers. Like all societies without States, pirates knew nothing of economics, possessions, or capital accumulation. Not that they were too stupid, lazy, or weak to develop such economics. Pirates, of all people, could have ended up among the richest men of that time, but riches meant little to a pirate. The reason was that modern economy consists in meaningless production for the sake of production, and therefore requires States, power, exploitation, class society. The pirate holds property in contempt, because it has nothing to do with his desire for freedom. Actually, it is an obstacle to that desire. The pirate is well aware of the danger that the accumulation of goods represents to a life in freedom and equality, meaning to the whole of pirate society.

Like primitive societies, pirates are "societies without economy out of a refusal of economy."[109]

War Machine

After the last sections we can say with some confidence that pirate crews were a type of primitive society: no State, no power, no modern economy. Primitive societies are not backwards or underdeveloped, but are characterised through a consistently anti-statist and anti-authoritarian character. Quite apart from any period of history, they are the societies of "society without the State"(as the title of Pierre Clastres' brilliant book directly conveys). We have already seen that statist organisation is the only true enemy of the pirate, an enemy that is fought with all force and mercilessness. Nowhere else is the thesis of the nomadic machinery of war, directed against the State by anti-statist societies, as manifest as it is in piracy.

Gilles Deleuze and Felix Guattari, the first to recognise

REASONS

For Reducing the

Pyrates at Madagaſcar:

AND

PROPOSALS *humbly offered to the Ho-*
nourable Houſe of Commons, for effecting the ſame.

THAT certain Pyrates having ſome Years ſince found the Iſland of *Mada-*
gaſcar to be the moſt Proper, if not the only Place in the World for their
Abode, and carrying on their Deſtructive Trade with Security, betook
themſelves thither ; and being ſince increaſed to a formidable Body are become a manifeſt Obſtruction to Trade, and Scandal to our Nation and
Religion, being moſt of them *Engliſh,* at leaſt four Fifths.

That *Madagaſcar* is one of the Largeſt Iſlands in the World, and very Fruitful, lies
near the Entrance into the *Eaſt-Indies,* and is divided into a great many petty Kingdoms
independant of each other, ſo that there is no making Application to any Supream Monarch (or indeed any elſe) to Expel or Deſtroy the Pyrates there.

That upon a general Peace, when Multitudes of Soldiers and Seamen will want Employment ; or by length of Time, and the Pyrates generating with the Women of the Country, their Numbers ſhould be increaſed, they may form themſelves into a Settlement of
Robbers, as Prejudicial to Trade as any on the Coaſt of *Affrica.*

For it's natural to conſider, That all Perſons owe by Inſtinct a Love to the Place of
their Birth : Therefore the preſent Pyrates muſt deſire to return to their Native Country ; and if this preſent Generation ſhould be once Extinct, their Children will have the
ſame Inclination to *Madagaſcar* as theſe have to *England,* and will not have any ſuch
Affection for *England,* altho' they will retain the Name of *Engliſh* ; and conſequently all
thoſe ſucceeding Depredations committed by them will be charged to the Account of
England. Notwithſtanding they were not born with us, ſo that this ſeems the only
Time for Reducing them to their Obedience, and preventing all thoſe evil Con-
ſequences.

It muſt therefore be allow'd to be a very deſirable and neceſſary Thing, that they
ſhould be ſuppreſſed in Time ; and that if it ever be effected, it muſt be either by Force
or Perſwaſion.

A2

Bill put before the British Parliament, 1704.

the nomadic war machine, basically argue as follows: as stateless societies, primitive societies face permanent threat from State units. The clan is always nomadic in the broadest sense of permanent mobility. Attacks from without, as well as the molar tendencies that always appear from within, subject it to constant danger. Meaning that the nomadic "war machine acts against the State, including potential States, whose rise needs to be hindered, and to an even greater extent against existing States, the destruction of which is made into a goal."[110] The consequence: "From the State's perspective the originality of the warrior, his eccentricity, necessarily appears to be negative, a stupidity, deformation, madness, impropriety, usurpation, sin. Dumézil analyses the three sins of the warrior in Indo-European tradition: he is against the King, against the priests, and against the laws issued by the State."[111]

The State and its enemies are at war, unavoidably and in every way. It is thus no cause for wonder when historians determine that during the "golden age" of piracy "thousands and thousands of pirates were waging de facto war on all the sea routes of the world."[112] Primitive society could not ever survive if it did not have institutions for dealing with a state of war. A nomadic war machine is a necessary element of an anti-statist society. "The war machine was a nomadic invention, for it was the essential element constitutive for smooth space."[113] Its full force is directed exclusively against everything rigid, limiting, dividing, ordering, and molar, in short: the State.

Since this war is waged on all fronts, the highest priority of the nomadic war machine is not war as slaughter and/or even combat, but the preservation of smooth space as the space of freedom: "just that is its only and genuinely positive goal."[114] "If war necessarily arises from that, then it is because the war machine runs into States and cities, meaning the forces [of enclosure] arrayed against the positive goal. From that moment the State, the city and the statist or city phenomenon become the enemy of the war machine, which sets out to destroy them. Here is where the war begins: to destroy the forces of the State, to destroy the statist form."[115] Nomadic war machinery functions molecularly: no arrangement, no uniformity, no command, no regulations, no supervision. No rigidity, not of language or of thinking, or of body or play, or of living and working together. In short: a defence of singularities, events, and nomadic (as opposed to despotic) unity, without compromises, using all available mechanisms.

We need now only compare this picture of the anti-statist war machine to that we have so far drawn of the pirates. We have seen that pirates are aptly described as nomads of the sea; that they are consistent enemies of the State; that they must attack merchant and war ships because it is a matter of "You or us! Despotism or freedom!" The entire organisation of their common life is oriented towards preventing power. They were anti-economists so as to allow no room for class society.

If the pirates do not represent a nomadic war machine, who ever did? Everything fits, for "one might say that every time that someone defends themselves against the State (by resisting discipline, through revolt, guerrilla war, or revolution) a war machine is revived; a new, nomadic potential arises; and thus the reconstitution of a smooth space or the life form of the smooth space."[116]

Guerrillas

The goal of the nomadic war machine is not war as a state of permanent physical violence or battle. This does not mean that violent exchanges are not held. The many pirate battles clearly demonstrate that their anti-statist war machinery could not get by without brutality.

But in place of bloodthirsty terror attacks, they operated much more by functionalising their reputation as merciless scoundrels in a kind of "non-violent" surprise tactic: "use of violence was far from their preferred mode of achieving an objective."[117] "Pirates were masters of psychology and took ship after ship without even striking a blow, simply by driving their victims into submission through fear and terror."[118]

> Suddenly a ship appears by the light of the moon. Sail and deck are drenched in blood. The figure of a woman stands at the bow. In her hand she holds a grappling hook dripping blood, and uses it to strike repeatedly at a human form. The ghostly ship quickly approaches the merchant brigantine. The merchant crew is frozen with terror. Without putting up any fight, they surrender their cargo to the attackers. The idea for this scenario was Anne Bonny's.[119] During the action she stood at the bow and struck at a stuffed mannequin with her hook. Previously she had drowned the puppet, hook, and ship in turtle's blood...Anne Bonny planned her attacks with cunning and fantasy. The horrible shows she staged spared her plenty of battles.[120]

Nonetheless occasional physical conflict could not be avoided altogether. "But there were also times when no threat bore fruit; and then an open sea battle would break out, causing the heavens to tremble, colouring the water with blood."[121] The nomadic or primitive (and thus also piratical) battle is of a very particular kind.

We might describe the basic characteristics of the guerrilla as follows: as far as the organisation is concerned, there is no fixed army of repression, no State legitimisation, and no institutionalised training. With regard to combat, there is permanent mobility in place of positional war: sabotage and sudden attacks with rapid withdrawals, within an unpredictable area of operations. Che Guevera, the epitome of the guerrillero, specifies:

> The guerrilla's attack has...its particularities. It begins with an attack that surprises the opponent in its intensity and ferocity. Its end comes just as unexpectedly to the enemy...suddenly a new attack is carried out at a different point...The main thing is that these attacks are unexpected by the enemy, and are carried out quickly."[122] "The most important quality of a guerrilla unit consists in its mobility. That allows it to withdraw far from the scene of battle within minutes if necessary. Thanks to mobility the unit can constantly attack the enemy in various places, and avoid being surrounded itself."[123] "We have already pointed out that combat exchanges must be carried out without hesitation, rapidly, and with the greatest possible effect. They should last only a few minutes. When they are over, the fighters must withdraw without delay."[124] "The strikes must follow upon one another without pause...By day or night, the opponent must have the impression of being encircled.[125]

THE LIFE OF

LAFITTE,

THE FAMOUS PIRATE OF THE GULF OF MEXICO.

Lafitte boarding the Queen East Indiaman.

With a History of the Pirates of Barrataria—and an account of their volunteering for the defence of New Orleans; and their daring intrepidity under General Jackson, during the battle of the 8th of January, 1815. For which important service they were pardoned by President Madison.

Shortly after being pardoned Lafitte and his crew returned
to their pirate activities.

Pirate crews were anything but fixed, never mind legitimated by a State. Their training occurred directly in combat, not at a barracks. They carried out no front war, which would have been impossible with their arms. The terror all sea travellers felt of pirates was based above all on their sudden, unpredictable, lightning-like attacks; this is everywhere confirmed. "In the main they carried out lightning attacks and employed corresponding tactics. Speed and surprise were of the essence."[126] Therefore "[the frigate] was preferred by the pirates because of its speed and manoeuvrability in comparison to all other ship types."[127] When boarding a ship, "the sea robber mostly used a short sable for dispatching his enemies. Pistols had the disadvantage that they could be fired only once during the [usually] short time of boarding, and could not be reloaded due to their length."[128] This theory of tactics had been forwarded two thousand years earlier by the Chinese philosopher Sun Tze: "War is a way of deception." "Speed is the most important thing in war."[129] And once the pirates took that to heart, "the fate of the attacked merchant ships was usually clear from the outset. Only seldom did the captain and crew of a merchant ship raided by pirates have any chance to defeat their attackers. The pirates already had superiority in hand-to-hand combat thanks to their better weaponry, the short sable and the grappling knife."[130]

Nomadic warriors are nothing other than true guerrillas. Anyone who wants to know what it means to be a guerrilla of the water must study the pirates and their battles.

Morality

To this day "revolutionary morality" is a subject of much discussion. What is the enemy of the State allowed to do, what not? How are enemies to be treated? A strict, moralist prohibition of any dealings with enemies represents the one extreme; the radical lack of conscience of a Nechayev makes up the other.[131] The pirates' choice in the matter was clear. If they could gain advantage through any kind of contact with representatives of the State, they didn't hesitate to do so. It hardly needs to be mentioned that pirates never held to any agreement if it was no longer fortuitous. After all, sea robbery for the State is the filibuster's domain. Pirates never did anything other than employ cleverness and deception to secure free space and avoid danger. State partners were always laughed at, mocked, and betrayed. As soon as pirates were truly forced to make any kind of concessions to State rulers, contact became unthinkable. State rulers were there to be deceived and betrayed; otherwise no deals were made. This corresponds to the particular individualism of pirates, and the difference they consistently maintained from their enemies. "A word of honour, an oath, is only valid for one whom I entitle to receive it."[132] It is self-evident that pirates do not so entitle rulers. Beyond this, playing with State rulers is naturally only possible as long as it is fun and helps in developing and strengthening the pirate way of life. According to Deleuze and Guattari, the god of the nomadic war machinery unleashed by pirates is surely Indra, the Indo-Germanic god of war. His most important characteristic: "he dissolves ties and breaks agreements."[133]

For a long time Blackbeard, one of the most famous pirate captains, made use of the conflict between the semi-independent American colonies and the English motherland. He was allowed to attack European merchant ships without disruption, and sell the booty in American ports under protection of the Governor of North Carolina. This should not be confused with the activities of the filibusters. Blackbeard had not been sent by the governor, nor did he remain loyal. He merely made use of a situation that favoured him. Any doubts should be dispelled when we consider that in the end, Blackbeard died in battle against an American governor's forces.

Like the revolutionaries in Brecht's play Measures, pirates had no compunctions about anything that served their cause. Any strong moral code would have made their task much more difficult, and subjected them to great dangers.

Pirate practice demonstrates that morality as a conscience-laden catalogue of rules, of "thou shalts" and "thou shalt nots," ultimately serves State units. Not only is it incompatible with a primitive, nomadic life; it in fact represents the beginning of the end for such a life. Pirates prove that responsibility must replace morality if freedom is to survive.

Parasites

Pirates produced nothing with which to earn their livelihood. They robbed others. Pirates accumulated no capital; they squandered everything. Their victims were mostly merchant ships. Pirates "caused such great damage to ship travel that normal commercial traffic, and even the economies of a few countries, were greatly endangered. It made no difference whether a ship flew under a Spanish, French, English, Indian, or Arabian flag. The pirates opposed all States, and any ship was acceptable as booty."[134] Pirates threatened capitalism. Instead of a circulation of production and consumption, they set up one of robbery and squander. What pirates did is comparable to the burning of a factory by autonomen;[135] except that in the process pirates also took everything they needed for survival. The basis of their livelihood was "redistribution." It comes as no surprise that the decisive campaign of extermination against the pirates was ultimately sounded by an association of English merchants.[136]

Commercial concerns are powerful, and belong to the society of the State. Capitalism is totalitarian. It is clear that the pirates, without naming it as their enemy, and certainly without analysing it, nonetheless had to fight it. They lived off the attempt to establish capitalism, at the same time blocking that attempt.

Why not just walk away from capitalism and build "something else," something "independent"(perhaps communes or something similarly libertarian and romantic)? Now that is easier said than done. In fact, it is as good as impossible. The combination of fighting capitalism while also exploiting it is admittedly far more exciting and intensive than mere escape.

But finally, it is in the nature of capitalism that there can be no escape; it will always catch up. "The potency of capitalism consists in a logic that is never saturated, and always prepared to add more axioms to the existing ones."[137] Thus: "let's go get'em and see what comes of it!"—the pirate as parasite. Such parasitic groups have always created relatively free spaces within capitalism, broken through its constitutive chains, established a connection to the outside, and allowed for (more or less) autonomous living. The question is not how capitalism can be done away with, nor that of what should replace it. The question is: how can I deal with it so as not to become a prisoner? Everything else will follow from that.

Pirates always behaved this way. Perhaps the only true forerunners to Caribbean piracy were the Hanseatic pirates grouped around Klaus Störtebeker (the "Vitalien brothers"). They too did not want to have their lives dictated by rulers and merchants. When these tried to consolidate their power in the Hanseatic area, Störtebeker and his friends made the North Sea into their home. The life they lived was not dictated by the Hanseatic order, but their livelihood was based upon Hanseatic trade: they robbed the merchants. "'Enemies of all the world, friends only of God,' according to the legend of the Vitalien brothers. At least this would mean that God was in favour of robbing rich merchants, of taking from the powerful that which they would probably not give freely."[138]

There is much talk about fighting capitalism. Pirates show us how to do it.

We have arrived at the end of our sketch of pirate life. I will be accused of glorification, and I don't care. Anyone who doesn't like what has been written here, doesn't like it. Enemies of pirates are friends of the State, and only rarely is there any help for them. Here an attempt has been made to demonstrate what we might gain by looking to the pirates today. Examining piracy helps us draw a picture of life in freedom, activity, and responsibility, of life without rulers, without State or economy. It shows us what it means to create that life against the opposition of State and economy. It confirms important theories, like that of the anti-statist society being a society without power, or of the necessity of a nomadic war machine. It teaches us to think differently about body, death, and religion. Perhaps it lends strength to a few who are rebelling. And perhaps—to a few who love the State, capital, and order—the calm hinterlands will appear a bit less secure.

NOTES

1. *Die Piraten* [The Pirates]. Amsterdam: Time-Life Books: 1980, p. 55.
2. Max Stirner, *Der Einzige und sein Eigentum* [The Ego and Its Own]. Stuttgart: Reclam, 1981, p. 392.
3. Salentiny, Ferdinand: *Die Piraten*. Wels: Welsermühl 1978, p. 12.
4. Francis Drake: born ca. 1541 in England. Empowered by Elizabeth I to undertake gigantic tours of plunder on all possible sea routes. Died 1596 in battle with the Spanish. Henry Morgan: Born 1635 in Wales. Under protection of Charles II and English governors, robbed Spanish ships and cities in the Caribbean. Finally became Lieutenant Governor and Commander-in-Chief of English forces in Jamaica. Died there as a rich plantation owner around 1700.
5. Ulrike Klausmann and Marion Meinzerin, *Pirate Women* (in this volume; see section on Caribbean, "The Golden Age of Piracy," Montréal: Black Rose Books, 1997.
6. *Die Piraten*, p. 44.
7. Friedrich Nietszche, *Zur Genealogie der Moral* [On the Genealogy of Morals], Munich and Berlin: Goldmann, 1988, p. 24.
8. Stirner, p. 261.
9. *Die Piraten*, p. 28.
10. Ibid., p. 29.
11. Salentiny, p. 36.
12. Klausmann and Meinzerin; see "The Woman and the Old Sea" in this volume.
13. Salentiny, p. 17.
14. Stirner, p. 181.
15. Ibid., p. 187.

16. Salentiny, p. 36.
17. Gilles Deleuze and Felix Guattari, *Tausend Plateaus* [A Thousand Plateaus], Berlin: Merve 1992, p. 671.
18. Ibid., p. 533.
19. *Die Piraten*, p. 55.
20. Deleuze and Guattari, p. 533.
21. Ibid., p. 664.
22. Paul Virilio and Sylvere Lothringer, *Der reine Krieg* [The Pure War], Berlin: Merve, 1984, p. 70.
23. Deleuze and Guattari, p. 525.
24. *Die Piraten*, p. 28.
25. Ibid., p. 20.
26. Deleuze and Guattari, p. 525.
27. Gilles Deleuze, "Nomaden-Denken" ["Nomadic Thinking"], in: Deleuze, Gilles, *Nietzsche-Lesebuch* [Nietzsche Reader], Berlin: Merve, 1979, p. 121.
28. Charles Bellamy: Operated in the early eighteenth century around the Antilles and New England. Hanged 1726 in Boston.
29. "Captain Charles Johnson" (Daniel Defoe). *A General History of the Robberies and Murders of the Most Notorious Pyrates, Vol. I & II*, Rivington: London, 1724-28, Vol. II, p. 220
30. Gilles Deleuze, *Nietzsche und die Philosophie* [Nietzsche and Philosophy]. Hamburg: eva, 1992, p. 95.
31. Ibid., p. 189.
32. Mission: Son of Provence nobility. First sailed around Martinique. Founded the "pirate's settlement" Libertalia on Madagascar, later destroyed by the islanders. Mission died soon after in a hurricane on the high seas.
33. Compare to the section below on "Organisation."
34. *Die Piraten*, p. 51.
35. Ibid., p. 47.
36. Salentiny, p. 34.
37. *Die Piraten*, p. 21.
38. Nietzsche, p. 31.
39. Michel Foucault, *Überwachen und Strafen* [Discipline and Punishment]. Frankfurt am Main: Suhrkamp, 1977, p. 174ff.
40. Baruch de Spinoza, *Die Ethik*. Stuttgart: Reclam, 1977, p. 159.
41. Salentiny, p. 35.
42. *Die Piraten*, p. 21.
43. Bartholomew Roberts: Born ca. 1682, probably in Wales. The last great pirate captain; commandeered about 400 ships from 1719-1722. Killed 1722 in battle with English warships. Klausmann and Meinzerin argue the well-founded thesis that Bartholomew Roberts was a woman (see the chapter on Bartholomew Roberts in the section on the Caribbean in this volume).
44. Klausmann and Meinzerin, "Sea Princess Bartholomew Roberts," in this volume.
45. Defoe, Vol. I, p. 173
46. Duerr, Hans Peter: *Sedna oder die Liebe Um Leben* [Sena or the Love of Life]. Frankfurt am Main: Suhrkamp, 1990, p. 235.

47. Ibid., p. 239.
48. Klausmann and Meinzerin, "Sea Princess Bartholomew Roberts," in this volume.
49. *Die Piraten*, p. 55.
50. Mary Read: Originally from England. Pretended to be a Dutch man so as to sail on a merchant ship to the Caribbean, where she hooked up with the group around Anne Bonny. Died 1720 of a fever in prison while awaiting her execution. (See the corresponding chapters in the section on the Caribbean, on "Anne Bonny" and "Mary Read" in this volume).
51. Defoe, Vol. I, p. 125
52. *Die Piraten*, p. 128.
53. Ibid., p. 128.
54. Caraccioli: A Dominican monk from Naples, joined Mission's crew (note 32).
55. Salentiny, p. 168.
56. Blackbeard (Edward Teach): English, appeared as a pirate in 1713 in the Caribbean, became the "epitome of the pirate himself," until he was killed by American soldiers in 1718.
57. *Die Piraten*, p. 174.
58. Ibid., p. 146.
59. See, for example, Vine Deloria Jr., *Gott ist Rot* [God is Red]. Munich: Trikont, 1984.
60. See Hans Reichhardt, *Die Germanen* [The Germanic Tribes]. Nuremberg and Hamburg: Tessloff, 1978, p. 27.
61. Jean-Francois Lyotard, *Apathie in der Theorie* [Apathy in Theory]. Berlin: Merve, 1979, p. 32f.
62. Deleuze and Guattari, p. 527.
63. Compare to the section on "Responsibility."
64. Salentiny, p. 24.
65. Ibid., p. 7
66. Deleuze and Guattari, p. 527.
67. See the essay on "Heidnische Unterweisungen" [Heathen Instruction] in Lyotard, pp. 7-71.
68. Deleuze and Guattari, p. 525.
69. Ibid., p. 704.
70. Ibid., p. 704.
71. Pierre Clastres, *Staatsfeinde* [Societies Without State], Frankfurt am Main: Suhrkamp, 1976, p. 45.
72. Ibid., p. 190.
73. *Die Piraten*, p. 29.
74. Ibid., p. 47.
75. Clastres, p. 48.
76. Defoe, Vol. I, p. 173
77. Ibid.
78. Clastres, p. 197.
79. *Die Piraten*, p. 47.
80. Ibid., p. 47.
81. Ibid., p. 47.

82. Clastres, p. 198f.
83. Low: Born in England; starting as a harbourside pickpocket, moved his way up to Caribbean pirate captain. His death is related here.
84. Salentiny, p. 141.
85. Clastres, p. 196.
86. Ibid., p. 38.
87. Ibid., p. 198.
88. Both Blackbeard and Bartholomew Roberts played themselves up into leaders and rulers, and over time were accepted as such by the "common pirates." "Suddenly Blackbeard cocked the pistol, blew out the candle and fired. Hands [a crew member] was hit in the knee and crippled for life. When Blackbeard was asked why he did this, he replied that if he didn't occasionally shoot a member of his crew, they would forget who he was" (*Die Piraten*, p. 148). This kind of behaviour by the captain would have been unthinkable on pirate ships until then. The same is true of Roberts: "The style of his clothing was meant to underline the difference between him and his men" (*Die Piraten*, p. 162). "On one journey a drunken crew member insulted the captain. Roberts, overcome with fury, killed the man on the spot. Many of the similarly intoxicated comrades of the drunken man were very resentful of this, especially one Thomas Jones. ...The tumultuous events set the whole ship in an uproar. One part of the crew took Roberts's side, the others sided with Jones. ...In the examination of the matter that followed, the majority of the crew was of the view that the captain's prestige had to be defended; since it was an honorary post, no crew member had the right to maltreat him" (Ibid., p. 163f.) In this story we see that despite voting procedures authority was by then considered an institution—and also that there was great resistance against this development on the part of many pirates. Perhaps this defeat of the insignificant pirate Jones sealed the end of piracy as a free form of life: he received 360 lashes of the whip, an otherwise inconceivable punishment among pirates. "This terrible punishment by no means convinced Jones that he was in the wrong. At the first subsequent opportunity he and a few of his friends left Roberts" (Ibid., p. 164).
89. Clastres, p. 203ff.
90. Ibid., p. 204.
91. *Die Piraten*, p. 47.
92. Salentiny, p. 35.
93. Deleuze and Guattari, p. 490.
94. *Die Piraten*, p. 47.
95. Stirner, p. 237.
96. Compare to the story of Captain Low, above.
97. *Die Piraten*, p. 47.
98. Compare to Clastres, p. 183ff. 5
99. Clastres, p. 185.
100. Ibid., p. 187.
101. Deleuze and Guattari, p. 680.
102. Clastres, p. 184.
103. Ibid., p. 189.

104. Ibid., p. 195.
105. Salentiny, p. 36.
106. Ibid., p. 36.
107. Ibid., p. 36.
108. Klausmann and Meinzerin; see"The Golden Age of Piracy," in this volume.
109. Clastres, p. 189.
110. Deleuze and Guattari, p. 492.
111. Ibid., p. 485.
112. *Die Piraten*, p. 6.
113. Deleuze and Guattari, p. 576.
114. Ibid., p. 576.
115. Ibid., p. 576.
116. Ibid., p. 532f.
117. *Die Piraten*, p. 55.
118. Ibid., p. 57.
119. Anne Bonny: Born in Ireland. Made the Caribbean unsafe for a few years together with Calico Jack Rackham, until she was sentenced to death in 1720. (See the chapter on Anne Bonny in this volume.)
120. Ibid.
121. *Die Piraten*, p. 57.
122. Che Guevera, *Guerillakrieg und Befreiungsbewegung* [Guerrilla War and Liberation Movement]. Dortmund: Weltkreis, p. 72.
123. Ibid., p. 68.
124. Ibid., p. 84.
125. Ibid., p. 65.
126. *Die Piraten*, p. 55.
127. Salentiny, p. 25.
128. Ibid., p. 28.
129. Compare to Virilio and Lothringer, p. 123.
130. Salentiny, p. 29.
131. Nechayev (1847-1882): Russian anarchist; wrote the "Catechism of an Anarchist" together with Michail Bakunin. Starved after ten years in a Russian dungeon.
132. Stirner, p. 339f.
133. Deleuze and Guattari, p. 483.
134. *Die Piraten*, p. 6.
135. Autonomen: Groups of squatters, punks, and urban youth with explicitly anarchist politics and an uncompromising anti-statism "against patriarchy and imperialism internationally." Arose in the seventies and eighties of the twentieth century, mostly in urban centres of the German-speaking countries. Best known for creating huge squatted cultural-residential centres and engaging in regular street clashes with the police, especially in Berlin, Hamburg, and Zurich—trans.
136. Compare to: *Die Piraten*, p. 139.
137. Gilles Deleuze and Felix Guattari, *Anti-Ödipus* [Anti-Oedipus]. Frankfurt am Main: Suhrkamp, p. 322; see especially pp. 286-338 as a comparison to the analysis herein.

138.	Dieter Zimmerling, *Störtebeker & Co.* Frankfurt am Main and Berlin: Ullstein 1988, p. 324. See also "On the Trail of Folka ten Broke" in this volume.

BIBLIOGRAPHY

Clastres, Pierre. *A Sociedade contra o Estado.* [Society Without the State: The Leader as Servant and the Humane Uses of Power Among the Indians of the America. New York, 1977].

Deloria, Vine Jr., *God is Red* [*Gott ist Rot*, Munich: Trikont, 1984].

Deleuze, Gilles and Guattari, Felix. *Mille Plateaux* [A Thousand Plateaus]. Paris: Ed. de Minnit, 1980.

Deleuze, Gilles and Guattari, Felix. *L'Anti-Oedipe* [Anti-Oedipus]. Paris, 1972.

Duerr, Hans Peter. *Sedna oder die Liebe zum Leben* [Sedna or the love of life]. Frankfurt: Suhrkamp, 1990.

Foucault, Michel. *Surveiller et punir* [Discipline and Punishment]. Paris, 1976.

Guevera, Ernesto ("Che"). *La guerra de guerrillas*, Havana, 1960. [*Guerilla Warfare*. New York, 1967].

Klausmann, Ulrike, and Meinzerin, Marion. *Woman Pirates and the Politics of the Jolly Roger.* Montreal: Black Rose Books, 1997.

Lyotard, Jean-Franscois. "De l'apathie théorique" [Apathy in theory]. In: *Critique* No. 333, February 1975.

Nietszche, Friedrich. *Zur Genealogie der Moral* [On the Genealogy of Morals]. Munich and Berlin: Goldmann, 1988.

Pirates. London: Time-Life Books, 1989.

Reichhardt, Hans. *Die Germanen.* Nuremberg and Hamburg: Tessloff, 1978.

Salentiny, Fernand. *Die Piraten.* Wels: Welsermühl, 1978.

Spinoza, Benedikt von. *Ethics.*

Stirner, Max. *The Ego and His Own* [*Der Einzige und sein Eigentum.* Stuttgart: Reclam, 1981].

Virilio, Paul and Lothringer, Sylvere. *Pure War.* New York, 1984.

Zimmerling, Dieter. *Störtebeker & Co.* Frankfurt and Berlin, Ullstein 1988.

Also published by

BLACK ROSE BOOKS

YEAR 501
The Conquest Continues
Noam Chomsky

A powerful and comprehensive discussion of the incredible injustices hidden in our history.

...Year 501 offers a savage critique of the new world order.
MacLean's Magazine
Tough, didactic, [Chomsky] skins back the lies of those who make decisions.
Globe and Mail
...a much-needed defense against the mind-numbing free market rhetoric.
Latin America Connexions

331 pages, index
Paperback ISBN: 1-895431-62-X $19.99
Hardcover ISBN: 1-895431-63-8 $48.99

GREEN GUERRILLAS*
Environmental Conflicts and Initiatives in Latin America and the Caribbean
Helen Collinson, ed.

This remarkable collection is just what we needed. Diverse viewpoints and a willingness to challenge received wisdom.
Richard Levins, Harvard School of Public Health
Challenges conventional stereotypes about the region's environmental crisis demonstrating both the diversity and dilemmas of local struggles.
Marcus Colchester, World Rainforest Movement

250 pages, index
Paperback ISBN: 1-55164-066-X $23.99
Hardcover ISBN: 1-55164-067-8 $52.99

THE POLITICS OF URBAN LIBERATION
Stephen Schecter

A wide-ranging libertarian evaluation dealing with political economy in an urban context, from France to Chile. it also examines the importance of the city in the history of social revolution.

203 pages
Paperback ISBN: 0-919618-78-2 $9.99
Hardcover ISBN: 0-919618-79-0 $38.99

BANKERS, BAGMEN, AND BANDITS
Business and Politics in the Age of Greed
R.T. Naylor

A collection of articles from the shadowy underworld of business, the shady side of politics, and the twilight zone they share.

Based on Naylor's widely read column, this book is designed to give the news behind the news, to put back into the stories the 'awkward' details the main stream media find more convenient to omit.

An eminently readable book, with outré insights into the corrupt underside of world affairs in each chapter.
Canadian Book Review Annual
Without exception, the essays make very interesting reading... Naylor's book is an exhilarating if sometimes frightening roller coaster ride through the real world.
The Alternative Voice

250 pages
Paperback ISBN: 0-921689-76-4 $18.99
Hardcover ISBN: 0-921689-77-2 $47.99

GEOGRAPHY OF FREEDOM
The Odyssey of Elisée Reclus
Marie Fleming

A solid addition to anarchist scholarship.
Choice
A good argument for the idea that anarchism of the last century was a remarkably stimulating haven.
American Historical Review
We have long needed a biography on this prominent geographer and anarchist.
George Woodcock

256 pages, bibliography, photographs
Paperback ISBN: 0-921689-16-0 $16.99
Hardcover ISBN: 0-921689-17-9 $45.99

WOLLASTON
People Resisting Genocide
Miles Goldstick

Natives' struggle in northern Saskatchewan to protect their homes from the effects of uranium mining.

These are important issues, and in raising them Goldstick does us a service.
Border/Lines

315 pages, photographs, illustrations
Paperback ISBN: 0-920057-95-0 $16.99
Hardcover ISBN: 0-920057-94-2 $45.99

PIERRE-JOSEPH PROUDHON
A Biography
2nd revised edition
George Woodcock

The first full-scale English-language biography of the prominent 19th-century social thinker and "father of anarchism."

A solid and workmanlike effort.
Times Literary Supplement
Woodcock makes a very good case for the consistency of [Proudhon's] teaching.
New York Times

295 pages, index
Paperback ISBN: 0-921689-08-X $19.99
Hardcover ISBN: 0-921689-09-8 $48.99

PETER KROPOTKIN
From Prince to Rebel
George Woodcock, Ivan Avakumovic

This biography surveys and analyzes the most significant aspects of Peter Kropotkin's life and thought: his formative years in Russia, 1842-1876, and the origins of his anarchist thinking; his years as an emigré in Western Europe, 1876-1917, and the ripening of his political thought; and his last years in the Soviet Union, 1917-1921.

490 pages, index, illustrated
Paperback ISBN: 0-921689-60-8 $19.99
Hardcover ISBN: 0-921689-61-6 $48.99

ECOLOGY OF FREEDOM
The Emergence and Dissolution of Hierarchy, revised edition
Murray Bookchin

The most systematic articulation of ideas.
San Francisco Review of Books
... a confirmation of his [Bookchin's] status as a penetrating critic not only of the ways in which humankind is destroying itself, but of the ethical imperative to live better.
Village Voice
Elegantly written, and recommended for a wide audience.
 Library Journal

395 pages, index
Paperback ISBN: 0-921689-72-1 $19.99
Hardcover ISBN: 0-921689-73-X $48.99
L.C. No. 90-83628

EUROPE'S GREEN ALTERNATIVE
An Ecology Manifesto
Penny Kemp, ed.

In a book which is both visionary and revolutionary, the authors propose a continent of autonomous regions which are economically decentralized, built on feminist principles, and underpinned by non-violent social structures.

200 pages, appendices
Paperback: 1-895431-30-1 $16.99
Hardcover: 1-895431-31-X $45.99
L.C. No. 92-70621

REGULATION OF DESIRE
Homo and Hetero Sexualities
Gary Kinsman

Kinsman imaginatively relates the production of sexual discourses to the power of the modern state.
Gender & History
Valuable for its research into an important history that has been overlooked or dismissed out of hand.
Books in Canada
The historical perspective serves as a very useful tool.
Globe and Mail
A substantial contribution to our understanding of the politics of same-gender sexual relations.
Fuse

423 pages, index
Paperback 1-55164-040-6 $23.99
Hardcover 1-55164-041-4 $52.99

EMMA GOLDMAN
Sexuality and the Impurity of the State
Bonnie Haaland

This book focuses on the ideas of Emma Goldman as they relate to the centrality of sexuality and reproduction, and as such, are relevant to the current feminist debates.

A model for "integrative feminism" that focuses on individuality rather than on rights.
Common Knowledge
In its focus on Goldman's ideas, Haaland's work stands out among other literature. What is most valuable about Goldman today, is not her ideas so much as what she did with her ideas.
Kinesis

201 pages, index
Paperback ISBN: 1-895431-64-6 $19.99
Hardcover ISBN: 1-895431-65-4 $48.99

RETHINKING CAMELOT*
JFK, the Vietnam War, and U.S. Political Culture
Noam Chomsky

For those who turn to Hollywood for history, and confuse creative license with fact, Chomsky proffers an arresting reminder that historical narrative rarely fits neatly into a feature film. A thoroughly researched background.

... a fascinating and disturbing portrait of the Kennedy dynasty.
Briarpatch
... a particularly interesting and important instance of media and power elite manipulation.
Humanist In Canada
... the most important contribution to the ongoing public and private discussions about JFK.
Kitchener-Waterloo Record

172 pages, index
Paperback ISBN: 1-895431-72-7 $19.99
Hardcover ISBN: 1-895431-73-5 $48.99

BAKUNIN
The Philosophy of Freedom
Brian Morris

This book confirms Bakunin was a holistic thinker and that his anarchism was dominated by a desire to achieve a unity of theory and practice.

Everything about him is colossal... he is full of a primitive exuberance and strength.
Richard Wagner

159 pages, index,
Paperback ISBN: 1-895431-66-2 $18.99
Hardcover ISBN: 1-895431-67-0 $47.99

BAKUNIN ON ANARCHISM
Sam Dolgoff, ed.

4th printing
The best available in English. Bakunin's insights into power and freedom, the new classes of specialists, are refreshing, original and often still unsurpassed in clarity and vision.
Noam Chomsky

453 pages
Paperback ISBN: 0-919619-06-1 $18.99
Hardcover ISBN: 0-919619-05-3 $47.99